MW00511368

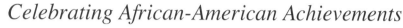

Celebrating African-American Achievements

WHO'S WHO
in BLACK
Detroit®
THE SECOND EDITION

Scenes from the 2006
Who's Who in Black Detroit® Unveiling Reception

Celebrating African-American Achievements

WHO'S WHO
IN BLACK
Detroit®
THE SECOND EDITION

Who's Who In Black Detroit®
is a registered trademark of
Briscoe Media Group, LLC

Purchase additional copies online at
www.whoswhopublishing.com

Corporate Headquarters
Who's Who Publishing Co., LLC
1650 Lake Shore Drive, Suite 250
Columbus, Ohio 43204

All Credit Cards Accepted
*Inquiries for bulk purchases for youth
groups, schools, churches, civic or
professional organizations, please call
our office for volume discounts.*

Corporate Headquarters
(614) 481-7300

**Copyright © 2007 by C. Sunny Martin,
Briscoe Media Group, LLC**

ISSN Number: 1935-9292

Photo Credits
C. Sunny Martin
David Watkins, Oxygen Photography

**ISBN # 1-933879-40-8 Hardback
$50.00 each-U.S. Hardback
Commemorative Edition**

**ISBN # 1-933879-39-4 Paperback
$34.95 each-U.S. Paperback**

Detroit's premier

FINE DINING AND JAZZ SUPPER CLUB

SERVING CONTEMPORARY CUISINE WITH AN INTERNATIONAL FLAIR

SELDOM BLUES HAS RECEIVED MANY PRESTIGIOUS AWARDS, INCLUDING:

◇ HOUR Detroit "2006 Best Restaurant General Excellence"
◇ Detroit Free Press "2006 Restaurant of the Year"
◇ Style Magazine "2006 Most Sophisticated Venue"
◇ Named one of America's Best Bars by Esquire Magazine
◇ Wine Spectator Award, 2005, 2006 and 2007

SELDOM BLUES

PLAY HERE

Hours: Mon. – Thurs: 11:30 a.m. to 10 p.m. | Fri.: 11:30 a.m. – 12 a.m.
Sat.: 5 p.m. – 12 a.m. | Sunday Brunch: 11:30 a.m. – 4 p.m.
313.567.7301 | 400 Renaissance Center, Detroit, Michigan | www.seldomblues.com

A Southern Hospitality Restaurant Group Property

Table of
CONTENTS

Scenes from the 2006
Who's Who in Black Detroit® Unveiling Reception

MEET THE TEAM

C. Sunny Martin
Founder & CEO

Carter Womack
Regional VP
Detroit Associate Publisher

Ophelia Twine-Henry

Fred Peeples

Marsha A. Brogdon

WHO'S who
PUBLISHING CO., LLC

Ernie Sullivan
Senior Partner

Paula Gray
VP Customer Care

Monica Lehman
Business Manager

Tamara Allen
Production Manager

Nathan Wylder
Senior Editor

Melanie Diggs
Executive Editor

Christina Llewellyn
Production Assistant
Graphic Designer

Diane Winters
Graphic Designer

Monica Sherchan
Graphic Designer

Sarah Waite
Webmaster

Adam DeDent
Copy Editor

Rachel Bobak
Copy Editor

Sarah Longacre
Receptionist

Alisha Martin
Executive Assistant

CORPORATE OFFICE
1650 Lake Shore Drive, Suite 250 • Columbus, Ohio 43204 • (614) 481-7300
Visit Our Web Site - www.whoswhopublishing.com

THIS BOOK WAS MADE POSSIBLE BY THE GENEROUS SUPPORT OF OUR

SPONSORS

PLATINUM SPONSORS

WHO'S who
OFFICIAL AIR LINE

Marriott.
DETROIT
AT THE RENAISSANCE CENTER

SHRG
Southern Hospitality Restaurant Group

DELTA

DIAMOND SPONSORS

CHRYSLER

National City.

Chrysler Financial

EMERALD SPONSORS

Wayne County
Robert A. Ficano
Wayne County Executive

Blue Cross Blue Shield of Michigan

A nonprofit corporation and independent licensee of the Blue Cross and Blue Shield Association

UNVEILING RECEPTION SPONSORS

OnWheels INCORPORATED

TRINITY HEALTH
Novi, Michigan

DBE

nielsen

Huntington

MEDIA PARTNERS

RADIO ONE
THE URBAN RADIO SPECIALIST

comcast.

MIX 92.3
WWW.MIX923FM.COM

MICHIGAN CHRONICLE

Foreword by
FRANK FOUNTAIN

I t is my privilege to welcome you to the second edition of *Who's Who In Black Detroit*®, where you will be introduced to people who are actively working to improve the quality of life in Detroit.

We just marked the 40th anniversary of that infamous night in July of 1967 when Detroit erupted in flames and violence, fueled by anger over deep poverty and isolation, the destruction of black neighborhoods, and the brutality that blacks endured from the police.

Five days came and went, in which the city experienced some of the deadliest and most destructive riots in U.S. history. More than 43 died, 1,100 injured and 7,000 arrested. The National Guard, as well as the Army's 82nd Airborne, was mobilized, and at least 2,000 buildings burned to the ground. The riots that happened that summer set the stage for a climate so tense, even 40 years later, our community still seeks to resolve the many problems that led to that fateful night in order to enhance the lives of all people who call Detroit home.

Our city has made remarkable progress in the past 25-30 years in addressing those problems. Yet today we face a new kind of threat, an economic threat that puts our futures at risk. Our city and our state are in dire financial straits. The auto industry, which turned the wheel of the local economy for decades, faces a challenge unlike any seen in decades as it transforms to compete in a global economy. Sometimes it takes a series of crises to see clearly what must be done to secure our future.

We must join together to affect change. The black community has gotten that message loud and clear. Our resources have been mobilized, and organizations from across the spectrum are working together. Businesses, laborers, churches, the political community and the social community have united with a clear shared vision: let's revitalize our city, our region and our state. We are getting it done with strong support from the mayor, county officials and state government. The future of our region is at stake, and we must position ourselves to make a comeback. I, for one, am optimistic about the future of Detroit. I see great things happening in our city and throughout the region. Many believe the city's future begins along the rapidly developing banks of the Detroit River, with the three-and-a-half-mile RiverWalk, complete with marinas, wetlands and even a carousel.

Also along the riverfront, Watermark Detroit, a $60 million development headed by NBA Hall of Famer and former Detroit Piston Dave Bing, promises 112 apartments, condos and townhouses. General Motors Corp. is planning 600 luxury condominiums in the shadow of its steel and glass world headquarters at the Renaissance Center. Selling for up to $1 million each, this ambitious project is one that will change the face of downtown. For more than ten years now, billions of dollars have been invested throughout the city by the corporate business and foundation communities in a wide range of projects that include corporate headquarters, new museums, new hospitals and world-class sporting events.

Moving away from the riverfront, two new stadiums sit side-by-side while three Detroit casinos attract visitors and new business. Hotels are going up again. Even the old Book Cadillac Hotel is being reclaimed.

Our neighborhoods, too, are on the move. In Detroit, more than 3,300 abandoned or burned out structures have been demolished over the past two years, and the city also has a five-year, $225 million neighborhood improvement plan.

The city is pushing to attract new, technology-based companies to its TechTown area near the Wayne State University campus, to join nearby Compuware, who chose Detroit for its corporate headquarters. Compuware's move to Detroit was made possible only by the reclamation of the former Hudson Building, where a part of the company now sits.

The business community along with countless other organizations has been working in earnest to revitalize the city. One D: Transforming Regional Detroit is a unifying force in that effort. It unites six Detroit-area groups in the quest to revitalize the region. It's comprised of New Detroit, the Detroit Regional Chamber, the Detroit Metro Convention & Visitors Bureau, Detroit Renaissance, United Way for Southeastern Michigan and the Cultural Alliance of Southeastern Michigan. One D allows for the collaboration necessary to ensure transformation is possible in a scope that encompasses the entire southeast Michigan region. It's focusing on establishing mass transit, restructuring the economy, and improving education and the region's quality of life.

A lot of this important work is being done by African-American leaders in government, business, education and the community. With so many talented men and women engaged in turning the tide to a new day, I believe that Detroit and the entire southeast Michigan region has never had a more promising future than today.

Yes, we are in the midst of what some would say are dire circumstances. But it is because of those circumstances that all forces have come together for the common good. Together, we have the collective intellect, the tenacity and the energy to turn the city, region and state around and put us on course to be one of the premier urban centers in the world.

The men and women you will read about in **Who's Who In Black Detroit** are the ones shaping our future. The accomplishments of each individual in this book tell a story that documents the perseverance of a people and the resurgence of a city. When you take this book home, put it to good use; give it to your kids. In it, they will discover real men and women just like them who succeeded against the odds, are making a difference in the lives of people and changing the face of their communities. In fact, they are changing the world. I hope that this book will be an encouragement to you as we continue to work together to revitalize our city.

Sincerely,

Frank Fountain

Frank Fountain
President, The Chrysler Foundation
Senior Vice President, Chrysler

Wayne County is proud to acnowledge the acomplisments and leadership of today

Please join us as we **Salute our Black Leadership**

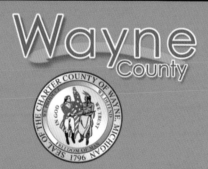

"Congratulations to all of this years honorees you are amoung the Best and Brightest, providing inspiration to us all."

Robert A. Ficano Wayne County Executive

w w w . w a y n e c o u n t y . c o m

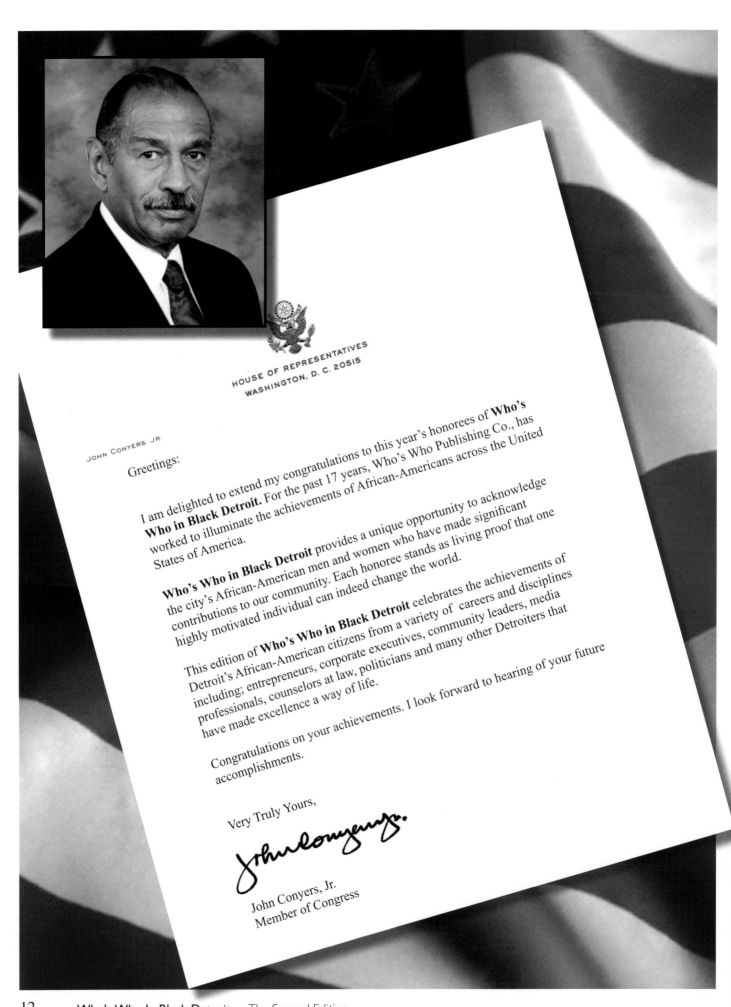

HOUSE OF REPRESENTATIVES
WASHINGTON, D. C. 20515

JOHN CONYERS, JR.

Greetings:

I am delighted to extend my congratulations to this year's honorees of **Who's Who in Black Detroit.** For the past 17 years, Who's Who Publishing Co., has worked to illuminate the achievements of African-Americans across the United States of America.

Who's Who in Black Detroit provides a unique opportunity to acknowledge the city's African-American men and women who have made significant contributions to our community. Each honoree stands as living proof that one highly motivated individual can indeed change the world.

This edition of **Who's Who in Black Detroit** celebrates the achievements of Detroit's African-American citizens from a variety of careers and disciplines including; entrepreneurs, corporate executives, community leaders, media professionals, counselors at law, politicians and many other Detroiters that have made excellence a way of life.

Congratulations on your achievements. I look forward to hearing of your future accomplishments.

Very Truly Yours,

John Conyers, Jr.
Member of Congress

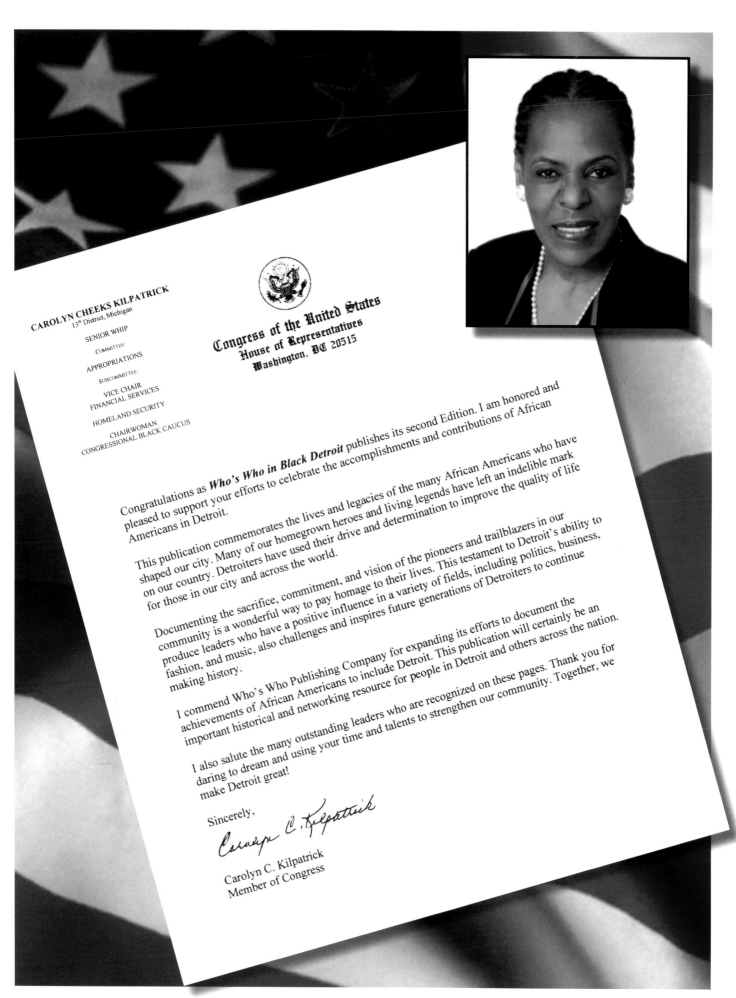

CAROLYN CHEEKS KILPATRICK
13th District, Michigan

SENIOR WHIP

COMMITTEE:

APPROPRIATIONS

SUBCOMMITTEE:

VICE CHAIR
FINANCIAL SERVICES

HOMELAND SECURITY

CHAIRWOMAN
CONGRESSIONAL BLACK CAUCUS

Congress of the United States
House of Representatives
Washington, DC 20515

Congratulations as *Who's Who in Black Detroit* publishes its second Edition. I am honored and pleased to support your efforts to celebrate the accomplishments and contributions of African Americans in Detroit.

This publication commemorates the lives and legacies of the many African Americans who have shaped our city. Many of our homegrown heroes and living legends have left an indelible mark on our country. Detroiters have used their drive and determination to improve the quality of life for those in our city and across the world.

Documenting the sacrifice, commitment, and vision of the pioneers and trailblazers in our community is a wonderful way to pay homage to their lives. This testament to Detroit's ability to produce leaders who have a positive influence in a variety of fields, including politics, business, fashion, and music, also challenges and inspires future generations of Detroiters to continue making history.

I commend Who's Who Publishing Company for expanding its efforts to document the achievements of African Americans to include Detroit. This publication will certainly be an important historical and networking resource for people in Detroit and others across the nation.

I also salute the many outstanding leaders who are recognized on these pages. Thank you for daring to dream and using your time and talents to strengthen our community. Together, we make Detroit great!

Sincerely,

Carolyn C. Kilpatrick

Carolyn C. Kilpatrick
Member of Congress

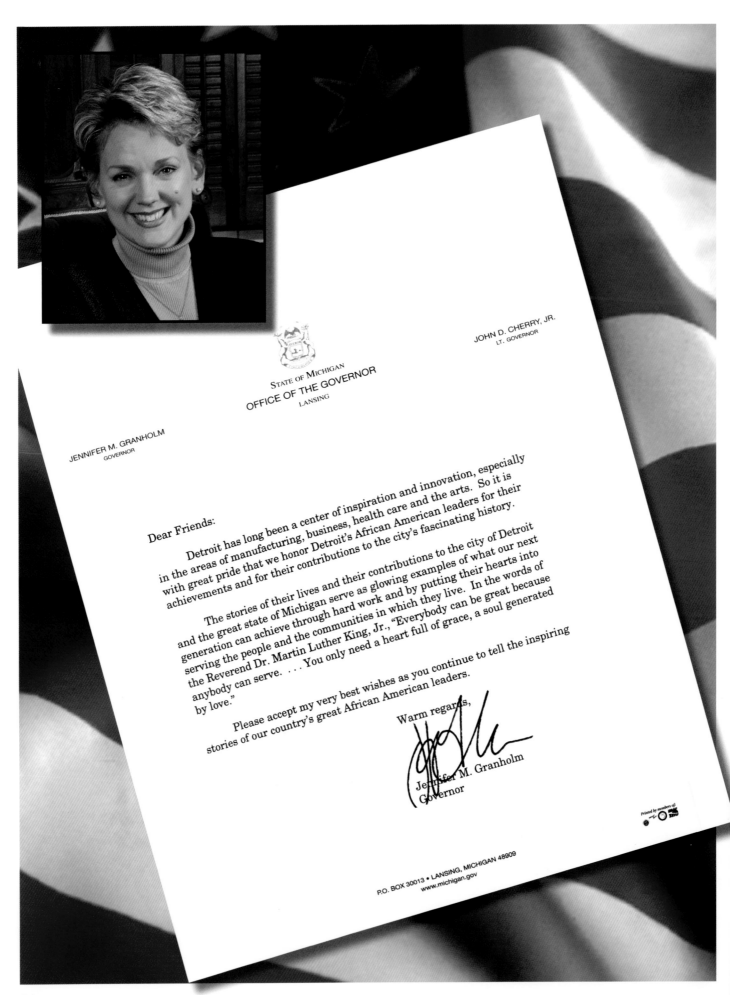

JOHN D. CHERRY, JR.
LT. GOVERNOR

STATE OF MICHIGAN
OFFICE OF THE GOVERNOR
LANSING

JENNIFER M. GRANHOLM
GOVERNOR

Dear Friends:

Detroit has long been a center of inspiration and innovation, especially in the areas of manufacturing, business, health care and the arts. So it is with great pride that we honor Detroit's African American leaders for their achievements and for their contributions to the city's fascinating history.

The stories of their lives and their contributions to the city of Detroit and the great state of Michigan serve as glowing examples of what our next generation can achieve through hard work and by putting their hearts into serving the people and the communities in which they live. In the words of the Reverend Dr. Martin Luther King, Jr., "Everybody can be great because anybody can serve. . . . You only need a heart full of grace, a soul generated by love."

Please accept my very best wishes as you continue to tell the inspiring stories of our country's great African American leaders.

Warm regards,

Jennifer M. Granholm
Governor

P.O. BOX 30013 • LANSING, MICHIGAN 48909
www.michigan.gov

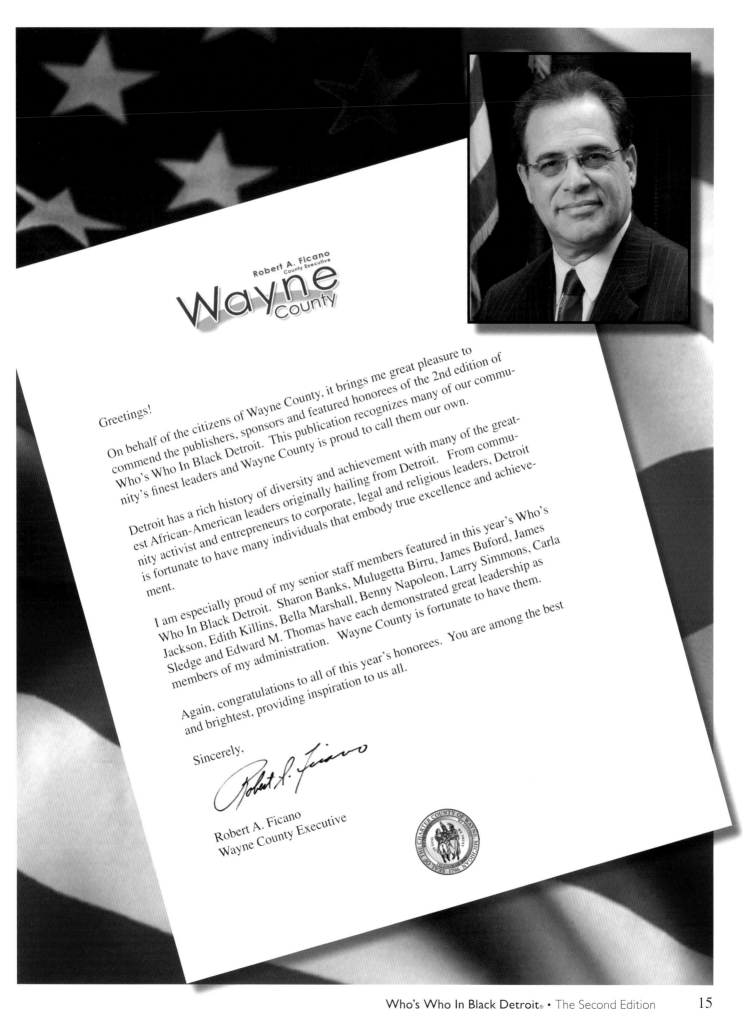

Wayne County

Robert A. Ficano
County Executive

Greetings!

On behalf of the citizens of Wayne County, it brings me great pleasure to commend the publishers, sponsors and featured honorees of the 2nd edition of Who's Who In Black Detroit. This publication recognizes many of our community's finest leaders and Wayne County is proud to call them our own.

Detroit has a rich history of diversity and achievement with many of the greatest African-American leaders originally hailing from Detroit. From community activist and entrepreneurs to corporate, legal and religious leaders, Detroit is fortunate to have many individuals that embody true excellence and achievement.

I am especially proud of my senior staff members featured in this year's Who's Who In Black Detroit. Sharon Banks, Mulugetta Birru, James Buford, James Jackson, Edith Killins, Bella Marshall, Benny Napoleon, Larry Simmons, Carla Sledge and Edward M. Thomas have each demonstrated great leadership as members of my administration. Wayne County is fortunate to have them.

Again, congratulations to all of this year's honorees. You are among the best and brightest, providing inspiration to us all.

Sincerely,

Robert A. Ficano
Wayne County Executive

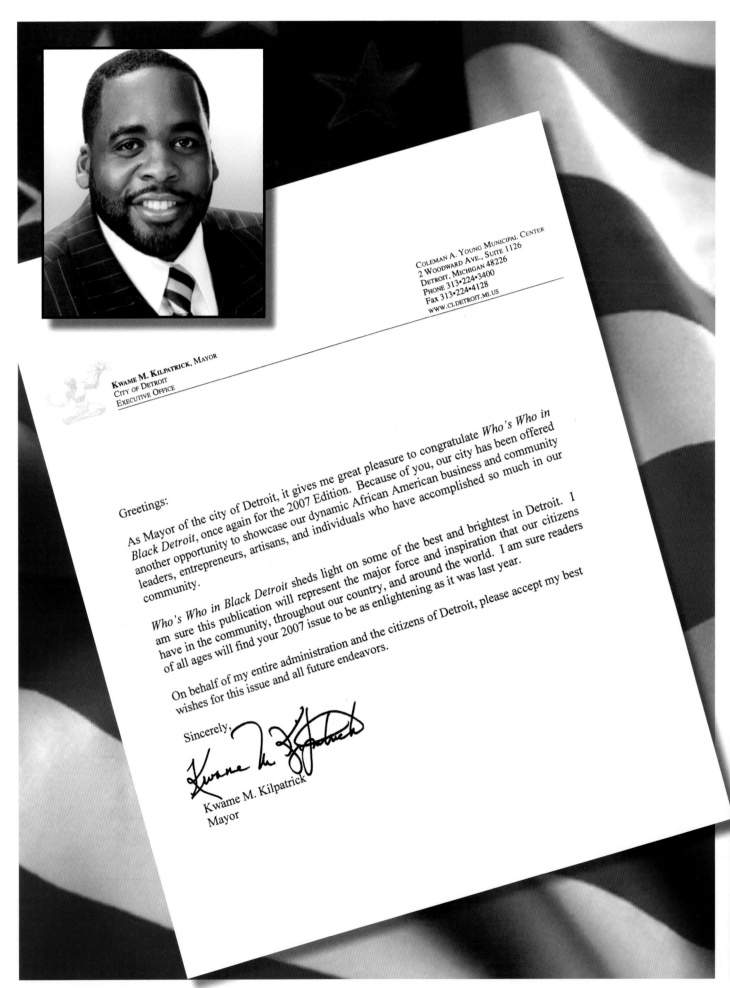

COLEMAN A. YOUNG MUNICIPAL CENTER
2 WOODWARD AVE., SUITE 1126
DETROIT, MICHIGAN 48226
PHONE 313•224•3400
FAX 313•224•4128
WWW.CI.DETROIT.MI.US

KWAME M. KILPATRICK, MAYOR
CITY OF DETROIT
EXECUTIVE OFFICE

Greetings:

As Mayor of the city of Detroit, it gives me great pleasure to congratulate *Who's Who in Black Detroit*, once again for the 2007 Edition. Because of you, our city has been offered another opportunity to showcase our dynamic African American business and community leaders, entrepreneurs, artisans, and individuals who have accomplished so much in our community.

Who's Who in Black Detroit sheds light on some of the best and brightest in Detroit. I am sure this publication will represent the major force and inspiration that our citizens have in the community, throughout our country, and around the world. I am sure readers of all ages will find your 2007 issue to be as enlightening as it was last year.

On behalf of my entire administration and the citizens of Detroit, please accept my best wishes for this issue and all future endeavors.

Sincerely,

Kwame M. Kilpatrick
Mayor

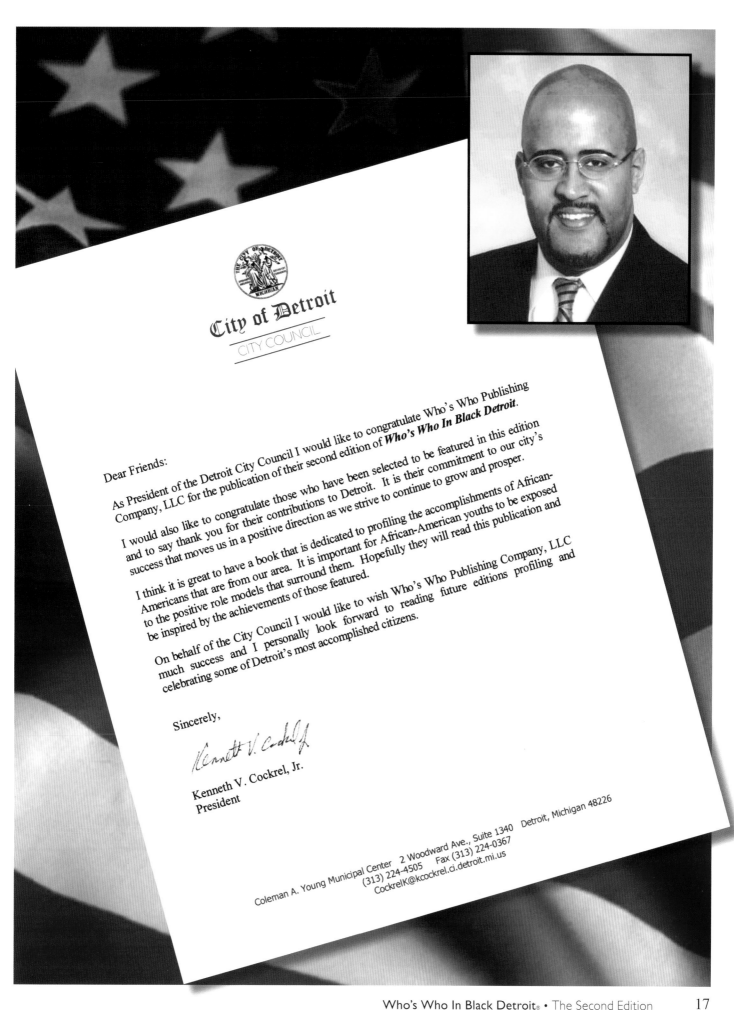

City of Detroit

CITY COUNCIL

Dear Friends:

As President of the Detroit City Council I would like to congratulate Who's Who Publishing Company, LLC for the publication of their second edition of **Who's Who In Black Detroit**.

I would also like to congratulate those who have been selected to be featured in this edition and to say thank you for their contributions to Detroit. It is their commitment to our city's success that moves us in a positive direction as we strive to continue to grow and prosper.

I think it is great to have a book that is dedicated to profiling the accomplishments of African-Americans that are from our area. It is important for African-American youths to be exposed to the positive role models that surround them. Hopefully they will read this publication and be inspired by the achievements of those featured.

On behalf of the City Council I would like to wish Who's Who Publishing Company, LLC much success and I personally look forward to reading future editions profiling and celebrating some of Detroit's most accomplished citizens.

Sincerely,

Kenneth V. Cockrel, Jr.
President

Coleman A. Young Municipal Center   2 Woodward Ave., Suite 1340   Detroit, Michigan 48226
(313) 224-4505   Fax (313) 224-0367
CockrelK@kcockrel.ci.detroit.mi.us

WHAT'S NEXT?

Being named Who's Who In Black Detroit more than an honor, it's a challenge. Your accomplishments and achievements got you here, but it's what you'll do tomorrow that is really exciting. We salute you for being named Who's Who, and can't wait to see what you do next.

That's a mission worth investing in.

huntington.com

A bank invested in people.®

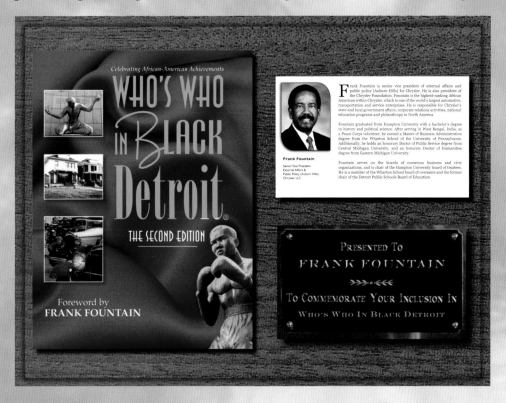

MIX 92.3

www.mix923fm.com

The Steve Harvey Morning Show
Mon-Fri 6am-10am

"The Mid-day MIX"
with Frankie Darcell
Mon-Fri 10am-3pm

"Love, Lust & Lies"
with Michael Baisden
Mon-Fri 3pm-7pm

"The Sweat Hotel"
with Keith Sweat
Mon-Thu 7pm-12am,

All Night MIX"
with Tracey McCaskill
Tue-Fri 3am-6am, Sat9am-12pm

"Back Jam" with Donafay
Fri 7pm-12am

"Midnight MIX" with Keil Lamont
Tue-Thu 12am-3am
Sat-Sun 12noon-3pm

Chris Boyd
Sat 3pm-7pm

"Saturday Night Live"
with Gerald McBride
Sat 7pm-12am

Rhythm & Praise
with Pastor Marvin Winans
Sun 6a-11a

"Talk of the Town"
with Frankie Darcell
Sun 11am-12pm

Ramona Prater
Sun 3pm-7pm

"Sunday Night Cruisin'
with Foody"
Sun 7pm-12am

Steve Harvey

Frankie Darcell

Michael Baisden

Keith Sweat

Keil Lamont   Donafay   Chris Boyd   Tracey McCaskill   Gerald McBride   Foody   Ramona Prater   Marvin Winans

Classic Soul & Today's R&B

A MESSAGE FROM THE
Founder
& CEO
C. SUNNY MARTIN

"Not failure, but low aim is sin." – Dr. Benjamin E. Mays

Detroit has always embodied the best of the human spirit, whether it is in the boardroom, the entertainment stage, the basketball court or in the awesome struggle for civil rights. People from Detroit have an unquenchable thirst to represent their homegrown style and skills to people all over the world.

For African Americans who visit Detroit, it always seems like home. Great food, cutting-edge fashions and a mix of extremely talented folks make Detroit an unforgettable place to visit. For example, the Charles H. Wright Museum of African American History is an extremely well-thought-out repository of black history.

The African-American entrepreneurial spirit evidenced through Don Coleman, Bill Picard, Don Barden and Dave Bing has certainly put Detroit on the map nationally. These men have figured out how to make the best of their God-given talents to drive commerce and sit at the table as major players.

Black folks have always had great black voices to represent them socially, politically and legally. From the late Mayor Coleman A. Young to today's leaders, such as Mayor Kwame Kilpatrick, Congresswoman Carolyn Cheeks Kilpatrick, Congressman John Conyers and Judge Damon Keith, Detroit has been blessed by their vision and community commitment.

There is a new renaissance taking place in Detroit. I'm sure that during this exciting time in the city's rebirth Generation Next will yield new leadership and dynamic new ways to represent Detroit on a world stage. It is imperative that we guide them and assist them to learn the lessons from the past so they can catapult Detroit to even greater heights!

Live life to the fullest,

[signature]

Criteria for Inclusion

Who's Who In Black Detroit® is an opportunity for us to afford a measure of recognition to the men and women who have made their mark in their specific occupations, professions, or in service to others in the Detroit community.

A sincere effort was made to include those whose positions or accomplishments in their chosen fields are significant and whose contributions to community affairs, whether citywide or on the neighborhood level, have improved the quality of life for all of us.

The names of those brief biographies included in this edition were compiled from customary sources of information. Lists of a wide variety were consulted and every effort was made to reach all whose stature or civic activities merited their inclusion.

In today's mobile society, no such publication could ever claim to be complete; some who should be included could not be reached or chose not to respond, and for that we offer our apologies. Constraints of time, space and awareness are thus responsible for other omissions, and not a lack of good intentions on the part of the publisher. Our goal was to document the accomplishments of many people from various occupational disciplines.

An invitation to participate in the publication was extended at the discretion of the publisher. Biographies were invited to contribute personal and professional data, with only the information freely submitted to be included. The editors have made a sincere effort to present an accurate distillation of the data, and to catch errors whenever possible. However, the publisher cannot assume any responsibility for the accuracy of the information submitted.

There was no charge for inclusion in this publication and inclusion was not guaranteed; an annual update is planned. Comments and other concerns should be addressed to:

C. Sunny Martin, CEO
Who's Who Publishing Co., LLC
1650 Lake Shore Drive, Suite 250
Columbus, Ohio 43204
Phone: (614) 481-7300

E-Mail: sunny@whoswhopublishing.com
www.whoswhopublishing.com

A MESSAGE FROM THE

Detroit

ASSOCIATE PUBLISHER

CARTER D. WOMACK

We are "building bridges" as our story continues. This is our second edition of **Who's Who In Black Detroit**®, and it is a continuation of the story that we started to tell in our inaugural 2006 edition. This edition brings to my mind the poem by Will Allen Dromgoole, "The Bridge Builder," because we have a special feature section that salutes Living Legends in the African-American community and the Detroit community at large. Truly the story continues as we salute these men and women who were and still are "building bridges."

In their lifetimes, these men and women have been subjected to racism, sexism, hard work, and denied the rights that were given and granted to others simply because they were black. This did not stop them from getting an education, participating in civil rights marches, or standing up for what is right and just. It did not stop them from supporting their families, and working in low-income jobs as they looked up to the heavens for bigger and better things. Their struggles and experiences lit flames of hope, faith and determination in their lives and the lives of their families. These men and women remind me of the old man in the poem who knew that he had a job to do and it needed to be done well. He also knew that he had a responsibility to the next generation, to help them be successful and build a strong bridge for future generations to cross. Our Living Legends have done just that—laid the foundation and built not just one, but many bridges that have allowed all of us to cross with less fear at twilight dim. Life for them and many like them "ain't been on crystal stairs," but because of them, I am and we all are able to celebrate African-American achievement in our great city of Detroit.

I want to thank Frank Fountain for his support and agreeing to write the foreword for this edition. To my local publishing team: Ophelia Twine-Henry, Fred Peeples, Marsha Brogdon, Monica Morgan, Donald James and Damon Autry, the success of this book would not have been possible without your support, thank you!

Please enjoy this second edition of **Who's Who In Black Detroit**®. Share it with others, for truly, the story continues as we build bridges for others to cross.

Sincerely,

Detroit Medical Center Living Legends

Detroit Medical Center offers an environment of mutual respect, cultural
diversity and healthcare excellence, where everyone has the opportunity to thrive and excel.
We are proud to be represented by these talented and influential African American physicians.

Barbara Anderson	Alma George	Ronald Little
William Anderson	George Gibson	Haywood Mabin
Arthur Bodie	Frank Glover	Nathan Pearson
James Brown	Gwen Gordon	Carol Pearson
Waldo Cain	George Hill	Alex Pickens
James Carter	Melvin Hollowell	Robert Sims
Frank Clark	Charles Innis	Natalia Tanner
Jack Clark	Frank Jackson	Lorna Thomas
Volna Clermont	William Jackson	Clarence Vaughn
James Collins	Cecil Jonas	Charles Whitten
Julius Coombs	William Kyle	Melisande Womack
Walter Everett	Felix J. Liddell	Claude Young
John Franklin	George Lightbourne	

DETROIT MEDICAL CENTER

1-888-DMC-2500
www.dmc.org

CHILDREN'S HOSPITAL OF MICHIGAN • DETROIT RECEIVING HOSPITAL
HARPER UNIVERSITY HOSPITAL • HURON VALLEY-SINAI HOSPITAL
HUTZEL WOMEN'S HOSPITAL • KRESGE EYE INSTITUTE
MICHIGAN ORTHOPAEDIC SPECIALTY HOSPITAL
REHABILITATION INSTITUTE OF MICHIGAN • SINAI-GRACE HOSPITAL

AAA's *The Safety Patroller* statue is a permanent symbol of our commitment to community service. The strength of our more than 1.6 million members supports the AAA School Safety Patrol and many other outreach programs and safety initiatives.

Our mission is clear: to educate, advocate, and involve the community in solutions that improve the safety and quality of life in all of the communities we serve.

Extending Our Reach to the Community

The Safety Patroller,© 1997 by Ed Dwight, an original work commissioned by The Auto Club Group

CHARLES H. WRIGHT

A SPECIAL TRIBUTE TO

The WRIGHT Man
Established Detroit's

MUSEUM OF AFRICAN-AMERICAN HISTORY

By Bamidele Agbasegbe Demerson, Director of Exhibitions and Research
Patrina Chatman, Curator of Exhibitions
Charles H. Wright Museum of African American History

Charles H. Wright, M.D., (September 20, 1918-March 7, 2002), visionary scholar, activist, and trailblazer, established Detroit's Musuem of African American History in 1965.

CHARLES H. WRIGHT, M.D. (September 20, 1918-March 7, 2002) achieved great success and satisfaction in his career as a physician. He also gained distinction as a professor of medicine at Wayne State University in Detroit, Michigan. As an accomplished author, he wrote articles for medical journals, penned books and articles on contemporary social history, and composed literary works on the dilemmas faced by humanity. Wright also supported causes related to social justice, quality medical care and education. Most regard him as a prominent obstetrician and gynecologist who delivered more than 7,000 babies in the Metropolitan Detroit community. However, many believe that among his greatest accomplishments was the establishment of a museum to educate the public about the history and culture of African Americans. Such an institution would illuminate the important role of blacks in the growth of this nation.

A native of Dothan, Alabama, Wright experienced the racial caste order of the Jim Crow era. Nevertheless, his religious and industrious parents instilled a sense of self-determination and self-reliance that empowered him throughout his lifetime. Wright completed undergraduate studies at Alabama State College, where he attained a Bachelor of Science degree in 1939; he later earned a medical degree from Meharry Medical School in 1943. During the course of his medical career, the physician was affiliated with Harlem Hospital in New York City; Cleveland City Hospital in Cleveland, Ohio; Woman's (now Hutzel), Harper-Grace, and Sinai hospitals in Detroit, Michigan. Each experience revealed the pernicious impact of social stratification in America, particularly in the access to medical care. Indeed Wright once remarked, "I never forgot the blatant racism of my Alabama origins, nor was I lulled into complacency with its more subtle manifestations in the North." He was compelled to social activism.

> "I never forgot the blatant racism of my Alabama origins, nor was I lulled into complacency with its more subtle manifestations in the North."

Wright demonstrated an abiding concern for abolishing racial restrictions and insuring human dignity. He traveled widely within the United States as well as in countries in Africa, Europe, South and Central America, and the Caribbean. During his journeys, the dedicated physician surveyed health care needs, provided medical care, visited cultural institutions and attended conferences. These field expeditions reinforced his appreciation for the interconnectedness of the struggles within the black world. He shared his newfound knowledge in many lectures delivered and articles published at home and abroad. For example, Wright spoke about "Medicine in Cuba" to the Detroit Medical Society; and in fluent Spanish, presented "La Lucha del Hombre Negro Para Libertad en los Estados Unidos" (The Struggle of the Black Man for Freedom in the United States) at The First Congress of Black Culture of the Americas in Cali, Columbia, South America. His published writings included both medical and social concerns such as "Opposition to the World Medical Assembly in South Africa, 1985," in *Journal of the National Medical Association*; and "Physicians Must Be Reminded of Their Economic Responsibilities," in *Michigan Medicine*.

While visiting West Africa—specifically towns and villages in Sierra Leone, Liberia, Dahomey (now Benin), and Nigeria—Wright would have seen public ceremonies at shrines, and rituals at private altars housing accoutrements that reflected long-held traditions. He visited small museums where communities made efforts to preserve their heritage. Inspired by their endeavors, he began to envision such an institution for African Americans in Detroit. An excursion to a memorial in Copenhagen, Denmark, which commemorated the role of Danish resistance workers during World War II, further motivated Wright. He realized the necessity of building institutions that ensured an accurate "first-voice" transmission of a people's history to future generations.

With the support of 32 civic-minded members of the community, Wright's dream of creating a museum became a reality in 1965. At that time, the doctor and his family resided at 1549 West Grand Boulevard. This location also served as his medical office. Given Wright's determination

The building at 1549 West Grand Boulevard, once Dr. Wright's residence and office, served as the original home of the Museum from 1965 to 1987.

to establish an enduring institution, it is not surprising that the basement of this building became the original home of the International Afro-American Museum. Later, when he moved his home and office to different locations, the once cramped Museum occupied the vacated upper levels of the unit, and thereafter expanded to include the adjacent house. During its formative years, the doctor contributed passion, time and financial resources to the development of the institution. In effect, Wright became the curator, historian, manager and chief promoter. A masterful organizer, he encouraged large numbers of people to volunteer their time in service to the growing Museum.

As an outreach project, Wright refurbished a 30-foot trailer as a "mobile museum." Operated by volunteers, its inaugural exhibition, *The History of Africa*, opened at the 1967 Michigan State Fair. Of the many exhibitions developed for the mobile unit, the most popular was one that focused on the accomplishments of African-American inventors. The Museum presented such developments as the steam engine lubricator by railroad employee Elijah "the real" McCoy, and prototypes of the traffic light and gas mask by Garrett Morgan. This exhibition charted a pathway into territory that in those years, no other museum dared to conceive or deemed worthy as a curatorial initiative. Thus, at a time when the civil rights movement made significant strides to end racial prejudices, stereotypes and discriminatory practices aimed at limiting African-American possibilities, the exhibition on black inventors also made significant statements. First, to the American society it demonstrated the phenomenal achievements of those who persevered in spite of racial adversity. Secondly, it dismissed a popular stereotype that African Americans were not mentally suited to work in the fields of science and technology. Thirdly, it served as a challenge and an encouragement to black public school children, especially in Detroit, that they had the capabilities to excel.

> *Thirdly, it served as a challenge and an encouragement to black public school children, especially in Detroit, that they had the capabilities to excel.*

In other words, mounting the exhibition was as much an astute political act as it was a significant curatorial effort.

Throughout the next two decades, this mobile unit traveled to schoolyards, church grounds and shopping malls. With this itinerary, the mobile unit reached a largely non-museum-going population. In doing so, the fledgling Museum gained community interest, support and an expanded audience for its exhibitions and educational programs, many of which were held at off-site venues. By 1975, the institution became known as the Afro-American Museum of Detroit, and on the eve of its 1987 move to a new, city-owned facility in the Cultural Center, the name changed again; it became the Museum of African American History. The growth and development of the institution was without question linked to community fundraising efforts that included fish fries, golf outings and art auctions. Clubs and organizations made pledges. Young students in the Detroit Public Schools participated in the buy-a-brick campaign for the Museum's new home. With no set price per brick, the democratized approach encouraged all to participate in building an institution that enshrined their heritage. And while the children bought bricks, the adults could join the Million Dollar Club. Wright was a fundraising strategist *par excellence.* He reasoned that although no one person in the community had $1 million to offer, with 1,000 persons each giving $1,000, the community could collectively raise money that was beyond the means of individuals. Of course the Museum also garnered support in the form of grants from government entities, foundations and corporations.

The move from the connected units on West Grand Boulevard to a new 22,000-square-foot building at 301 Frederick (later designated Frederick Douglass) was a major step. Yet, soon after the Museum settled into the location, some considered the space too small and advocated for a larger and more impressive structure. Wright prudently expressed concerns regarding the tremendous funding required for the operation, maintenance and professional staffing of such a venture. Even so, he recognized the sentiments of those favoring further expansion. The electorate of the City of Detroit authorized the sale of bonds for the design and construction of a new edifice nearby, at 315 East Warren

The Museum in 1987 relocated to the Detroit Cultural Center where it occupied a new building designed by Sims-Varner & Associates. The Museum remained at 301 Frederick Douglass for ten years.

Avenue. In 1997 the Museum moved once more, this time to a 120,000-square-foot facility. Renamed in honor of the founder in 1998, the Charles H. Wright Museum of African American History became a major icon anchored in the Detroit Cultural Center.

Many years ago Wright cogently articulated, "We are dedicated to one of the most important tasks of our times, to ensure that generations… to come, will be aware of, and take pride in the history of their forebears and their remarkable struggle for freedom."

In 1997 the Museum moved to 315 East Warren Avenue. The new edifice, a major icon in the Cultural Center, was also designed by Sims-Varner & Associates.

This credo continues to guide the exhibitions, educational offerings and public programs of the Museum. Indeed, the Museum is the largest and one of the oldest institutions dedicated to telling the stories of blacks in the United States, other parts of the Diaspora, and the African continent. Over time, its exhibitions and educational initiatives have focused on such diverse topics as African art and architecture, the African presence in Mexico, the Haitian revolution, the Underground Railroad in Michigan, Paul Robeson, blacks in the U.S. military, spiritual traditions and much more. And the annual three-day African World Festival, organized by the Museum on the Downtown waterfront, has long been regarded as a stellar celebration of the music, art and cuisine of blacks globally. Not surprisingly, many consider that the Wright Museum sets a standard among cultural institutions.

Far from content with establishing a black museum only in Detroit, Wright wanted to support other such institutions as they emerged in various cities throughout the country. Partnering with Dr. Margaret Burroughs, co-founder of the DuSable Museum of African American History in Chicago, Illinois, he also organized the forerunner of the Association of African American Museums. They are affectionately known as the "mother and father" of the African American Museum Movement, which has been a catalyst for establishing and supporting more than 200 black museums and cultural institutions nationally.

Charles H. Wright was a scholar, activist, cultural trailblazer and ambassador for the promotion of African-American history. This beloved visionary will always be remembered as the "Wright" man who established Detroit's Museum of African American History.

> *"We are dedicated to one of the most important tasks of our times, to ensure that generations… to come, will be aware of, and take pride in the history of their forebears and their remarkable struggle for freedom."*

This essay has been developed in part from the Memorial, published by the Charles H. Wright Museum upon the passing of its founder; the "Charles H. Wright Museum of African American History Fact Sheet" that is part of the institution's press packet; and the indispensable book, *The Wright Man: A Biography,* authored by Wilbur C. Rich and Roberta Hughes Wright, published in 1999 by CHARRO BOOKS of Southfield/Detroit.

The quotations by Dr. Wright are from *The Wright Man*.

All photos courtesy of the *Charles H. Wright Museum of African American History*.

RADIO ONE DETROIT

Detroit's Best R&B from the 70's, 80's, and Motown

www.KissDetroit.com
Request Line: 313.298.1059

NEWSTALK 1200 WCHB AM

www.WCHB1200.com
Talk Line: 313.298.1200

HOT 102.7
interactive hip hop and r&b

www.Hot1027Detroit.com
Contests & Requests: 313.298.1027

3250 Franklin St.
Detroit, MI 48207

General Info: 313.259.2000
Fax Line: 313.259.7011

RADIO ONE
THE URBAN RADIO SPECIALIST!

DIVERSITY IS NOT JUST A HEADLINE.
IT'S THE FULL STORY.

Television viewing habits vary from person to person, household to household and city to city. As the TV ratings company, we work hard to accurately measure the differences in television viewership. That's why, at Nielsen, having a workforce reflective of these differences is a priority.

nielsen
· · · · · · ·
Every view counts.

National Newspaper Publishers Association
Publisher of the Year

Sam Logan

The Michigan Chronicle salutes Sam Logan, honored by the National Newspaper Publishers Association as 2007 Publisher of the Year. We congratulate him for his dedication to the Michigan Chronicle and the community it serves.

The National Newspaper Publishers Association (NNPA), also known as the Black Press of America, is a 67-year-old federation of more than 200 Black community newspapers.

VOICE OF THE COMMUNITY SINCE 1936

MICHIGAN CHRONICLE

Detroit's

LIVING
LEGENDS

- A DETROIT LIVING LEGEND -

BEATRICE WESSON

102 Years Old and Counting

By Donald James

Upon meeting Beatrice Wesson, it becomes amazingly clear that this lady is not your average 102-year-old centenarian. Her mind is sharp, her voice is strong, her words are knowledgeable, her demeanor is confident, her movements are sophisticated, and her handshake is impressive.

Do you want to talk with Wesson about the war in Iraq? How about the policies of President Theodore Roosevelt or those of President Bill Clinton? Can Senator Barack Obama win the presidency in 2008? What challenges did the NAACP face in 1925, or what are its present challenges? What were the real contributions of W.E.B. Dubois to black America? What were race relations like in Detroit in 1927 or 1947 or 1967? The Jena 6? If inquiring minds want to know, Wesson is ready to teach.

Born in Caddo Parish, Louisiana, on September 17, 1905, Wesson, whose maiden name was Williams, was the tenth of 12 children. She moved to Detroit on May 20, 1924, and began working as an elevator operator at the Fort Shelby Hotel on June 27, 1924.

Vastly aware of the brewing racial climate in Detroit and the nation, Wesson joined the Detroit Branch of the NAACP in 1925 to make a positive difference. She quickly demonstrated the ability to raise money for the organization, which supported the efforts of both local and national endeavors, most notably, the NAACP Legal Defense Fund. Wesson's effective communication skills made her successful at selling NAACP life memberships. She later was a key component in establishing the first Detroit NAACP Fight for Freedom Fund Dinner in 1956, which has become an annual event to raise money for the civil rights organization. Wesson, a life member of the NAACP, also served on the organization's board of directors for a number of years.

In 1935 Wesson joined the League of Women Voters of Detroit. Although she first voted in 1926, Wesson was concerned that other women, especially women of color, were not exercising their rights to vote, and were not fully informed on many issues facing the nation. "I joined the League because it was, and still is, a nonpartisan organization that has the ability to be influential in the political and legislative process in the country," says Wesson. "I continue to be better informed about government and political issues and candidates through my participation."

In 1940 Wesson married Maurice Wesson, a physician. Two children were born from their union, Leatrice and Maurice. Dr. Wesson died in 1973.

The beat, however, goes on for Beatrice Wesson. While this lady doesn't bother anyone, and won't allow anyone to bother her, Wesson's philosophy on living is simple. "I treat people the way I want to be treated," says Wesson. "I think for myself by forming my own opinions, but I always give and demand respect."

Wesson loves watching such informative television news outlets as CNN and CSPAN. An avid reader, she also keeps up on world issues by reading books on politics, social justice, and autobiographies and biographies written on political and social activists.

- A DETROIT LIVING LEGEND -

THE HONORABLE DAMON J. KEITH

A Crusader for Justice...He'll be the Judge of That

By Donald James

It's difficult not to be amazed when entering the chambers of the Honorable Damon J. Keith, judge of the United States Court of Appeals, Sixth Circuit. Upon stepping over its threshold, one is immediately inundated with hundreds of photographs mounted on the walls, all capturing an era, a movement and many of the people who shaped history during the last 50 years.

There are photos of Keith welcoming President Nelson Mandela of South Africa to Detroit; pictures of the judge with President John F. Kennedy at the White House; several still shots of Keith with Rosa Parks; and a few photos of him with Thurgood Marshall. Upon further observation, there are photos of the judge with Colin Powell, Aretha Franklin, Lena Horne, Bishop Tutu, Gov. Jennifer Granholm, Willie Horton, Muhammad Ali, Max Fisher, Coleman A. Young, Oprah Winfrey, and many more.

Walking deeper into the maze-shaped outer chambers and into the judge's back chambers, there are countless awards, honors, resolutions, framed historic news articles, earned and honorary degrees, as well as other cultural and legal artifacts, all systematically painting a picture of this living legend.

Although the impressive wall displays make a valiant effort to define Keith, perhaps the 1974 *Ebony* magazine article "Crusader for Justice," written about the judge, offers the best answer. The article is preserved and mounted over the inside doorway of Keith's private chambers. The article's headline is in big, bold black letters.

As a member of the federal judiciary since 1967, Keith has been a relentless crusader for justice when defending the U.S. Constitution and civil rights of all people. Over his long career on the bench, he has ruled on hundreds of cases against companies, governmental agencies, school districts and other entities, who have violated the United States Constitution. The case most associated with the judge, however, is known as "The Keith Case."

"That's the case where I told President Richard Nixon and Attorney General John Mitchell that they could not wire tap without prior judicial approval," recalls Keith. "The case went to the Supreme Court and the Supreme Court unanimously affirmed me."

Born and raised in Detroit, Keith developed a "total commitment to the struggle." He was also taught that one person can make a difference. After receiving a Bachelor of Arts degree from West Virginia State College in 1943, he went on to earn a juris doctorate degree from Howard University Law School, where he was elected chief judge of the Court of Peers. He also earned a Master of Laws degree from Wayne State University.

It's impossible to chronicle all the many accomplishments and contributions of Keith's long and distinguished career. However, The Damon J. Keith Law Collection of African-American Legal History, which is housed at Wayne State University, is a prime example of his deep commitment to freedom and justice for all. The collection, which was created to meet the need for a central repository for the nation's African-American legal history, is the only compilation of its kind in the United States.

- A DETROIT LIVING LEGEND -

THE HONORABLE
CAROLYN CHEEKS KILPATRICK

Dynamic and Influential Leadership

By Damon Autry

As a Detroit Public School teacher in the mid-1970s, Congresswoman Carolyn Cheeks Kilpatrick remembers watching and being moved by the historic keynote speech of the late Congresswoman Barbara Jordan during the 1976 Democratic National Convention. "She was a strong, tall and articulate black woman," Congresswoman Kilpatrick recalls. And though she followed Jordan's career for many years, watching the Texas congresswoman that evening was an epiphany. "I said that when my kids get older—which they didn't until I finally ran for office—I'm going to go into politics." Several years later, she was elected to the Michigan State House of Representatives and served there for 18 years, in the process becoming the first African-American woman to serve on the Michigan House Appropriations Committee—an experience that would serve her well down the road. Kilpatrick then decided to take her political proficiency to Washington, D.C., and in 1997 won her current seat in Congress.

For ten years, Kilpatrick has demonstrated her dynamic and influential leadership qualities as the representative of the 13th Congressional District of Michigan, and many of her colleagues on Capitol Hill have taken notice, as confirmed by her peers-appointed position to the powerful House Appropriations Committee. Kilpatrick helps authorize spending for all levels of the federal government in this capacity, a responsibility that includes handling an $850 billion budget. Such an important position allows Kilpatrick to maintain a finger on the pulse of the nation's checks and balances; it also ensures her home state isn't ignored financially. "I've brought home over half a billion dollars to the state of Michigan," Kilpatrick says proudly. "Being able

to bring dollars home is invigorating. We don't get our fair share of our tax dollars that we send to Washington; my job is to make sure that we do."

Kilpatrick's day-to-day roles and responsibilities as a congresswoman, coupled with all the required ancillary duties, keep her busy indeed: vice chair of the newly created Financial Services Subcommittee of the Appropriations Committee; chairwoman of the Congressional Black Caucus; Homeland Security Subcommittee member; various meetings with constituents, groups and committees—all shoehorned between an exhaustive travel schedule. While Kilpatrick truly enjoys representing and serving the people of the state of Michigan, she says there is nothing that matches the delight of being around her two children and five grandchildren. "They are the epitome of my being," she glows. Kilpatrick says watching her family grow is motivating, and she remains thankful for the opportunity to serve. "I'm blessed with what God and my family has given me, and what my supporters and staff have helped me to become." Kilpatrick will continue to urge young people to be leaders, and inform and remind them that the kind of America their children will live in depends on what they do now.

Kilpatrick received a bachelor's degree from Western Michigan University and later earned a master's degree from the University of Michigan. She has one daughter, Ayanna, and a son, Kwame, who is serving his second consecutive term as the mayor of Detroit. Kilpatrick is also the proud grandmother of five grandsons, including two sets of twins.

CHARLIE SANDERS

A Hall of Fame Class Act

By Donald James

As a 6'4", 230-pound rookie for the Detroit Lions in 1968, tight end Charlie Sanders was an unstoppable force. His combined attributes of speed, power, a superb leaping ability, great hands and punishing blocking skills, quickly earned him respect around the league, and a selection to the Pro Bowl in his first magical season. During a ten-year career with the Lions, Sanders went on to earn seven Pro Bowl honors.

After retiring in 1977, Sanders had amassed 336 career catches for 4,817 receiving yards, thus ranking him as one of the greatest tight ends in NFL history. Earlier this year (2007), Sanders was voted into the Pro Football Hall of Fame, an honor that is the crown jewel of his spectacular career. "I was more excited for my family than I was for myself," said Sanders, about his induction. "I was excited because of what it took from them for me to even play in the NFL."

A native of Richlands, North Carolina, Sanders didn't begin playing organized football until he was in the 10th grade, where he played both tight end and defensive end. After graduating from high school, Sanders was recruited by the University of Minnesota, where he excelled in both football and basketball. In 1968, the Detroit Lions made him their third round draft choice.

While the city of Detroit and the world of football have marveled at the greatness of the Hall of Famer, Sanders' magnificent football career as a Detroit Lion almost didn't happen. On the heels of the riots that ravaged the city of Detroit in 1967, Sanders, a country boy by his own admission, wasn't sure if the Motor City was the best place for him at the time. Although drafted by the Lions, Sanders was close to opting to play in Canada for the Toronto Argonauts. "I was about four miles from hitting the tunnel to Canada," says Sanders. "I stopped by the office of Russ Thomas, (the Lions' general manager at the time), on my way to Toronto. He made me another offer, and my agent convinced me to sign with Detroit. And as they say, the rest is history."

After his playing days were over in 1977, Sanders could have moved and lived anywhere in America. However, his love for Detroit and the Lions has kept him in the region for a total of 39 years, where he and his wife, Georgianna, have raised nine children. One of their six daughters is Mary Jo, a six-time professional boxing champion. Sanders and his wife have ten grandchildren and two great-grand kids.

Currently, Sanders serves as assistant pro personnel director for the Lions, which entails evaluating professional players in the NFL, designed to assist the team with free agency acquisitions and players available through the waiver wire. Additionally, Sanders stays busy doing charity work with children in the region through his Charlie Sanders Scholarship Foundation. He also authored a book in 2005 entitled, *Charlie Sanders' Tales from the Detroit Lions*, in which the Hall of Famer chronicles the many fascinating stories about his ten-year pro football career.

THE HONORABLE ERMA L. HENDERSON

Pioneer for Empowerment and Change

By Donald James

As the first African-American woman to be elected to Detroit City Council, and the first female, black or white, to become its president, the Honorable Erma L. Henderson has never backed away from a challenge. Elected in 1971, just four years after the infamous Detroit Riots of 1967, and two years before Coleman A. Young was voted Detroit's first black mayor, Henderson masterfully developed and sponsored hundreds of resolutions, ordinances and programs that addressed such issues as redlining, unemployment, domestic violence, civil rights and equal justice.

Additionally, Henderson was instrumental in establishing the City Planning Commission, Neighborhood Opportunity Fund, Mini Police Stations, Citizens District Councils and Farm-a-Lot. "I wanted to change the environment in which people lived," says Henderson, who holds a Master of Social Work degree from Wayne State University. "I wanted to take them from fear, worry, want and pain, caused by limited knowledge and other practices against people–especially African-American people–to places where they could be empowered." Henderson retired as president of City Council in 1989.

Before Henderson ever took the oath of office, she was already respected in communities and organizations around Detroit, as someone who cared about helping people politically, socially, spiritually and educationally. In fact, Henderson was an activist for change as far back as high school, when she demanded that the school's administration bring in black speakers, not just white speakers, to address general assemblies. Years later, she helped secure venues in Detroit for concert singing great Paul Robeson, when theaters across America barred him because of his political, civil and human rights beliefs.

With that type of mindset, it is not surprising that Henderson organized the Equal Justice Council, a court-watching and community monitoring mechanism of the criminal justice system in Detroit. She also organized and led numerous protests and demonstrations against police brutality, demanding a greater black representation in the Detroit Police Department. Henderson also founded the Women's Conference of Concerns, a powerbase entity in Southeastern Michigan, which is still going strong.

Henderson, also an ordained minister, is humbled to have helped so many people as a politician, minister, social worker, coalition builder and civil rights activist. During the last six decades, she has received a multitude of local, regional, state, national and international awards and honors.

However, on a hot and muggy afternoon in August of 2007, hundreds of people gathered at Cobo Hall in downtown Detroit, to honor and wish Henderson a happy 90th birthday. Many of those gathered were people who had benefited from Henderson's community, civic and political endeavors throughout the years. In addition, numerous political, civic, community, corporate, education and religious advocates and leaders, as well as family and friends, came to salute the Honorable Erma L. Henderson, easily one of Detroit's most beloved public figures, ever.

"I was overwhelmed by the marvelous accolades and honors that I received on that day," recalls Henderson, who moved to Detroit from Florida in 1918. "I can't describe how good it made me feel to see so many wonderful people, officials and non-officials, come out to wish me a happy birthday. I'm truly grateful for it."

THE HONORABLE JOHN CONYERS JR.

A Steadfast Dedication to Social Justice

By Damon Autry

Few things speak to one's ability to lead more than being chosen to lead on a consistent basis. Such is the case with Congressman John Conyers Jr., who in November of 2006 received 87 percent of the vote and won a remarkable 21st term. Conyers represents Michigan's 14th Congressional District, which includes Highland Park, Hamtramck, large portions of Detroit and Dearborn, and several Downriver communities.

The Detroit native was educated in the city's public school system, and later served in the Korean War as part of the U.S. Army Corps of Engineers. Conyers returned to Michigan and, driven by an unwavering desire to earn a college degree, enrolled at Wayne State University. He received a bachelor's degree in 1957, and a year later, earned a juris doctor degree. Conyers worked as a legislative assistant to Detroit Congressman John Dingell from 1959 to 1961, and from 1961 until 1964 as a politically appointed referee of the Michigan Workmen's Compensation Department. Then in 1964, Conyers decided to run for Congress and won the election by more than 110,000 votes.

As a 43-year veteran of Congress, Conyers is the second-most senior member in the House of Representatives—second only to his mentor, Congressman Dingell. During his more than four decades as a congressman, Conyers has introduced and endorsed legislation that ensures all citizens receive social justice. He has also maintained a steadfast dedication to improving the lives of Americans in general and Michigan residents in particular.

Conyers' accomplishments are plentiful; they are tangible evidence of a leader dedicated to making a difference, of a leader empathetic to the needs of his constituents. They include the Violence Against Women Act of 1994, the Motor Voter Bill of 1993, the Martin Luther King Holiday Act of 1983 and the Alcohol Warning Label Act of 1988. He was also the driving force behind the Help America Vote Act of 2002. Conyers even secured an appropriation totaling more than $1 million for the Detroit Medical Center, with Hutzel Women's Hospital receiving $800,000 and the Rehabilitation Institute of Michigan receiving $450,000. Further, in an effort to strengthen the ability of African-American lawmakers to address the legislative concerns of African Americans and other minority citizens, he and 12 colleagues founded the Congressional Black Caucus in 1969.

Conyers is a well-respected figure on Capitol Hill, and many of his colleagues speak of him in glowing and reverent terms. His election by his congressional peers to the chairman post of the House Committee on the Judiciary is a direct reflection of that deference. The influential Judiciary Committee oversees the Department of Justice, including the FBI, and has jurisdiction over copyright, constitutional, consumer protection and civil rights issues. Conyers' involvement in the committee dates back as far as 1974, when he was a committee member during its 1974 Watergate hearings.

Conyers is married to Detroit City Councilwoman Monica Conyers and together they have two sons, John III and Carl Edward.

- A DETROIT LIVING LEGEND -

GLENDA D. PRICE, PH.D.

A Passion for Education

By Damon Autry

"I always loved school. I absolutely adored being in the classroom." That is what Glenda D. Price remembers most from her days growing up in Harrisburg, Pennsylvania. She says learning was enjoyable, and while her parents and other adult family members constantly stressed education's importance, Dr. Price was self-motivated by the inherent virtues of learning. "I didn't need a lot of encouragement because it was fun," she says. "School was just plain fun."

That passion for learning helped propel her toward earning a bachelor's degree in medical technology from Temple University in Philadelphia. She also received a master's degree in educational media and a Ph.D. in educational psychology from Temple. While pursuing her advanced degrees, Price remained at Temple and worked in both faculty and administrative capacities. She left Philadelphia in 1986 for the University of Connecticut. Price remained at UConn for six years before heading south to Spelman College in Atlanta, where she served as provost for six years. In 1998 she moved to Detroit's Marygrove College and became the Catholic school's first African-American president.

Immediately upon arriving in Detroit, Price began bridging the gulf between the school and the community, a circumstance she feels was due in part to Marygrove being an undervalued gem in the city. "Marygrove is a unique institution," she says. "It is serving this community in a way that no other institution is, and too few people recognize that." In an effort to reverse that trend, she immersed herself in the community,

feverishly promoting the school every chance she got. "I talked at the Rotary and I talked at storefront churches," she recalls. "I talked at the Kiwanis and I talked at the Girl Scouts. I went everywhere and talked to everyone."

In addition to her ambassadorial efforts promoting the school, Price introduced various initiatives aimed at making Marygrove more attractive to prospective students, including a study abroad program, an honors program and the Women's Leadership Institute, which encourages and guides students to become leaders in their chosen fields of endeavor. She also revived the sports program, reopened the lone residential hall on campus and implemented a program called Marygrove Griots (pronounced gree-oh), an initiative designed to increase the number of African-American men entering the teaching profession.

Price's can-do spirit and focused approach on issues relating to bettering the learning experience of students placed her in high regard among everyone associated with the college. She retired from Marygrove in June of 2006, but not before leaving a lasting and positive impression on how the community views the institution. Price will enjoy retirement by remaining an active member of the community and engaging in an array of volunteer activities. She will also continue her role as board member for numerous organizations, including Compuware, Detroit Receiving Hospital, Focus: HOPE, Mercy Education Project, YES Foundation and many others.

- A DETROIT LIVING LEGEND -

WILLIE HORTON

"You can be successful at anything."

By Damon Autry

As a 20-year-old rookie attending spring training for the first time, Detroit Tiger Willie Horton experienced the ugliness of the Jim Crow South. Needing a ride from the team hotel in downtown Lakeland, Florida, to the training facility, he summoned a taxi but was told it was for whites only. Furious, he began the eight-mile trek on foot in the searing Florida heat. "That walk was the beginning of me getting involved with things off the field," he says.

Four years later, in 1967, the Detroit native received a crash course in community involvement when he intervened during one of the deadliest urban uprisings in American history. Still dressed in his Detroit Tiger uniform, he raced from Tiger Stadium after a game and drove himself toward the billowing black smoke on the horizon, toward a throng of rioters determined to uncork years of frustration. "I thought the world was coming to an end," he recalls. The Detroit Riot of 1967 was in full swing.

Once he arrived on the scene, Horton, who was later called the "People's Champion" for his commitment to the community, tried playing peacemaker. "I found myself standing on top of a car trying to talk to the people," he states. "What amazed me was that they were more concerned about my safety than their own."

Though his presence did little to quell the violence, Horton and his teammates gave assistance of a different kind the following year: they won the 1968 World Series. If only temporary, that championship was credited with galvanizing the region and giving everyone—regardless of race—a common rooting interest. Horton's 36 home runs led the team that year, and his overall stellar play solidified his nickname of "Willie the Wonder."

The importance of that championship was not lost on Horton. "God put us here to heal the city," he said at the time.

Horton played professional baseball for 18 years, the first 14 in Detroit. After retiring in 1981, he took various coaching assignments with several major league teams before returning home to assist then-Mayor Coleman Young with the Police Athletic League (PAL). He later left PAL for the corporate world but returned to the Tigers in 2000 as special assistant to the president, where he remains today.

The youngest of 21 kids, Horton thanks those closest to him for believing in his abilities and offering sound advice during his formative years, including his parents and Judge Damon Keith. "God put the right people around me who understood what I could do," he said. "All I did was play, and I enjoyed it."

Horton's numerous honors include having October 18th proclaimed Willie Horton Day in Michigan by Governor Jennifer Granholm; receiving the Order of St. Maurice from the National Infantry Association for his tireless work with the United States Army Infantry; and perhaps his most meaningful: the 13-foot statue in his likeness erected beyond the left-centerfield fence at Comerica Park.

"I look at that statue as a sign that there's hope; that if you put your mind to it and work hard and treat people right, you can be successful at anything."

Horton and his wife, Gloria, share seven children and 19 grandchildren.

- A DETROIT LIVING LEGEND -

DR. ARTHUR L. JOHNSON

Champion of the Struggle

By Donald James

For more than 57 years, Dr. Arthur L. Johnson has been a relentless champion of civil rights, education and other issues confronting black people living in Detroit. After migrating to Detroit in 1950 from Fisk University in Nashville, Johnson, a 24-year-old former research fellowship appointee, boldly took the reigns of executive secretary of the Detroit Branch of the NAACP. Thus, Johnson began an impressive 14-year term that saw him successfully fight such racial injustices as police brutality and blatant segregation in housing, schools, hospitals and businesses. Johnson later served as president of the NAACP's Detroit Branch.

Additionally, Johnson conceptualized and wrote the proposal for the creation of the NAACP Freedom Fund Dinner, which was first held in 1956. The annual Detroit extravaganza is now touted as "The largest sit-down dinner of its kind in the world." According to Johnson, the creation of the Freedom Fund Dinner was no easy sell to his peers, or to the organization's growing membership. "There were two political issues raised in relationship to the first dinner," explains Johnson. "One was that we couldn't have a $100 ticket affair, which would be against the organization's principles, and two, the organization could not afford such an event. I argued that we could afford the event and we should have it. The first dinner was held at Latin Quarters, and was attended by about 600 guests."

Following his impressive tenure with the NAACP, Johnson accepted the position of deputy director of the Michigan Civil Rights Commission, a job that would allow him to continue to put his fingerprints on issues related to civil rights. While content, Johnson could not turn down the opportunity to become assistant superintendent of the Detroit Board of Education, a job he maintained for six productive years. Johnson ultimately accepted a faculty position at Wayne State University, where he served for 23 years.

A 1948 graduate of Morehouse College, where he was good friends with a young Martin Luther King, Johnson went on to earn a master's degree in sociology from Atlanta University. He accepted a research fellowship to Fisk University before heading north to Detroit. During his illustrious career, Johnson has had numerous honors and awards bestowed upon him, including three honorary doctorate degrees, respectively from Morehouse College, the University of Detroit Mercy and Wayne State University.

Now 81-years-old, Johnson knows that the struggle for equality continues, and he vows to keep fighting until he is no longer breathing. Education remains a critical issue with Johnson.

"The part of the struggle that touches me, touches my heart, stirs my emotions, is what I know black youngsters are not getting in the schools today," says Johnson. "There is nothing more important for us to do than to get our schools straight and give our black children the chance they deserve."

Johnson is currently completing his autobiography, which will be published by Wayne State University Press. The book is expected to be released in late 2007, or in early 2008. Johnson will dedicate the book to Chacona, his wife of 27 years.

THE HONORABLE CLAUDIA HOUSE MORCOM & THE HONORABLE ANNA DIGGS TAYLOR

Champions for Justice

By Donald James

The Honorable Claudia House Morcom, a retired judge from Wayne County Circuit Court, was 11 years old when she decided that one day she would become a lawyer and champion of human rights. After earning an undergraduate degree in psychology and a juris doctorate degree from Wayne State University, Morcom, in the early 1960s, lived her childhood dream as she became an associate member of the first integrated law firm in America, Goodman, Crockett, Eden, Robb and Philo.

The Honorable Anna Diggs Taylor, senior United States District judge of the Eastern District of Michigan, decided that she wanted to become an attorney after earning a degree from Barnard College in 1954, and after hearing about the famous *Brown v. Board of Education* case. This landmark case and ruling motivated the Washington, D.C., native to earn a law degree from Yale Law School.

After moving to Detroit in 1960, Diggs and Morcom met and became friends. The two had several things in common, most notably, they were young, black female lawyers functioning in a predominately white male dominated field, living in a racially divided city and country. Additionally, they both wanted to use their professional law skills to fight for civil rights.

With that mindset, Morcom and Diggs boldly went down South to volunteer their legal services as part of the Mississippi Freedom Summer of 1964. The two attorneys, after arriving in Jackson, were met with news of the mysterious disappearance and murder of three civil rights workers, James Chaney, Andrew Goodman and Michael Schwerner. Deeply shaken by the deadly developments, the two refused to return immediately to Detroit. In the face of constant danger, Morcom served as southern regional director of the National Lawyers Guild Committee for Legal Assistance in the South in Jackson for a significant part of 1964 and all of 1965. "Mississippi was America's South Africa," says Morcom. "I represented people who were being arrested on trumped up charges; people who were often arrested on the steps of courthouses and other buildings where they had gone to register to vote."

"Upon arriving in Jackson, I drove with George Crockett up to Philadelphia, Mississippi, to help look for the three missing civil rights workers," says Diggs Taylor. "We didn't know that they had been murdered. There were huge crowds there, pushing us and shouting racial epitaphs as we questioned Sheriff Rainey about the missing men. It was scary."

Several years after returning to Michigan, Diggs Taylor worked as assistant U.S. attorney for the Eastern District of Michigan, followed by an array of other high profile law positions. In 1979 she was appointed to the bench of the Eastern District of Michigan by President Jimmy Carter. She served as chief judge for two years before functioning in her present capacity of senior United States District judge, Eastern District of Michigan.

Morcom, after returning from Mississippi, served as founding director and program administrator for Neighborhood Legal Services in Detroit. She later served as administrative law judge for the State of Michigan, Department of Labor, and Bureaus of Worker's Disability Compensation Court. Morcom sat on the judicial bench of Wayne County Circuit Court for 15 years before retiring in 1998. Since leaving the bench, Morcom has continued to champion human rights around the globe.

- DETROIT LIVING LEGENDS -

DELORES AND DAVID WINANS

The Mom and Pop of Gospel's First Family

By Donald James

The surname Winans has long been synonymous with world class gospel music. When brothers Ronald, Marvin, Carvin and Michael Winans mesmerized the world in 1981, with the release of the mega contemporary gospel album, *Introducing the Winans*, it was clear, a new day in gospel music had arrived. Following in the footsteps of the four brothers, were siblings Daniel, Benjamin (BeBe), Priscilla (CeCe), Angelique (Angie) and Debra Winans, all of whom have enjoyed successful gospel careers over the past two decades. David Jr., a guitarist and singer, has also reached high plateaus in several genres of music. And the beat goes on, as yet another generation of Winans has made major inroads into the music industry.

However, long before any of the aforementioned Winans ever took stage, Delores and David Winans, the matriarch and patriarch of this first family of gospel music, were creating a signature gospel sound and style of their own. Mom Winans, as the former Delores Ransom is now affectionately called, met David "Pop" Winans in the late 1940s, when the two native Detroiters were members of the Lemon Gospel Chorus, an ensemble that performed around the country. She also played piano for the gospel group.

While singing with the Lemon Gospel Chorus, Pop Winans also performed with the Nobelaires, a gospel quartet influenced by the Mighty Clouds of Joy and the Soul Stirrers. His good friend was the lead vocalist for the Soul Stirrers, before leaving the gospel group for a secular music career. The friend's name was Sam Cooke.

In 1953, Delores and David married. The two continued to sing at worship services and special events at their home church, Zion Congregational Church of God in Christ on Detroit's east side. When children began to populate the family, and demonstrated incredible vocal abilities, the couple raised them to sing for the Lord. Through the sacrifice and guidance of Mom and Pop Winans, the singing talents of their ten offspring started to take shape, and ultimately culminated into multiple recording careers.

Finally, in 1989, it was Mom and Pop Winans' turn, as the matriarch and patriarch released their debut CD, appropriately titled *Mom and Pop Winans*, on Sparrow Records. The CD earned a Grammy nomination for Best Traditional Soul Gospel Album. The couple's second CD, *For the Rest of My Life*, was released in 1991. As a solo artist, Mom Winans has recorded two CDs, *It's Been an Affair to Remember* and *Hymns From My Heart*. Pop Winans' debut solo CD, *Uncensored*, earned him a Grammy nomination.

These days Mom and Pop Winans continue to perform; just not as much as they once did. Pop Winans is also an evangelist. Both Winans are members of Perfecting Church in Detroit, where their son, Marvin, is founder and pastor.

While Mom and Pop Winans are happy about their own success, they'd rather speak about their children's prosperity in gospel music. "I am so proud of each and every one of my children," says Mom Winans. "I'm proud to know that they live the type of life they sing about." Pop Winans adds, "Praise the Lord for blessing all my children. I'm their biggest fan."

- A DETROIT LIVING LEGEND -

SAM LOGAN

"I do what I do to make a difference."

By Damon Autry

The leadership philosophy of Sam Logan, publisher of the *Michigan Chronicle*, is summed up in two words: follow me.

That guiding principle was born during his time in the U.S. Army as a paratrooper in the 1950s. He recalls General Ridgeway, an older white gentleman, small in stature with bright white hair who often joined Logan's squad on jumping missions from airplanes. "We'd approach the drop zone and he'd get up and walk toward the door, look us young guys in the eye and say 'follow me, men,'" Logan recalls. "What he was showing us was he wouldn't ask us to do anything he wouldn't do."

Logan later adopted that approach and soon realized it increased productivity and set an example for his staff. "I get more done by doing it this way," he states. "Just follow me; if I work, you work. Why should I want somebody else to work if I'm not willing to work?"

For more than 40 years, Logan has called the *Michigan Chronicle* home. Though he started as a commission-only general salesman, he had the foresight to think big, so much so that early in his employment, he proclaimed to bosses and co-workers alike that one day they would all report to him. Twenty years later, his vision became reality. Not only were they reporting to him, but in January of 2003, he and several other African-American investors formed Real Times, LLC and purchased the *Michigan Chronicle* along with four other publications, including the *Michigan FrontPAGE*, the *Chicago Defender*, the

New Pittsburgh Courier and the *Memphis Tri-State Defender*.

Logan earned a bachelor's degree in marketing from the University of Detroit (now U of D Mercy) in 1971, but his educational pursuit did not come without challenges. He often questioned the need for a degree, especially considering his fairly lucrative sales career at the time. But frequent talks with local businessman Frank Stella helped Logan maintain course. "He is the main reason why I persevered and graduated," he admits. Ultimately, Logan realized the eternal link between prosperity and a college degree. "There is no such thing as a viable economic life without education, especially in today's society."

Logan fully understands the role and responsibility of the modern-day black press and its purpose in the community. "The black press has to take the lead," he says. "We've got to educate. We've got to inform and continue to motivate and inspire our people. We have a moral obligation to do that."

It is that leadership, that level of commitment to what he feels is right that has brought Sam Logan recognition from organizations throughout the country. His office is full of plaques, trophies and commendations, all tangible signs of the level of respect others have for his leadership. "These awards are all nice," he says, "but I don't do what I do for a pat on the back. I don't even do what I do for money. I do what I do to make a difference."

INTERNATIONAL DETROIT BLACK EXPO, INC

PRESENTS

BUY **BLACK** WEEKEND

Economic, Policy and Entrepreneurship Conference

May 25-28, 2008

AT THE  **COBO**
CONVENTION CENTER
DETROIT

Sponsorship & Vending
Opportunities are Available

Today!

info@buyblackweekend.com | 313.309.3215

Over 76,000 **in attendance for 2007**

714 **Exhibitors**

100 **Entrepreneurship Workshops**

Largest African American Consumer Expo in the Country

COMING SOON!

www.buyblackweekend.com

COMPUWARE
CONGRATULATES OUR LEADERS FOR
BEING RECOGNIZED IN THE

Who's Who in Black Detroit

Patricia Bennett
Vice President,
Professional Services

Diane Jones
Program Director,
Professional Services

Terrina Murrey
Director,
Human Resources

Leanora Weaver
Regional Director,
Professional Services

Deborah Williams
Director,
Human Resources

COMPUWARE®

Saluting the *accomplishments* that make a healthier *community*

profound

captivating

DETROIT'S

Interesting

INTERESTING PERSONALITIES

distinct

impassioned

original

inspiring

remarkable

individual

prodigious

Chrysler Fin[ancial]

WILLIAM F. JONES JR.

Values of Financial and Social Responsibility

By Amber Gowen

Born and raised in Hampton, Virginia, William F. Jones Jr. draws his inspiration from his father and mother. His father worked two jobs to support his family, while his mother was the center of all activities. Jones recalls his father as "a man of modest means; always moving, always engaged. He set an example for me—in wanting to make things better for family and community."

William continues to gain strength and inspiration from his family. With a tremendous partner in his wife, Marion, he is most proud of raising three boys, William III, Johnathan and Malcolm. "All three boys are hardworking students, athletes and Boy Scouts." In addition to his duties as father, William is an active Scoutmaster and especially enjoys the camping and hiking trips. In his limited free time, he loves to play golf, indulge in a good book, listen to straight ahead jazz, and root for the Detroit Pistons.

Favorite vacations for the Jones' are spent on the family farm in Woodville, Virginia. The farm has been in the family for 125 years, and William's mission is to preserve and keep it in the family.

Early on, his hard work and commitment to education were realized with his acceptance to Columbia University, where he earned a Bachelor of Arts degree in psychology and an MBA. "The early 70s were turbulent on Columbia's campus but provided a great environment to learn to think critically and explore a wide range of ideas."

William is currently the chief operating officer for Chrysler Financial. He has been instrumental in the continued success of Chrysler Financial's partnerships with nonprofit and community organizations across the U.S. Community partners, such as The National Urban League, Congressional Black Caucus Foundation, ASPIRA, SER-Metro and Univision, work with the community to spread the word about financial empowerment.

Thanks to his modest upbringing, the values of financial and social responsibility continue to be important in his life. His personal commitment to sharing with others comes as no surprise as he was truly affected by the devastation of Hurricane Katrina. After visiting multiple Chrysler dealerships affected by the storms, William came back to the office and asked, "Is there something more we can do?" He and his staff brainstormed ideas for a relief concert to benefit displaced victims. Chrysler Financial partnered with Habitat for Humanity of Oakland County and raised more than $500,000 from a special Country Cares concert for hurricane relief efforts.

William is actively engaged at Focus: HOPE as chairman of the board and on the board of trustees of Walsh College. True to his giving nature, Jones says when he leaves the corporate world he would like to continue giving back by providing his business and management skills to a nonprofit organization.

"I am a child of the 60s and early 70s and old enough to remember and participate in the civil rights movement. A tremendous debt is owed to those who opened up the doors so that I could walk through. I recognize and accept that I have an obligation to open up opportunities for others."

His advice to young people who want to be future leaders is to "Dream big! Have a plan, and listen more than you talk." Those are the words he lives by.

Photo By: MONICA MORGAN PHOTOGRAPHY LLC

Dr. Sophie J. Womack & Rev. Dr. Jimmy Womack

A Passion for Helping Others

By Damon Autry

Dr. Sophie J. Womack and husband Rev. Dr. Jimmy Womack met in 1978 as first-year medical students at Meharry Medical College in Nashville, Tennessee. After graduation, both returned home to begin their medical residencies—Jimmy to Detroit, and Sophie to Texas. Little did Sophie realize, however, that she would soon pick up the telephone and hear Jimmy ask, "Will you marry me?"

She accepted, and almost 25 years later, the Womacks have become one of Detroit's most influential power couples. Sophie practices medicine as a neonatologist and is currently the vice president of medical affairs for Harper University Hospital and Hutzel Women's Hospital—the first woman to hold this position in the Detroit Medical Center. Jimmy, a retired anesthesiologist, accepted what he labeled a "higher calling" to the ministry after practicing medicine for eight years. He is the assistant minister of health and wellness at Plymouth United Church of Christ and associate pastor at St. John St. Luke United Church of Christ. He also serves as president of the Detroit Board of Education.

The Womacks share an innate conviction that has undoubtedly helped guide them to where they are today: a passion to help others. That noble tenet has been present in both since they were young, so pursuing medical careers was a natural manifestation of that desire. "Helping people," Jimmy says. "That's what motivates me. I like helping the underdog...that's the biggest adrenaline rush for me."

In an effort to give back in a more personal way, the Womacks founded the Coalition Inc. - Circle of Hope in 1992, a nonprofit organization designed to raise money for home health care for infants. Coalition Inc. also funds smaller community groups, provides money for summer camp experiences for children, purchases Bibles for school-based Bible studies and many other worthwhile charitable acts.

The Womacks have also teamed with the 21st Century Club, a group devoted to raising funds for children of domestic violence victims who find themselves in domestic violence shelters. "They're generally there for 90 days," Sophie says. "And during that time, there isn't any funding to get counseling for the children. So we raise money for the shelters that exist in Wayne County to ensure the children receive the treatment they need." If that's not enough, the Womacks once had a 20-year stretch where off and on they would offer the comfort of their home as shelter to literal strangers who were battling through a myriad of life's challenges. It was a gracious gesture, to be sure, but Jimmy states solemnly: "We can't do that anymore; that's very stressful emotionally."

Jimmy knows all too well what it means to battle through challenges. His life has been spent fighting through attention deficit disorder, and though it manifests itself throughout his daily existence, he has not allowed it to prevent him from succeeding. "I'm a *functioning* attention deficit disorder individual," he says through a hearty burst of laughter.

The Womacks reside in Detroit as empty nesters and are the proud parents of two adult daughters.

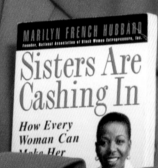

MARILYN FRENCH HUBBARD
Founder, National Association of Black Women Entrepreneurs, Inc.

Sisters Are
Cashing In

How Every
Woman Can
Make Her

MARILYN FRENCH HUBBARD, PH.D.

A Legacy of Empowerment

By Damon Autry

There is an affable quality to Marilyn French Hubbard that instantly brightens a room. She smiles often and laughs easily. She is happy and possesses a deep-rooted love for her career as corporate vice president and chief diversity officer with Henry Ford Health System. "Many times I come to work and at the end of the day, I feel I should pay them," she says.

Dr. Hubbard's approach to work can be traced back to the influence of her parents, especially her mother, Mabel. Watching her mother work long hours as a mortgage banker provided Hubbard the foundation upon which to build a successful career of her own. She began as a court reporter, and while lucrative, the position left her depressingly unfulfilled. As a result, she sought an alternative career in the form of self-employment, providing career advice and business development consultations to individuals and corporations, respectively. Soon after making that choice, in 1980 she founded the National Association of Black Women Entrepreneurs, Inc. (NABWE) at the suggestion of *Black Enterprise* publisher Earl Graves. The group was created in response to a lack of supportive resources designed to assist African-American women entrepreneurs.

"Through Black Women Entrepreneurs, I'm able to improve the economic status, health, well-being and quality of life of women, their families and their communities," Hubbard shares. "I want to bring out the best in women and help them to see that they can make a living by using their unique gifts and talents, and once they become successful, they have a commitment to give back."

Hubbard began doing less consulting as the years passed, but later secured employment with Health Alliance Plan (HAP), a subsidiary of Henry Ford Health System. During her tenure at HAP, she penned Sisters Are Cashing In, a book that provides strategies for living a healthy, well-balanced and prosperous life. Hubbard moved up the ranks at HAP in record time, culminating in her present position where she is responsible for leading the organization's responsiveness to all the diverse communities it serves, including ensuring cultural competence and sensitivity to and respect for diversity in language, religion, customs, values and traditions.

Hubbard has enjoyed a thorough and diverse career thus far. She is recognized by local and national organizations as an authority on entrepreneurship, marketing, leadership and women's issues, and has even been appointed to federal leadership positions by Presidents Carter, Reagan and Clinton. Additionally, her role as an International Coach Federation master-certified coach provides her with the opportunity to continue her life's mission of helping individuals craft the futures they desire, and with plans to expand the scope of the NABWE in 2008, Hubbard has the infrastructure in place to do so. "I really would like to leave it (NABWE) as my legacy, to show women that they can be empowered and go out there and do what they need to do."

The single mother of one adult son serves on numerous boards and committees, including the board of trustees for Central Michigan University, and the board of directors for the Detroit Youth Foundation and the Booker T. Washington Business Association, among others.

DARRELL MIDDLETON

Making an Impact

By Donald James

Darrell Middleton is living proof of the old adage, "where there's a will, there's a way." As senior vice president of human resources for Blue Cross Blue Shield of Michigan, Middleton consistently finds creative ways to facilitate HR functions that impact more than 8,000 company employees throughout Michigan.

On any given work day at Blue Cross, Middleton demonstrates the will to creatively implement, facilitate, evaluate and oversee an array of HR issues, in such areas as employee benefits and compensation, organizational development, corporate administration, employee relations, employee services, performance management, labor relations, hiring, recruitment, training and development, and workforce diversity. "What I like most about my job is that while I'm fully a part of the company, I also have an opportunity to make a personal impact on its employees," says Middleton. "I actually get a chance to really help people!"

A career in human resources was not on the radar screen for Middleton, when he graduated from Kent State University with a degree in industrial engineering and industrial management. After graduation, he accepted an operational management position with General Tire and Rubber in Akron, Ohio. Following a transfer to Phoenix, the company offered him an interim assignment in its human resources department. Middleton accepted the temporary position, and proceeded to learn the intricacies and nuances of HR. He saw how beneficial the department was to the success of the company, and at the same time, he experienced how rewarding human resources was in assisting

employees and their families in a multitude of areas. Middleton decided that human resources would be his new career, a decision that would ultimately take him across America.

Since leaving General Tire and Rubber, Middleton has held a number of high-level HR management positions with several companies including, MCI in Denver and Phoenix, PepsiCo in Santa Ana, California, Honeywell in Phoenix and Minneapolis, and Johnson Controls in Milwaukee. He was recruited by Blue Cross Blue Shield of Michigan in 2006. While many companies across the nation describe their own HR departments as "the last line of defense between the company and confusion," Middleton continues to advance strategies and systems that effectively and harmoniously bridge Blue Cross Blue Shield with its employees.

Although Middleton's job is extremely demanding, he always spends quality time with his wife, Lynn, and their three children. Not afraid to put God first in his life, Middleton believes in volunteering his time and talents to the church. "I believe if you honor God, God will honor you," says Middleton. Over the years, he has taught numerous financial classes from a biblical prospective at various churches, and has organized and facilitated several men's ministries.

In addition, Middleton finds time to work with kids. He is one of the directors for a local youth basketball program, where more than 500 youngsters, not only learn how to play the game, but they also acquire valuable practical life skills, such as self-esteem and confidence.

THE HONORABLE GREG MATHIS

The Judge of Transformation

By Donald James

Judge Greg Mathis, television's cool talking, law dispensing, no-nonsense man on the bench, is seen daily by millions of viewers on his award-winning syndicated court show, *Judge Mathis*, now in its ninth season. Powerfully dressed in the traditional black robe, with the mallet of justice close by, the bespectacled Mathis leaves no doubt that in his courtroom, he is large and in charge.

While Mathis is the authority of law, order and justice that plaintiffs in his courtroom must face, as a youth, Mathis often found himself facing a judge for various transgressions against society. It is this amazing story of, "from the jailhouse to judgeship in the courthouse" that makes Mathis an inspiration to millions of inner-city youth across America.

Growing up in Detroit, Mathis, despite his mother's strong influence and love, learned many of his early life lessons on the streets of the Motor City, where thoughts of fast money meant a crime waiting to happen. As a teen, he was on a fast track to nowhere after joining a gang, dropping out of school and being arrested time-after-time for an array of crimes.

The great turnabout for Mathis came in 1977 when, as a 17-year-old in trouble, he promised his beloved mother that he would turn his life around. So instead of continuing a life of crime, with the possibility of going to prison always lurking, Mathis chose to study for a GED.

After earning a GED, Mathis enrolled at Eastern Michigan University, where he developed a thirst for civil rights, social and economic justice issues. In addition, he was extremely impressed with the work of civil rights advocate Rev. Jesse Jackson. Following graduation from Eastern Michigan,

Mathis joined the staff of Detroit City Councilman Clyde Cleveland, and later served as manager of Detroit Neighborhood City Halls, under Mayor Coleman A. Young.

Additionally, Mathis worked as a political operative, managing numerous political campaigns, and was a significant force in 1984, when presidential candidate Rev. Jesse Jackson won Michigan in historic fashion. Jackson holds the distinction of being the only black presidential candidate in American history to win a northern state primary.

While active in political and civic affairs, Mathis earned a juris doctorate degree from the University of Detroit School of Law. In the mid-1990s, Mathis made history when he became a judge for Michigan's 36th District Court, making him the youngest judge to be elected to the aforementioned court. In the late 1990s, Warner Bros. Domestic Television offered Mathis his own dispute resolution television show.

When not ruling in his televised courtroom, Mathis lectures on civil rights and equal justice issues. Not one to forget his roots, Mathis, along with his wife, Linda, co-founded Young Adults Asserting Themselves, a nonprofit agency that helps youth ages 17 – 25. Through the years, Mathis has raised or donated more than $2 million for numerous civil rights, political, church and youth causes. He currently serves as the national vice president of RainbowPUSH, and is a national board member of the Southern Christian Leadership Conference.

"I'm living proof that people can change," Mathis once told a reporter. "My being on the bench will show some of these black children that they can achieve, that they don't have to be in the street."

The Honorable JoAnn Watson

Power to and for the People

By Donald James

In her own words, Detroit City Council Member JoAnn Watson describes herself as "an absolute Detroiter to the bone," and "a child of the activist movement," and "a freedom fighter." Such self descriptions come in earnest, as Watson grew up in Detroit, astutely watching the growth of city-born black movements, such as the Nation of Islam, Shrine of the Black Madonna and the Republic of New Afrika. At the University of Michigan, where she earned a Bachelor of Arts degree in journalism, Watson was an activist with the Black Panther's Free Breakfast for Children Program, and was founder of the Black Action Movement. "Activism, in a real sense, has always been in my blood," says Watson. "It was my coming of age."

It is this coming of age that has propelled Watson to stand tall for the people of Detroit. As a councilwoman, she has sponsored more than 600 pieces of legislation, all drawing from her background as a licensed social worker, community activist and freedom fighter. Watson is considered one of the most productive members of Council, who relentlessly seeks ways to improve the quality of life for Detroiters.

Now in her second term, Watson's life goal was not to become a member of City Council. Following the death of Councilwoman Brenda M. Scott in 2002, however, a seat on Council needed to be filled. Watson didn't plan to run in the special election, but was influenced when two of her mentors spoke to her.

"Both former Council presidents, Erma Henderson and Maryann Mahaffey, met and talked with me on a number of occasions," recalls Watson. "They demanded that I run. I greatly respect both women, so I had no choice but to run."

And run she did. Watson pulled off a stunning victory to complete Scott's term, and she repeated the feat with a victory to a second term. Her reluctance to run for City Council was not due to her lack of interest in Detroit affairs; it was because she was already making a powerful impact on the city, especially as it relates to African Americans, in other capacities.

Prior to serving on Council, Watson worked as public policy liaison for Congressman John Conyers, where she tackled such issues as reparations, universal health care, hate crimes, violence against women and children, and more. She was, and still is, national president of the National Anti-Klan Network.

Additionally, Watson has also held an array of other influential positions, which include first female executive director of the Detroit Branch of the NAACP; assistant executive director of the national YWCA; and she hosted her popular radio talk show for many years. She also chaired numerous commissions, committees and organizations that addressed issues impeding the progress of people of color. Over the last 35 years, Watson has received hundreds of awards and honors, including an honorary doctorate degree from Lewis College of Business.

The mother of four adult children, Watson has made young people a top priority through her mentorship and advocacy outreach for quality education.

Photo By: MONICA MORGAN PHOTOGRAPHY LLC

REGINALD M. TURNER

For the Good of the Public

By Donald James

Reginald M. Turner, a law partner and executive committee member with Clark Hill PLC in Detroit, is not one to boast of accomplishments or accolades pertaining to his brilliant career as a lawyer. While Turner's modesty is commendable, it is difficult to overlook his tremendous success as one of America's best and most talented attorneys.

Highly regarded by his peers, Turner has been featured six times in the respected national law publication *The Best Lawyers in America*, and has been selected twice to appear in *Super Lawyers*. Additionally, Turner was listed in *Michigan Lawyers Weekly* as one of the publication's Lawyers of the Year for 2005. He is also a life fellow of the American Bar Foundation, an honor bestowed on less than one percent of practicing attorneys in each state across America. In 2004, Turner, a past president of the State Bar of Michigan, was voted to serve as president-elect of the National Bar Association, and subsequently served as the organization's president from 2005 to 2006.

Since completing law school at the University of Michigan in 1987, where he was salutatorian, Turner, a Cass Technical High School and Wayne State University graduate, has been on a mission to take on tough cases in civil rights, ethnic diversity, education, public policy matters, and labor and employment law. He has vowed to never turn his back on people whose civil rights and civil liberties have been breached, even if the individuals are not able to pay for his services.

"In my view, the most respected lawyers distinguish themselves by breathing life into the Lawyer's Oath," says Turner. "One of the great traditions embodied in the Lawyer's Oath is the tradition for 'pro bona publico' legal services. Pro bona in Latin means, 'for the good of the public.' My involvement with the Lawyer's Oath is that I shall never reject the causes of the defenseless or oppressed."

True to the pro bona credo, Turner has taken on a number of civil rights and educational cases, at no charge, so that the defenseless, the oppressed, women and people of color can participate in the main stream of society. One such instance was the historic affirmative action case involving the University of Michigan, where Turner was counsel to the coalition of civil rights organizations identified as Citizens for Affirmative Action's Preservation. Attached to this case were 17 African-American and Latino students.

After the case was litigated in the United States District Court, the United States Court of Appeals, and ultimately in the United States Supreme Court, Turner was victorious. The November 2, 2006 passage of Proposition 2 (the Michigan Civil Rights Initiative), however, now bans affirmative action in the state.

For Turner, however, the beat goes on. When he is away from his busy law practice, he can be found at home with his wife, Marcia, and their two daughters. The Turner family worships at Fellowship Chapel, under the leadership of Rev. Wendell Anthony. Turner also finds time to play golf, a game he describes as "a work in progress."

Jon E. Barfield

Staying Power

By Damon Autry

As chairman and president of Livonia-based Bartech Group, Jon E. Barfield continues a family legacy that for 30 years has been a leader in the human capital industry. Founded in 1977 by his parents, John W. and Betty Barfield, the Bartech Group has blossomed from a small, ambitious and forward-thinking startup into one of America's largest independent human capital staffing and outsourcing firms.

Barfield joined the family business in 1981 after a four-year stint practicing law in Chicago. "I wanted to make an impact," he says. "I was determined to help grow the business and bring in processes that would help fuel that growth. I also felt that having been the beneficiary of a fine education that my parents purchased for me, I had an obligation to give back to the family business."

Barfield's "giving back" has not been limited to business practices. During the fall of 2006, he traveled around the state on behalf of affirmative action and debated proponents of the controversial Proposal 2, an initiative that stood to alter the landscape of hiring processes and college admissions statewide. "I think the passage of Proposal 2 has set our entire state back," he states. "But we're proud of the effort that we made to combat the initiative."

Such principled intelligence and commitment to being exemplary corporate citizens have aided Bartech with not only its highly regarded status in the community, but its staying power as a 30-year-old quality-focused services supplier, a particularly admirable trait considering the countless number of competing staffing firms that have receded during the past decade. But it is the visionary leadership of Barfield that has helped Bartech grow and diversify its customer base; it is also due to his extraordinary business acumen that the firm has expanded its service offerings through strategic acquisitions and other tactical business ventures. Barfield even decided to bring professional managers into the fold to help the family build the business, in addition to appointing an outside board of directors—both unique approaches for a family-owned business. "Had we not made those moves, I suspect we wouldn't have had the success that we've had over the past 15, 16 years," he says.

While Bartech has enjoyed tremendous success under Barfield's leadership, there are simple business philosophies to which Barfield subscribes that help guide his vision: attract great talent, provide his staff with strong incentives to be successful, communicate openly and candidly with his staff and perhaps the most important, the ability to take risks. "If you don't take enough risks," he says, "sooner or later your business will reach its Waterloo. If you're not taking enough risks, you're not trying hard enough to meet your company's objectives."

Barfield's expertise extends to his service on the board of directors for National City Corp., headquartered in Cleveland, Ohio. In this role, he shares his business philosophies and vision with the leadership of the $140 billion financial services company.

Barfield graduated with honors from Princeton in 1974 and received his juris doctor degree from Harvard Law School in 1977. He is married with two adult children.

LINDA D. FORTE AND TYRONE DAVENPORT

The Power of Two

By Donald James

She is senior vice president of business affairs for Comerica, Inc. He is chief operating officer for the Charles H. Wright Museum of African American History. Together, Linda D. Forte and Tyrone Davenport form one of the most interesting husband and wife professional teams in Detroit. While jealousy can often be a destructive force in a relationship, for Forte and Davenport, their 15-year marriage remains strong and devoid of professional envy or resentment. "We knew from the beginning of our marriage that we wanted each other to be successful," says Davenport. "I knew exactly what was required of me and her to make our marriage work."

Forte agrees. "We support each other's success because we knew each other extremely well before we married," says Forte, who has worked for Comerica for more than three decades. "We knew all the elements of support that were needed from each other for our marriage and professional careers to succeed."

As a high-ranking executive with Comerica, one of the world's leading banks (in excess of $53.3 billion in assets), Forte defines and drives internal and external diversity strategies, to positively impact the company's management workforce and customer base. In addition, she oversees corporate contributions, the Comerica Charitable Foundation and all civic affairs.

A native of Painesville, Ohio, Forte graduated from Bowling Green State University with a degree in education, but not before a college professor convinced her that she had the right mathematical and analytical qualities to do well in business. Heeding the professor's advice, Forte, after graduation, moved to Detroit in 1974, where she began working for the former Detroit Bank and Trust Co.

Meanwhile, Davenport was making a name for himself in the banking industry in his native Detroit, after graduating from Wayne State University with a degree in accounting. He later graduated from the School of Bank Administration at the University of Wisconsin. Throughout his long career in banking, Davenport has held numerous senior level positions with the old National Bank of Detroit and First Chicago NBD. Davenport retired in 2001 from Bank One Corp., as senior vice president of technology risk management.

Shortly after retirement, he took on the challenges of chief operating officer of the struggling Charles H. Wright Museum of African American History. In this capacity, Davenport is responsible for the overall operations of the museum, including all exhibits and education programs. Under his innovative management and leadership style, the museum has stabilized and is considered one of the best institutions of its type in America.

Although Forte and Davenport are extremely busy with their respective careers, the couple consistently finds time to volunteer together for several charities, including the United Negro College Fund. Forte and Davenport also love traveling together to national and international destinations, but always look forward to returning to the Motor City, where they enjoy spending time with family and friends.

"We are both passionate about Detroit, and will continue to invest in its growth," says Forte. Davenport agrees wholeheartedly. "We love this city, and we really want to be here."

Kenneth L. Harris

"We are a powerful people."

By Damon Autry

Kenneth L. Harris has a vision for the city of Detroit that prompts an almost daily self-interrogating rhetorical inquiry: Why can't Detroit become the next black Wall Street?

That question is the underlying goal of the 33-year-old entrepreneur who in 2004 founded the International Detroit Black Expo, Inc. (IDBE) as a nonprofit economic empowerment agent for African-American businesses in Michigan. The organization, a consortium of companies designed to showcase African-American businesses to the community, has in the space of three years grown to more than 20,000 member companies under Harris' leadership.

His role as founder, president and chief executive officer of the IDBE is simply the continuation of a journey that has found the Detroit native in positions where he wields considerable influence. After earning an undergraduate degree in psychology and a master's degree in counseling psychology, both from Clark Atlanta University, Harris returned home and landed one historical position after another: first African-American chief of staff in Southfield's history, first African-American director of Greek affairs at Wayne State University, and the first African-American director of minority business development and strategic initiatives for the Michigan Minority Business Development Council, Inc.

In the process of advancing his professional career and securing history-making positions, Harris founded the IDBE. He also dedicated himself to putting into motion the inaugural Buy Black Weekend 2007, held during Memorial Day weekend. The four-day marketplace exposition, which Harris plans to make a yearly staple at the Cobo Center, was designed to celebrate the successes of African-American businesses, as well as become a natural networking opportunity for those business owners operating multimillion-dollar corporations and those toiling in relative obscurity. "That was an exciting event for the community to see that we are a powerful people," he says. And the name of the event, according to Harris, says it all. "We've been buying everyone else for 400 years," he admits. "I felt it was important that we start buying black, but more importantly, that other cultures begin looking at some of the quality products and services that African Americans provide and that they start spending their money with us."

Harris speaks incessantly of the passion he has for what he does. He emits an air of enthusiasm, an aura of confidence and eternal optimism that's palpable, almost infectious. When having a conversation with Harris, however brief, one comes away with the notion that his vision of a black Wall Street in Detroit is within reach.

"We need to continue educating entrepreneurs on how to be the best, how to compete globally, how to network and how to support each other," he says. "Once we start making that a common thread in our community, we'll start seeing dramatic changes."

Harris is currently a Ph.D. candidate at Bernelli University in Virginia, and holds several board positions, including the National Pan-Hellenic Council, the Ira Newble Foundation, the Derrick Coleman Foundation and the NAACP-Detroit Branch. He is also a member of Omega Psi Phi Fraternity, Inc. and the Detroit Regional Chamber of Commerce, to name a few.

Harris is single and the father of 8-year-old Kenneth Jr.

Photo By: MONICA MORGAN PHOTOGRAPHY LLC

ROBERT SHUMAKE

From Squatter to CEO

By Damon Autry

To say Robert Shumake has overcome adversity would deny him full due. As a 9-year-old kid growing up in Detroit, he witnessed the drowning death of his 8-year- old brother. His parents' marriage crumbled as a result, leaving Shumake, his mom and three remaining siblings homeless. The family eventually found an abandoned house, removed the boards from the windows and lived as squatters for more than seven years. "That situation taught me perseverance," he says. "And it helped develop who I am today."

Despite being a frontline witness to the ravages of poverty, Shumake, a severe asthmatic as a child, remained positive and dreamed big. After graduating from Denby High School in 1986, Shumake earned a track scholarship to Ferris State University. He later transferred to Morehouse College but returned home permanently to help care for his ailing grandmother. In need of a full-time job to supplement his budding entrepreneurial dreams, Shumake began working as a janitor at Ford Motor Company. But it was frequent chats with an old college buddy that helped turn the tide for Shumake. His friend was in the real estate business and never worked on Fridays, choosing instead to play golf. Shumake wanted in. "I had read a lot of books on real estate and my aunt was in the business," he says. "So I figured I could cut my teeth at it."

He then began negotiating deals and secured his first transaction with $1 in his pocket. "I left work on my lunch break to buy a house for $18,000," he remembers. "The bank gave me $28,000, so I made a $10,000 profit." Sensing the infinite possibilities in real estate, he walked away from Ford and started First Equity Holdings, a lending and investment company. "Literally, within four hours of leaving [Ford] I generated $20,000 in business," he recalls. In 1999, Shumake was awarded a Department of Housing and Urban Development (HUD) contract that called for First Equity Holdings to manage 85 percent of the HUD inventory in Michigan. He later broke away from First Equity and his partners to start Inheritance Capital Group, a real estate investment firm that specializes in purchasing and managing net lease properties.

Besides presiding over a multimillion-dollar organization, Shumake is heavily involved in the community. In 2004, he started the Robert Shumake Scholarship Relays, a track meet that pits high school athletes from Michigan against one another. The event is an officially-sanctioned USA Track & Field meet and stresses scholastic achievement as much as physical prowess; thousands of dollars in college scholarships have been paid out to participating students whose winning 250-word essays on the importance of education, homeownership and entrepreneurship stood out from the rest.

Shumake has been a board member of numerous organizations, but perhaps the most significant is his appointment to the board of directors of the Federal Home Loan Bank. "It's quite a blessing to go from not having a home to sitting on a board that focuses on setting the policy for homeownership," he says. "It's a blessing; I could not have written this story."

Robert Shumake is the divorced father of three ambitious children, ages 15, 13 and 11.

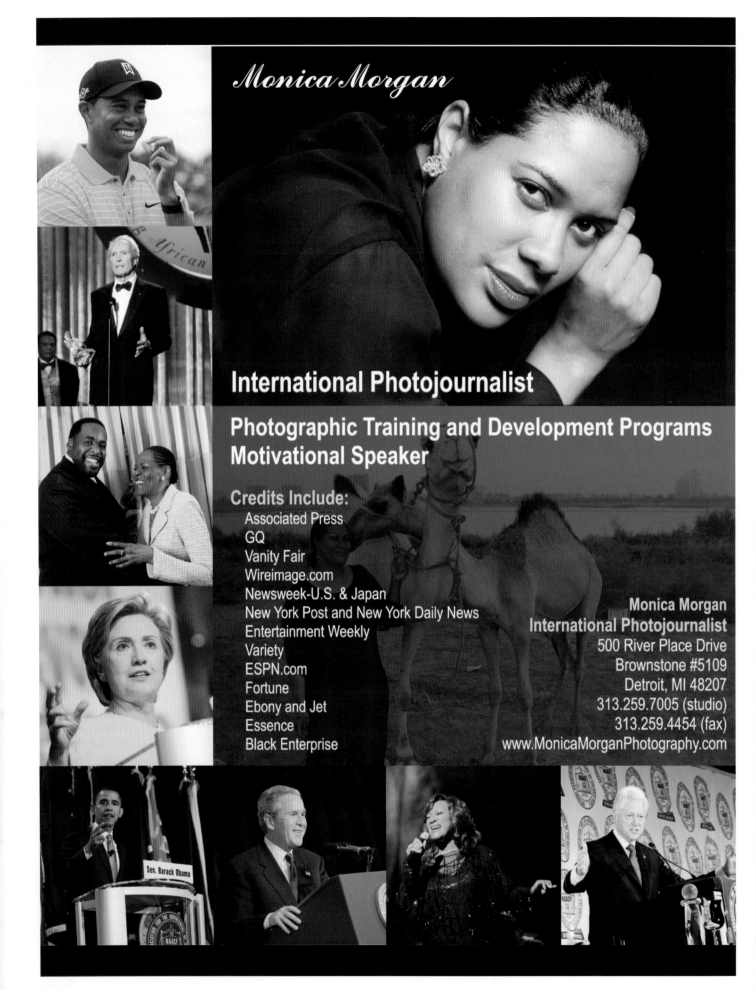

Monica Morgan

International Photojournalist

Photographic Training and Development Programs
Motivational Speaker

Credits Include:
Associated Press
GQ
Vanity Fair
Wireimage.com
Newsweek-U.S. & Japan
New York Post and New York Daily News
Entertainment Weekly
Variety
ESPN.com
Fortune
Ebony and Jet
Essence
Black Enterprise

Monica Morgan
International Photojournalist
500 River Place Drive
Brownstone #5109
Detroit, MI 48207
313.259.7005 (studio)
313.259.4454 (fax)
www.MonicaMorganPhotography.com

D eshawn Johnson is the Director of Human Resources at Lawrence Technological University where she incorporates progressive Human Resources practices with an emphasis on policy development and administration.

With the growth of Lawrence Tech's student body, advanced employee processes and leadership programs play a major role in the success of the university. Johnson designed and implemented the foundational infrastructure of the Human Resources department to align with the university's mission of developing leaders through innovative and agile programs. She implemented a multi-million dollar HRIS system and directed the development of Lawrence Tech's internal leadership training program to augment employee expertise and enhance their skill sets.

Johnson is a member of the Society of Human Resources Association; Human Resources Association, Greater Detroit Chapter; American Association for Affirmative Action; and Delta Sigma Theta Sorority, Inc. She received her bachelor's degree from Spring Arbor College, Michigan, and earned her master's degree from Central Michigan University. In 2000, she was nationally certified as a Professional of Human Resources by the Society of Human Resources Management.

Buildings may have a story or two.

But neighborhoods have many more.

Key Community Development is committed to the growth of economically challenged communities, and always has been. Our dedication to low- to moderate-income urban areas is visible in the $100 million we invest and $300 million we lend annually to affordable housing projects, small business and other urban neighborhood enhancements.

Our experienced, dedicated team brings together creativity and a variety of financing sources, including debt and equity financing, public sector loans, foundation grants, government guarantee programs and tax credits to craft specialized financing packages for urban communities.

For more information, contact Burner Crew at 216.689.5710. Or visit us online at key.com/publicsector. For lending opportunities, please contact Tom Walker at 734.452.5491. Or, visit us online at key.com/cdl today.

powerful

effective

DETROIT'S

Most Influential

guiding

prominent

momentous

significant

authoritative

leading

meaningful

Jeanette M. Abraham

President &
Chief Executive Officer
Detroit Heading, LLC

Jeanette M. Abraham is majority owner, president and chief executive officer of Detroit Heading, LLC. Detroit Heading has been ranked on *Black Enterprise*'s BE 100s list annually since 2002. Abraham was featured in *Black Enterprise* in 2003 as one of the top eight women CEOs.

Before acquiring Detroit Heading in 2000, Abraham was an executive for General Motors Worldwide Purchasing for 32 years. In 2001 she founded JMA Logistics, LLC. JMA was formed to manage all of the packaging and distribution of products manufactured by Detroit Heading.

Abraham is co-chair of the National Association of Black Automotive Suppliers' Scholarship Fund board, a certified member of the Michigan Minority Business Development Council, and chair of the board for Detroit Heading. Additionally, she is a member of Word of Faith International Christian Center in Southfield.

A native of Detroit, Abraham earned a bachelor's degree from Wayne State University and a master's degree from Central Michigan University. She enjoys travel, jazz, working out and being with friends and family. Abraham resides in Farmington Hills and has an adult son, Evan.

The Honorable Deborah Ross Adams

Judge, Family Division
3rd Judicial Circuit Court

The Honorable Deborah Ross Adams is a judge in the 3rd Judicial Circuit Court Family Division. She was elevated to this position by appointment of Governor Jennifer Granholm on April 10, 2006. Adams previously served nine years as an outstanding judge in the 36th District Court, where she was the top vote getter in two citywide judicial races. She also served three years as a respected magistrate in that court as well, following a distinguished career as a trial attorney in the law department of the City of Detroit.

Adams received an undergraduate degree from the University of Michigan and a law degree from Georgetown University Law Center. She is active in numerous civic and community organizations, serving on boards that promote child advocacy, women's rights and mental health issues. A frequent lecturer at schools across metropolitan Detroit, she has mentored many children throughout her career.

Adams has been married to Detroit Deputy Mayor Anthony Adams, Esq. for 28 years. They have three lovely children.

Following a distinguished and impressive 30-year tenure with Accenture, Kedrick D. Adkins Jr. joined Trinity Health in January of 2007 to become its first president of integrated services. His responsibilities encompass the complete span of financial services, information services, supply chain management, and insurance and risk management.

While at Accenture, Adkins was a senior partner, most recently serving as U.S. country managing director and chief diversity officer. He is well known and highly respected within the health care community, and is considered to be one of Accenture's pioneers and experts in the managed care industry.

His experience includes strategy development, technology planning, systems design, installation and process reengineering for hospitals and health systems, physician-based organizations, national and international managed care companies, indemnity health insurers, numerous Blue Cross Blue Shield plans and government health agencies.

Adkins holds a bachelor's degree in industrial engineering, and a Master of Business Administration degree in accounting and finance from the University of Michigan. He is a licensed certified public accountant, and currently serves on the corporate advisory board of the University of Michigan's College of Engineering.

Kedrick D. Adkins Jr.

President, Integrated Services
Trinity Health

Larry Alexander is president and chief executive officer of the Detroit Metro Convention & Visitors Bureau (DMCVB). A 31-year veteran of the hospitality and tourism industry, Alexander has transformed the bureau into the leading organization for facilitating tourism economic development in metro Detroit. His introduction of a ten-year tourism vision for the region has led to several efforts to achieve regional beautification that are now underway, service training of hospitality industry workers and infrastructure improvements.

Alexander efficiently runs the 50-person bureau and its $12 million budget. He leads an innovative, multi-award-winning convention sales, marketing and convention services effort that often exceeds CVB industry standards for performance.

Alexander navigated the efforts to land some of the world's most coveted sporting events, including Super Bowl XL in 2006 and the 2009 NCAA Men's Final Four. He created and led the Detroit Metro Sports Commission, a DMCVB subsidiary responsible for landing the 2003 AAU Junior Olympic Games. He also contributed to the 2008 Women's International Bowling Congress, and the successful bid for the 2005 MLB All-Star Game.

Larry Alexander

President &
Chief Executive Officer
Detroit Metro Convention &
Visitors Bureau

Charles E. Allen

President & Chief Executive Officer
Graimark Realty Advisors, Inc.

Charles E. Allen is president and chief executive officer of Graimark Realty Advisors, Inc., a real estate development company in Detroit. Prior to founding Graimark, he held various senior level positions in commercial banking, and was president and chief executive officer of First Independence National Bank of Detroit.

Allen serves on the boards of directors of the Auto Club Group, AAA Michigan and Gartmore Mutual Funds of Nationwide Insurance Company. He was also the first African-American chairman of AAA.

Allen's civic involvement includes serving on the board of directors for the Detroit Economic Club and as chair of the Hartford Head Start Agency.

A graduate of Morehouse College, Allen received an MBA from The University of Chicago. He is a recipient of the DuSable Award from The University of Chicago, an honorary Doctor of Laws degree from Benedict College, the Martin Luther King Jr. Award for Distinguished Achievement in economics, the Outstanding Business Leader Award from Northwood University, and the *Crain's Detroit Business* Real Estate Excellence Award.

Allen is a member of Omega Psi Phi Fraternity, Inc., Nu Omega Chapter.

N. Charles Anderson

President & Chief Executive Officer
Detroit Urban League

N. Charles Anderson was reappointed president and chief executive officer of the Detroit Urban League in January of 1997. He also served in this capacity from October of 1987 to January of 1994. Anderson is the sixth and eighth person to serve as the agency's chief executive officer since its founding in 1916.

One of 100 affiliates of the National Urban League, the Detroit Urban League has an operating budget of more than $5.5 million and works to enable African Americans and other people of color to cultivate and exercise their fullest potential on par with all other Americans.

From 1994 to 1997, Anderson served as executive director of the city's Department of Human Services, fulfilling his appointment by former Mayor Dennis W. Archer. From 1983 to 1987, he was on the NAACP national staff as director of the seven-state Midwest region. He also worked for the Detroit Branch of the NAACP as youth director from 1981 to 1983, and he was a sales and marketing representative and district sales manager for the American Tobacco Company from 1974 to 1981.

Vernice Davis Anthony is president and chief executive officer of the Greater Detroit Area Health Council (GDAHC). Leading the region's most influential health care coalition, she has provided leadership in developing strategies to address regional health care delivery through her active involvement in the creation of the Save Lives, Save Dollars Initiative and the Detroit Wayne County Health Authority. She has a proven track record in developing collaborative models to improve health care quality, cost and access. In January of 2007, GDAHC was recognized as a Community Leader for Value Driven Healthcare by the U.S. Department of Health and Human Services.

Anthony is the recipient of the Wayne State University Distinguished Alumni Award, the Michigan Association of Business and Professional Women Award, the Michigan Women's Foundation Humanitarian Award and the Anti-Defamation League's Women of Achievement Award. She was named one of the Most Influential Women by *Crain's Detroit Business* and one of Michigan's Most Influential African Americans in *Corp!* magazine.

Anthony received a Master of Public Health degree from the University of Michigan, and a bachelor's degree in nursing from Wayne State University.

Vernice Davis Anthony

President &
Chief Executive Officer
Greater Detroit Area
Health Council

Dennis Archer is chairman of Dickinson Wright PLLC, a Detroit-based law firm with 225 attorneys, and offices in Michigan and Washington, D.C.

Dennis served two four-year terms as mayor of the City of Detroit (1994-2001), and earned national and international respect for his success in changing Detroit's image and direction. He is currently chairman of the Detroit Regional Chamber of Commerce.

A graduate of the Detroit College of Law, Dennis has long been active in the organized bar. He was the first person of color elected president of the American Bar Association (2003-2004), as well as the State Bar of Michigan. He has also served as president of the Wolverine Bar Association and the National Bar Association. Dennis is a life member of the Fellows of the American Bar Foundation, the National Bar Association and the Sixth Circuit Judicial Conference. He is also a fellow of the International Society of Barristers, and the College of Law Office Management.

Dennis serves on the boards of directors of Masco Corporation, Johnson Controls, Inc. and Compuware Corporation.

Dennis Archer

Chairman
Dickinson Wright PLLC

Anita Baker

Jazz &
Rhythm & Blues Vocalist

Born in Toledo, Ohio, but raised in Detroit, Grammy award-winning Anita Baker began singing in a Baptist church choir at age 12. Along with high school friends, she joined a band called Humanity at age 16. In 1975 Baker joined the popular Detroit group Chapter 8. After a few years, the band landed a record deal with Ariola, later purchased by Arista. Following a disappointing review of her singing by Arista executives, Baker returned to Detroit and took jobs as a bar waitress and with a law firm as a receptionist.

Baker was approached to record a 1983 album for upstart California label Beverly Glen. The resulting album, *The Songstress*, revealed her as a developing star and attracted the attention of Elektra Records, which signed Baker to her first major label deal. Subsequent albums include *Rapture*, *Giving You the Best That I Got* and *My Everything*, to name a few. Her music has garnered her multiple Grammys, as well as American Music and NAACP Image awards.

Baker is married to Walter Bridgeforth, and the couple has two sons, Walter Baker and Edward Carlton.

Don H. Barden

Owner, Chairman &
Chief Executive Officer
Barden Companies, Inc.

Don H. Barden is owner, chairman and chief executive officer of Barden Companies, Inc., the Majestic Star and Fitzgeralds Casinos and Hotels, and Waycor Development Company. His conglomerate operates in the casino, real estate development and entertainment industries from his corporate headquarters in Detroit.

Recognized as one of the top black entrepreneurs in the country, Barden has guided Barden Companies and its affiliates from earnings of $600,000 to 2005 revenues of more than $519 million, making it one of the largest African-American-owned businesses. The 2005 acquisition of Trump Indiana, now Majestic Star II, positioned the company to become the most competitive gaming operation in the Chicagoland market.

Before establishing Barden Companies, Barden became the first elected black city council member in Lorain, Ohio, and served two terms. He also founded a weekly newspaper, the *Lorain County Times*, and served five years as publisher and editor. Additionally, he spent 11 years as an on-air personality in Ohio, and owned and operated five radio stations in Illinois.

Born in Detroit, Barden attended Central State University, and holds three honorary doctorate degrees.

M arvin Beatty has shareholder interest in Greektown Casino and is secretary of the Greektown Casino management board. He represents the casino and its community relations committee.

Beatty served with the Detroit Fire Department for more than 22 years. In 1994 he retired as Detroit's first African-American deputy fire commissioner. He served as executive director at the Wadsworth Community Center in Detroit. In 1995 the Detroit City Council appointed him to the Board of Zoning Appeals, on which he still serves. Beatty's "Women in the Fire Service" was included in an NFPA publication.

Beatty attended Osborn High School, and earned a Bachelor of Arts degree in urban management at California Coast University. He completed the National Fire Academy Executive Development Program.

He serves on boards for the NAACP, the Detroit Area Council of the Boy Scouts of America, Boys Hope Girls Hope, the Coleman A. Young Foundation and the Downtown Detroit Partnership, among other nonprofits.

Beatty and his wife, Maxine, formed New Millennium Consultants. They live in Detroit, and have two children and three grandchildren. Beatty's hobbies include golf and travel.

Marvin Beatty
Owner & Manager
Greektown Casino

P atricia "Pat" Bennett serves Compuware as vice president of healthcare and government for the company's Professional Services Division. She joined Compuware in January of 1979 and began her career as a consultant, providing technical services to Compuware customers throughout the metropolitan Detroit area. In her current role, Pat drives the growth of Compuware's partnerships with health care and government clients in southeastern Michigan. Her duties include directing a sales, management and technical team of more than 500 employees.

As a lifelong supporter of Detroit's cultural institutions, Pat has worked to sustain the Detroit Institute of Arts, the Detroit Historical Society, the Museum of African American History and the Detroit Repertory Theater. She is a member of the Black Data Processing Association, and serves as treasurer of the Water Access Volunteer Effort, a philanthropic organization that assists Detroit residents with the payment of delinquent water bills.

A past recipient of Crain's Black Business Leaders award, Pat is a proud, longtime member of the High School of Commerce Alumni Association. A Detroit native, she and her husband reside in the city and have two children.

Patricia Bennett
Vice President
Healthcare & Government
Professional Services Division
Compuware Corporation

The Honorable June E. Blackwell-Hatcher

Judge
Wayne County Probate Court

The Honorable June E. Blackwell-Hatcher was appointed to the Wayne County Probate Court bench in 1992, and is the first woman in the court's history to sit in the Estates Division.

Blackwell-Hatcher earned a Bachelor of Arts degree from Syracuse University, and earned a juris doctorate degree from American University in Washington, D.C. She is a past president of the Association of Black Judges of Michigan, immediate past president of the Greater Wayne County Chapter of The Links, Inc. and a member of numerous other organizations.

Blackwell-Hatcher served as the co-chair of ABJM's Adopt-A-School Project and a mentor for five years. She coordinated the delivery of more than 500 Easter baskets to children at COTS and the Doorstep Shelter for seven years. She has received numerous awards, including the Golden Gavel Award from the Wayne County Probate Bar Association and the Role Model of the Year Award from Alternative for Girls.

Blackwell-Hatcher speaks frequently in the community to seniors, community organizations and schools. The judge is the proud mother of two daughters, Amari and Kari Hatcher.

VeLois Bowers

Senior Vice President
Diversity & Inclusion
Trinity Health

As senior vice president of diversity and inclusiveness, VeLois Bowers is focused on ensuring that all employees have an opportunity to contribute and succeed. She provides leadership in the development of a culturally competent environment that thrives with a diverse and inclusive group of associates, medical staff and business partners serving in the healing ministry of Trinity Health.

Before joining Trinity Health in 2007, Bowers served as the Kellogg Company's vice president of diversity and inclusion for two years. Additionally, she led Whirlpool Corporation's diversity strategies and initiatives as its vice president of global diversity. Her career experience also includes human resources positions at Western Michigan University.

Bowers holds a bachelor's degree in business administration from the University of Arkansas at Pine Bluff. She is a member of the National Association of African Americans in Human Resources, the Diversity and Inclusion Food Group Industry Council, the Network for Executive Women and the University of Arkansas Pine Bluff Foundation Board. She is a founding member of the Council for World Class Communities, and the chair of the Conference Board – Diversity and Inclusion Council.

The Reverend Dr. Marsha Foster Boyd was installed as the fourth president of Ecumenical Theological Seminary (ETS) on October 7, 2006. As such, she is the second African-American woman to assume the presidency of an Association of Theological Schools (ATS) member school.

Previously, Boyd had served for seven years as director of accreditation and leadership education at ATS, academic dean of Payne Theological Seminary, and associate professor of pastoral care and counseling at United Theological Seminary. In each of these five positions, she has been the first African-American woman to serve.

Boyd received a Bachelor of Arts degree in elementary education from Tufts University, a Master of Divinity degree from the Interdenominational Theological Center, and a Doctor of Philosophy degree in religion and the personality sciences from the Graduate Theological Union.

Boyd was ordained an itinerant elder in the African Methodist Episcopal Church in 1978. In April of 2007, she was awarded the James H. Costen Award for Education.

The mother of one adult daughter, she is married to the Reverend Kenneth Boyd, a financial consultant.

Rev. Marsha Foster Boyd, Ph.D.

President
Ecumenical Theological Seminary

Charles Briggs is senior vice president at Marsh USA risk consulting services. His clients are in various fields such as construction, public entity, higher education, government, manufacturing and health care.

Charles is the current president of the Michigan chapter of the National African American Insurance Association (NAAIA). NAAIA's mission is to enhance the position and strengthen the careers of minority professionals in the insurance and related industries to the benefit of the companies they represent and the multicultural communities they serve.

He serves as a board member, and is the current treasurer for the Detroit Hispanic Development Corporation, a nonprofit organization that provides bilingual information and direct services to individuals through programs centered in the community.

Charles graduated from Moravian College in Pennsylvania, and received a law degree from Howard University School of Law in Washington, D.C.

Charles Briggs

Senior Vice President
Marsh USA

William C. Brooks

Chairman, President &
Chief Executive Officer
United American
Healthcare Corporation

Bill Brooks is chairman, president and chief executive officer of United American Healthcare Corporation. He is a member of the board of directors of the Detroit Economic Growth Corporation and the Detroit Downtown Development Authority.

Brooks is chairman and CEO of Detroit's African American Business Alliance. He is also chairman of the United Negro College Fund's Michigan Campaign. A retired U.S. Air Force officer and vice president of General Motors Corporation, he is a former board chairman of the Detroit Regional Chamber of Commerce and chairman of the Detroit Public Schools Board of Education.

Brooks was nominated by President Bill Clinton on August 10, 1995, and was confirmed by the U.S. Senate to serve as a member of the Social Security Advisory Board in 1996. He was also nominated by President George Bush and confirmed by the U.S. Senate on July 27, 1989, to be the assistant secretary of labor for the Employment Standards Administration.

Brooks was the commencement speaker at Florida A&M University and awarded an honorary Doctor of Humane Letters degree. He received the 1997 NAACP's Image Award.

Ken Brown

Franchise Owner
McDonald's Restaurant
Life Coach
Ken Brown International

Ken Brown is an all-American success story. He is one of the youngest African-American owners and operators of a McDonald's restaurant, purchased with no capital of his own. Additionally, Ken is a talented author, and speaks regularly to businesses, churches, schools and nonprofit organizations affecting lives in a profound way. In addition to his speaking ministry, he teaches at colleges and universities.

A Chicago native and graduate from Southern Illinois University, Ken released his first book, *From Welfare to Faring Well*, where he shares his amazing story. He has appeared in numerous newspaper and magazine articles, and has appeared on national television and radio programs. Broadcaster Tavis Smiley has featured Ken's story in his bestseller, *Keeping the Faith: Stories of Love, Courage, Healing and Hope from Black America*.

Ken's mantra is, "Life is 10 percent of what happens to you and 90 percent of how you choose to respond to it." He did not inherit his professional status, nor was it an accident. His discipline in using his guiding principles that he teaches—Focus, Ownership, Purpose, Passion and Attitude (FOPPA)—have steered his success.

Ella M. Bully-Cummings is chief of police for the City of Detroit. When Mayor Kwame M. Kilpatrick appointed her on November 3, 2003, she became the Detroit Police Department's first female chief in its 138-year history. Leading more than 4,700 sworn officers and civilian employees, Bully-Cummings commands the tenth-largest police department in the nation. Throughout her stellar career, she has always held issues affecting Detroit citizens in the highest regard.

Bully-Cummings received a bachelor's degree with honors in public administration from Madonna University and earned a law degree, cum laude, from the Detroit College of Law at Michigan State University. She was sworn into the State Bar of Michigan in 1998.

Bully-Cummings also belongs to the National Bar Association, the Wolverine Bar Association, the International Association of Chiefs of Police, the National Organization of Black Law Enforcement Executives and the Michigan Association of Chiefs of Police. She is a graduate of Detroit Leadership XX.

She resides in Detroit with her husband, William Cummings, a retired Detroit Police Department commander.

Ella M. Bully-Cummings

Chief of Police
City of Detroit

Dr. Connie Kennedy Calloway is general superintendent of the Detroit Public Schools. She was appointed to this position in July of 2007, and is responsible for leading and managing the total operation of the school district, which has more than 17,000 employees and more than 110,000 students.

A native of Alabama, Calloway was raised in the belief that education changes the course of one's life. She earned a Bachelor of Science degree from Sarah Lawrence College in Bronxville, New York; a Master of Arts degree in teaching from Harvard University in Cambridge, Massachusetts; and a Doctor of Philosophy degree in leadership and curriculum from Ohio University in Athens, Ohio.

Calloway spent one life-changing year of teaching and study at the University of Ghana in West Africa, and later moved to West Germany, where she taught for several colleges and the military. Subsequently, she served as superintendent of the Trotwood-Madison City School District in Trotwood, Ohio, and the Normandy Public Schools in Normandy, Missouri.

The mother of one daughter, Calloway is an avid quilter and gourmet cook.

Connie L. Kennedy Calloway, Ph.D.

General Superintendent
Detroit Public Schools

**The Honorable
Irma Clark-Coleman**

Senator, District 3
Michigan Senate

The Honorable Irma Clark-Coleman lives life with a purpose. Born in rural Georgia, she migrated to Detroit as a child. She serves on the Senate Appropriations Committee, and is minority vice chair of the Community Colleges and History, and the Arts and Libraries subcommittees. She also is a member of the Capital Outlay, K-12, School Aid and Education subcommittees.

Clark-Coleman's public service began in 1967, when she joined the Wayne County Road Commission. For seven of her 31 years with the county, she served on the Detroit School Board, where she was president for three years. In 1998 she retired from the county and ended her tenure on the board. That same year, she was elected to the Michigan House.

Clark-Coleman's honors include the Women of Wayne State University Alumni Association 1997 Headliner award and the 1997 List of 150 Most Influential Black Women in Metro Detroit. Additionally, her community service includes the NAACP, God Land Unity Church, Alpha Kappa Alpha Sorority, Inc. and the United Way.

She earned bachelor's and master's degrees in communications at Wayne State University.

**The Honorable
Eric L. Clay**

Judge
U.S. Court of Appeals, 6th Circuit

The Honorable Eric L. Clay is a judge on the U.S. Court of Appeals for the 6th Circuit, where he has served since his appointment to the federal bench by President Clinton in 1997. Clay previously practiced with the Detroit law firm of Lewis, White & Clay, P.C., where he chaired the litigation department. He began his career as a law clerk for U.S. District Court Judge Damon J. Keith, and currently serves with Keith on the U.S. Court of Appeals.

Clay has served as a member of the Executive Committee of the Yale Law School Association and on the board of visitors for The University of North Carolina. He has received numerous awards for his community involvement, including the 2004 Trailblazer Award from the D. Augustus Straker Bar Association in recognition of his pioneering efforts to promote diversity, equality and justice.

A native of Durham, North Carolina, Clay graduated Phi Beta Kappa from The University of North Carolina at Chapel Hill, and received a juris doctor degree from Yale Law School.

Karla M. Cole is president of James H. Cole Home for Funerals, Inc., located in Detroit. She has been in charge of the daily operations and continued success of the business since her father, James H. Cole Jr., passed in 1991. She is also the third generation of the family-owned business.

Cole graduated from the Cincinnati College of Mortuary Science in 1979, and received her license in mortuary science from the State of Michigan in 1980. She currently participates in countless community activities, and is an active member of the Eugene Applebaum College of Pharmacy and Health Sciences board of visitors at Wayne State University.

Born and raised in Detroit, Cole is married to Arthur Green III, and the mother of two boys, Antonio and Brice Green.

The James H. Cole Home for Funerals was founded by James H. Cole Sr. in 1919, and under the leadership of Karla Cole, continues to uphold its motto of "Servicing the Community."

Karla M. Cole

President
James H. Cole Home
for Funerals, Inc.

Nathan G. Conyers is president of Jaguar of Novi. He has the unique distinction of being the second-longest tenured African-American retail vehicle dealer in the industry.

Born in Detroit, Conyers received a law degree from Wayne State University in 1959, and began a civil rights law practice. In 1970 he decided to pursue a family dream of becoming a successful entrepreneur and opened a Ford dealership. He became involved in the formation of and held leadership positions in several minority dealer organizations in the 1970s and 1980s. An advocate for equity and parity for African-American dealers, Conyers continues to remain an active voice as the "Dean of African-American dealers."

In 2002 Conyers opened the third African-American-owned Jaguar dealership in the country. Jaguar of Novi received the prestigious Pride of Jaguar Dealer Excellence Award for sales and service excellence for three consecutive years.

Conyers has been married to Diana for 51 years, and has five adult children and ten grandchildren.

Nathan G. Conyers

President
Jaguar of Novi

The Honorable Julian Abele Cook Jr.

U.S. District Court Judge
Eastern District of Michigan

The Honorable Julian Cook Jr. was appointed to the U.S. District Court on September 25, 1978, by President Jimmy Carter. He served as chief judge of the Eastern District of Michigan from 1989 to 1996.

Cook currently serves as chair of the fellows of the Michigan Bar Foundation. Since 1986 he has served as chair of the 6th Circuit Committee of Standard Criminal Jury Instructions. He has served as an instructor at the Harvard University trial advocacy workshop, the Trial Advocacy Institute at the University of Virginia School of Law and the Criminal Trial Advocacy Program for the Department of Justice. Cook has received numerous accolades and awards for his professional and civic contributions.

A graduate of The Pennsylvania State University and Georgetown University Law School, Cook holds a master's degree in law from the University of Virginia. He also holds honorary Doctor of Laws degrees from Georgetown University, the University of Detroit Mercy, Wayne State University and Michigan State University.

Cook and his wife, Carol, are the proud parents of three children.

The Honorable George C. Cushingberry Jr.

State Representative, District 8
Michigan House of Representatives

The Honorable George C. Cushingberry Jr. represents the 8th District of the Michigan House of Representatives. He is chairman of the Appropriations Committee and chairman of subcommittees.

Cushingberry was the youngest person elected to the Michigan House of Representatives at age 21, serving from 1975 to 1982. He served 16 years as a member of the Wayne County Board of Commissioners, and is a historian for the Michigan Legislative Black Caucus.

Cushingberry is principal attorney for George Cushingberry Jr. and Associates PLLC. He is also active with the NAACP, the Concerned Citizens Council Youth Task Force and the Afro-American Museum of Detroit.

Cushingberry received a bachelor's degree, with distinction, in black studies and political science; a master's degree in political science, urban politics, policy and administration; and a juris doctorate degree from the University of Detroit Mercy. He is also a Doctor of Philosophy degree candidate in political science at Wayne State University.

A lifelong Detroit resident, Cushingberry is married to Maria Hazel Drew Cushingberry, and has two children, George III and Brandon.

Donna Darden-McClung is executive vice president of James Group International, a two-time recipient of the General Motors 2007 Supplier of the Year award. She manages a $600 million annual parts delivery budget, and is responsible for leading global development of company initiatives. She has held positions in two of North America's automotive manufacturers, General Motors and Ford.

Donna received the Sojourner Award for her distinguished service in the community, and the Manufacturing Worklife and Diversity Award from Ford Motor Co. She was also named the Woman to Watch by the Professional Women's Network, Women in Manufacturing.

Donna is a member of numerous organizations, including The Sojourner Foundation, Women Helping Women; Big Brothers Big Sisters of Detroit; and MMBDC. She sits on the advisory board of CAPA (Council of Asian Pacific Americans). Additionally, she is the Frasernet local director for Detroit. Frasernet is a global networking movement that brings together diverse human resources to increase opportunity for people of African descent.

Donna received an MBA from Fontbonne College in St. Louis, and a bachelor's degree in business from Tarkio College.

Donna Darden-McClung

Executive Vice President
James Group International

Donald Davis is chairman of First Independence Bank, Michigan's oldest African-American-owned commercial bank. He leads a bank with more than $220 million in assets, making it the 12th-largest black bank in the United States, according to *Black Enterprise*.

A lifelong entrepreneur, Davis has been acknowledged as a leader in Detroit's business community for four decades. He is known for pioneering efforts in the music industry, as a proponent of community development through housing and banking, and as an innovative supplier of services to major corporations.

His success in financial and business ventures followed his departure from the music industry two decades ago, where he enjoyed an exceptional career as a music publisher, three-time Grammy winner and record producer.

A native Detroiter, Davis attended Central High School, where his love of music was nurtured. He is an active patron of the arts and advocate of charitable organizations. He also serves on the boards of Detroit Renaissance, the Detroit Economic Club and the Booker T. Washington Business Association.

Davis and his wife, Kiko, are the proud parents of one daughter.

Donald Davis

Chairman
First Independence Bank

Kirkland Dudley
Founder, Chairman & CEO
Tedra Butler Dudley
Vice Chair &
Chief Communications Officer
GVCwinstar

Entrepreneurs Kirkland and Tedra Dudley are partners in business and in life. As the founders and owners of GVCwinstar, the first minority-owned telephone company in the U.S., they manage a nationwide telecom network with more than 100 employees and offices in most major U.S. cities, including the company's headquarters in Detroit.

An entrepreneur at heart, Kirkland has brought his dream of owning a telephone company to reality. GVCwinstar is a major force in the telecom industry, and is the largest independent provider of telecom services to the federal government. He serves as the company's chairman and chief executive officer, while Tedra is vice chair and chief communications officer. After separate and successful careers, the two joined forces, and together this dynamic duo orchestrates the company's activities.

Previously, Kirkland owned several successful telecom and technology companies. Tedra has worked nationally in public relations, television production and corporate communications. Together for 17 years, the Dudleys have three children, four grandchildren, and have helped to raise their nephew. They are active members of Plymouth United Church of Christ, and support many charitable initiatives nationwide.

**The Honorable
Fred Durhal Jr.**

Former Representative, District 9
Michigan House of Representatives

The Honorable Fred Durhal Jr. has a long, distinguished public service record that includes serving as state representative, executive assistant to Mayor Coleman A. Young and district director for Congresswoman Barbara Rose Collins. He has also served as legislative aide to Wayne County Commissioner Bernard Parker, deputy director of the Detroit Charter Revision Committee, and legislative aide to state senators Arthur Cartwright and Jackie Vaughn III.

Durhal has served as communications analyst for the Michigan House of Representatives Democratic staff, executive director of the Michigan Legislative Black Caucus and executive director of the Virginia Park Citizens Council. Additionally, he is a past president of the New Center Community Mental Health board of directors, the Coalition On Temporary Shelter (COTS) and numerous community organizations.

Durhal has served as the first African-American political organizing director for the Michigan Democratic Party. He is currently program manager for the Michigan Land Bank Fast Track Authority.

He attended Detroit Public Schools, Wayne County Community College, Wayne State University and the University of Phoenix.

Married with five children, Durhal is a 32nd degree Mason and Shriner.

Byna Elliott is a community reinvestment professional with 14 years' experience, including administering all aspects of consumer compliance programs and Community Reinvestment Act initiatives. She began her career at the Office of the Comptroller of the Currency in 1993, moved into the financial services industry in 1998, and is currently vice president and director of Fifth Third Bank's Community Development Department. Elliott and her team are instrumental in the community development projects funded by the bank in the city of Detroit to include affordable housing and initiatives to help small businesses to open and flourish.

Elliott is involved in Habitat for Humanity of Michigan, Northeast Village CDC, the Local Initiatives Support Corporation (LISC) Loan Committee, the Detroit Community Initiative, the Macomb County and Oakland County CRA Association, the Michigan Compliance Officers Association and Delta Sigma Theta Sorority, Inc.

Elliott continues to build strategic partnerships with successful nonprofit developers as well as established organizations to help small businesses. She believes that government, corporations and community organizations can make a difference by thinking creatively of how to use our resources together.

Byna Elliott

Vice President & Director
Community Development
Fifth Third Bank

The Honorable Edward Ewell Jr. was born and raised in Detroit. He pursued a master's program through Atlanta University, and became an intern to Georgia Senator Julian Bond. In 1985 he graduated from Wayne State University Law School, and clerked for the Honorable Damon J. Keith of the 6th Circuit Court of Appeals for two years.

Ewell was an associate at the law firm of Pepper, Hamilton & Scheetz before working as a criminal prosecutor in the U.S. Attorney's Office, Eastern District of Michigan.

In 1997 he became general counsel for Wayne County. He oversaw a team of 35 lawyers who handled lawsuits and claims against Wayne County departments, such as Detroit Metropolitan Wayne County Airport, Community Mental Health, Wayne County Commission, and the Sheriff's Department and the jail.

Governor Jennifer Granholm appointed Ewell to Wayne County's 3rd Judicial Circuit Court, Criminal Division in August of 2003. He was retained in November of 2006, and currently sits as presiding judge.

Ewell lives in Detroit with his wife of 19 years, Florise Neville Ewell, and their two children, Edward and Simone Alyse.

**The Honorable
Edward Ewell Jr.**

Judge
3rd Judicial Circuit Court

Dr. A.V. Fleming

Executive Director &
Chief Executive Officer
Ford Motor Minority
Dealers Association

Dr. A.V. Fleming is executive director and chief executive officer of the Ford Motor Minority Dealers Association. His main charge is to level the playing field for all minority dealers under the Ford umbrella.

Fleming worked in senior management for Ames and Rose's department stores for ten years. He served as executive director for the Northeast Indiana SBA/Small Business Development Center for seven years. He also served as an adjunct professor of business for 12 years at Indiana Institute of Technology.

Fleming is founder of the Fleming Group, LLC. He participates in chess tournaments around the country as a Category A player, and holds the rank of high expert/master in postal chess.

Fleming was president and chief executive officer of the Fort Wayne Urban League for seven years. He was committed to strengthening the agency's core programs in the areas of advocacy, employment, economic development and youth services.

W. Frank Fountain

Senior Vice President
External Affairs &
Public Policy (Auburn Hills)
Chrysler LLC

W. Frank Fountain is senior vice president of external affairs and public policy (Auburn Hills) for Chrysler. He is also president of the Chrysler Foundation. Fountain is the highest-ranking African American within Chrysler, which is one of the world's largest automotive, transportation and service enterprises. He is responsible for Chrysler's state and local government affairs, corporate relations activities, national education programs and philanthropy in North America.

Fountain graduated from Hampton University with a bachelor's degree in history and political science. After serving in West Bengal, India, as a Peace Corps volunteer, he earned a Master of Business Administration degree from the Wharton School of the University of Pennsylvania. Additionally, he holds an honorary Doctor of Public Service degree from Central Michigan University, and an honorary Doctor of Humanities degree from Eastern Michigan University.

Fountain serves on the boards of numerous business and civic organizations, and is chair of the Hampton University board of trustees. He is a member of the Wharton School board of overseers and the former chair of the Detroit Public Schools Board of Education.

The Honorable Sheila Gibson is a Wayne County 3rd Judicial Circuit Court judge of the Family Division, where she handles domestic, neglect and juvenile cases. She has served as presiding judge of the Family Division's Domestic and Juvenile sections. She was previously assistant corporation counsel for the City of Detroit and assistant general counsel for Blue Cross Blue Shield of Michigan.

Gibson obtained a Bachelor of Arts degree from the University of Michigan in 1980 and a law degree from the University of Pittsburgh School of Law in 1983. She has legal affiliations with the Michigan Judges Association, the Association of Black Judges, the Wolverine Bar Association and the Women Lawyers Association, and is chair of the Michigan Judges Association Family Law Committee.

Gibson developed and serves as director for the Wayne County Juvenile Drug Court Program, and handles the school truancy docket. She has served as chair or co-chair of the Detroit Association of University of Michigan Women, the American Corporate Council, Alpha Kappa Alpha Sorority, Inc., Oak Grove A.M.E. Church scholarship committees and several other private scholarship committees.

The Honorable
Sheila Ann Gibson

Judge, Family Division
3rd Judicial Circuit Court

Carol A. Goss is president and chief executive officer of the Detroit-based Skillman Foundation, a private, independent foundation whose mission is to improve the lives of children in southeast Michigan by strengthening their schools and neighborhoods.

Involved in philanthropy for the past 20 years, Goss joined The Skillman Foundation in March of 1998 as a senior program officer. She was named president and chief executive officer of the foundation in 2004. *Crain's Detroit Business* named Goss as one of Metro Detroit's Most Influential Women of 2008, and she received the 2007 James A. Joseph Lecturer Award.

Goss has worked as a program officer at the Stuart Foundation in San Francisco, and as program director at the W.K. Kellogg Foundation in Battle Creek, Michigan. Her professional career includes nearly 20 years' experience in child welfare, family services and youth development in Detroit and Oakland, California.

A native Detroiter, Goss has a Bachelor of Arts degree in sociology and a Master of Social Work degree from the University of Michigan.

Carol A. Goss

President &
Chief Executive Officer
The Skillman Foundation

Louise G. Guyton

Vice President &
Community Reinvestment Manager
Comerica Bank

Louise G. Guyton is a vice president in the Public Affairs Department at Comerica Bank. She manages community outreach initiatives in Detroit on behalf of the bank. Her primary focus is to partner with nonprofit organizations engaging in housing and economic development projects. *The Detroit News* cited Louise as one of six African-American women at Comerica Bank who is helping to shape Detroit in a positive direction.

Louise serves on the board of directors for New Hope Community Development Housing Corporation, the Black Caucus Foundation and the Southern Christian Leadership Conference. A life member of the NAACP, she sits on the Lewis College of Business (LCB) board of trustees, and is a member of Delta Sigma Theta Sorority, Inc.

Louise earned a bachelor's degree from the University of Detroit Mercy, and received an honorary doctorate degree from LCB.

Affectionately called the "Church Lady" by her colleagues and friends, Louise is an active member of Greater Burnette Baptist Church. She chairs the board of trustees, and is a Bible class instructor.

She is the proud mother of a daughter, Patrice, and a son, Curtis.

Ronald E. Hall

President & Chief Executive Officer
Bridgewater Interiors &
Renaissance Alliance

An entrepreneur and longtime business and civic leader, Ronald E. Hall is the president and chief executive officer of Bridgewater Interiors and Renaissance Alliance. He is also chairman and chief executive officer of New Center Stamping.

Hall is known for turning the Michigan Minority Business Development Council into one of the premier minority business organizations in the country, more than doubling its minority business and corporate memberships.

Maintaining board involvement in the Amateur Athletic Union (AAU) and the Boy Scouts of America, Hall is very active in youth organizations. He serves as an AAU boy's national basketball commissioner, donating time during the summer to conduct national tournaments. He also serves as chairman of the ADA of Michigan. Hall was elected to serve as a delegate at the White House Conference on Small Business. Additionally, Hall is a national board member for the American Diabetes Association (ADA).

Hall earned a Bachelor of Science degree in mathematics from Western Michigan University, and a Master of Business Administration degree from Wayne State University.

George Hamilton is president of Dow Coating Solutions, a business unit of The Dow Chemical Company. He is responsible for the company's profit and loss, global business strategies and organizational health.

Hamilton joined The Dow Chemical Company in 1977 as a seller of plastics, and has held a variety of positions in sales, marketing, application development and business operations during his 30 years with the company. Prior to joining Dow Coating Solutions in 2007, he served as president of Dow Automotive since 2003.

Hamilton is a member of the board of directors for the National Paint and Coatings Association, and is a member of The Executive Leadership Council. Additionally, he is a board member of Montreat College in Montreat, North Carolina, and the visitor's board for the North Carolina Central University School of Business.

Hamilton and his wife, Jill, reside in Rochester and have three children. He holds a Bachelor of Science degree in business administration from North Carolina Central University in Durham, North Carolina, and is a life member of Kappa Alpha Psi Fraternity, Inc.

George Hamilton

President
Dow Coating Solutions

Rainy Hamilton Jr., a graduate of the University of Detroit Mercy School of Architecture, established his own Detroit-based architectural firm as solo practitioner in 1993. Since that time, Hamilton Anderson Associates has grown to include partner Kent Anderson, a landscape architect and more than 120 employees. The firm has been active in rebuilding the economic and physical fabric of Detroit, with such projects as MGM Grand Detroit, Detroit Lions' Ford Field, the Detroit School of Arts and YouthVille.

Rainy's dedication to architecture is illustrated by his professional activities. He has served continuous appointments on the Detroit Historic District Commission during Mayor Dennis Archer's administration and currently for Mayor Kwame Kilpatrick. In the past, he was appointed to the Michigan Board of Architects and the Michigan Board of Land Surveyors. Additionally, Rainy was elected the first African-American president of the Detroit Chapter of the American Institute of Architects in 2001. He has also been active with the National Organization of Minority Architects (NOMA), winning their most prestigious design award the last two years and spearheading the formation of the NOMA Detroit Chapter.

Rainy Hamilton Jr.

President
Hamilton Anderson Associates

The Honorable
Judy A. Hartsfield

Judge
Wayne County Probate Court

The Honorable Judy A. Hartsfield was appointed by Governor Jennifer M. Granholm to the Wayne County Probate Court, where she hears child abuse and delinquency cases.

Before joining the bench, Hartsfield worked for more than 15 years for the State of Michigan Office of the Attorney General. In 1997 she became the first African-American female to head a division in the history of the attorney general's office when she became head of the Child Abuse and Neglect Division in Detroit.

Hartsfield is frequently a guest lecturer in child welfare law at Wayne State University and Marygrove College. She is currently on the board of directors for the Children's Aid Society, the Children's Charter of the Courts of Michigan and the Association of Black Judges of Michigan. She also serves on the Governor's Task Force for Children's Justice.

Hartsfield graduated with honors from Detroit Central High School and the University of Michigan, and earned her law degree from the University of San Diego. She is a member of the state bars of California and Michigan. She is married with one daughter.

Joyce Hayes-Giles

Senior Vice President
Customer Service
DTE Energy

Joyce Hayes-Giles is senior vice president of customer service for DTE Energy subsidiaries Detroit Edison and Michigan Consolidated Gas Company. She has held several leadership positions with the company, including vice president of corporate resources at MCN Energy Group.

Hayes-Giles earned a bachelor's degree in psychology from Knoxville College, a master's degree in business from the University of Detroit and a law degree from Wayne State University.

Hayes-Giles serves as vice president of the Detroit School Board and as a member of the Music Hall board. She was also appointed to the Mentor Michigan Leadership Council by Governor Granholm. An active member of the NAACP and the Urban League, she belongs to Delta Sigma Theta Sorority, Inc. and The Links, Inc.

Additionally, Hayes-Giles was recognized by the Fannie Lou Hamer Political Action Committee with the Political Service Award, and by *Corp!* magazine as one of Michigan's Extraordinary African American Achievers. She was also recognized by *Crain's Detroit Business* in 2007 as one of Metro Detroit's Most Influential Women, and previously as one of Metro Detroit's Most Influential Black Business Leaders.

The Honorable Beverly Hayes-Sipes, a judge in the 36th District Court, is dedicated to the principle that "justice is where law and compassion meet."

Hayes-Sipes received a Bachelor of Science degree from Wayne State University and a juris doctorate degree from the Detroit College of Law at Michigan State University.

An attorney of 25 years, Hayes-Sipes practiced in Michigan and Massachusetts. She served in Massachusetts as the first African-American assistant district attorney in Springfield, an assistant attorney general and general counsel of the health department.

Hayes-Sipes participates in many organizations. She has served as president of the Association of Black Judges of Michigan, who hosted the Judicial Council of the National Bar Association (NBA) at its 81st Annual Conference. Hayes-Sipes is also a member of the board of directors of the Judicial Council. She was awarded an NBA President's Award and a Judicial Council Chair's Award for 2006.

Hayes-Sipes is the wife of Victor L. Sipes, with three wonderful children, Valencia, Martin (Karen) and David (Michele), and seven grandchildren. She is a member of Hartford Memorial Baptist Church.

The Honorable
Beverly J. Hayes-Sipes

Judge
36th District Court

Darryl B. Hazel was appointed senior vice president of Ford Motor Company and president of the Ford Customer Service Division, in March of 2006. In this role, he is responsible for customer service, parts sales, distribution and logistics in North America, vehicle service and technical support operations.

Previously, Hazel was vice president of marketing for Ford Motor Company, and was responsible for Ford, Lincoln and Mercury marketing. In April of 1997, Hazel was appointed general marketing manager for the Ford Division, a position he held until he joined the Ford Customer Service Division in 1999 as executive director. Before that, he was general sales manager for the Lincoln Mercury Division. In August of 2002, he served as president of the Lincoln Mercury Division, and in April of 2005, he became president of the Ford Division.

Hazel earned a bachelor's degree in economics from Wesleyan University and a master's degree in economics from Northwestern University.

Additionally, Hazel serves as a board member of Think Detroit/Police Athletic League, Alliant Energy, Oakland Family Services, the Congressional Black Caucus Foundation and Wesleyan University.

Darryl B. Hazel

Senior Vice President
Ford Motor Company

The Honorable Denise Page Hood, a graduate of Yale University and Columbia University School of Law, presently serves as United States district judge for the Eastern District of Michigan. She was nominated by President Bill Clinton and confirmed by the Senate in 1994. Hood presides over numerous criminal and civil matters. She has served on the state court benches of the 36th District Court, the Recorder's Court and the Wayne County Circuit Court, and has worked as assistant corporation counsel in the City of Detroit Law Department.

An active member of several professional organizations, Hood chairs the Michigan State Planning Board for legal services, and is a member of the State Bar Pro Bono Initiatives Committee and the Detroit Metropolitan Bar Association Foundation board. She is past president of the Detroit Bar Association and the Association of Black Judges of Michigan. Additionally, Hood serves as a volunteer in various community groups, including as vice president of the Olivet College board of trustees, and as a member of the Harper-Hutzel Hospital board of trustees and the InsideOut Literary Arts Project board.

The Honorable
Denise Page Hood

Judge
U.S. District Court
Eastern District of Michigan

In November of 2002, the Honorable Karen Fort Hood made history when she became the first African-American woman elected to the Michigan Court of Appeals. Prior to this position, she was elected to the Detroit Recorder's Court bench in 1992, and in January of 1999, she became presiding judge of the Wayne County Circuit Court, Criminal Division.

Before being elected to the bench, Hood was a special assistant prosecutor in Wayne County Juvenile Court. She later transferred to the Appellate Division of the Prosecutor's Office. She was first elected to the bench in 1992.

The Honorable
Karen Fort Hood

Judge
Michigan Court of Appeals

Since serving as the fifth president of New Detroit, Inc., Paul Hubbard has held several management and community positions.

Hubbard is a life member of the NAACP. He is the past national vice president of the Association of Black Social Workers. Hubbard serves on several boards including Diversified Youth Services, Franklin-Wright Settlements, Goodwill Industries, the Detroit Science Center, Marygrove College, Grand Valley State University, WTVS Channel 56, the executive board of the Boy Scouts of America, Harper Hospital, and the National Urban League.

Hubbard has written several editorials for *The Detroit News*, the *Detroit Free Press*, *Crain's Detroit Business* and the *Michigan Chronicle*. He has received more than 100 awards, plaques and honors in recognition for his achievements in the community and civic service.

Currently, Hubbard is chairman of Alpha Restaurant Group, owners of Captain D's Seafood in Detroit.

Paul Hubbard

Chairman
Alpha Restaurant Group

The Honorable Tupac A. Hunter represents the 5th Senate District, which comprises northwest Detroit, Dearborn Heights and Inkster. As a freshman senator, he has been bestowed the high honor of serving as the assistant Democratic leader. Also, he has been appointed the ranking member on the Banking and Financial Institutions Committee, and the Homeland Security and Emerging Technologies Committee. Hunter is a proven leader in economic development, consumer protection and financial services.

Hunter has also been a leader in the effort to increase youth literacy, having donated more than 10,000 books to children across the metro area through his Leaders Are Readers program. He is a member of the Democratic Leadership Council State Legislative Advisory Board and the Travelers Aid Society board of directors.

Hunter earned a Bachelor of Arts degree in urban studies and public policy from Morehouse College in Atlanta, Georgia. Currently, he is simultaneously pursuing a master's degree in business administration from Wayne State University and a master's degree in public administration from Oakland University.

Hunter resides in northwest Detroit with his wife, RaShawn, and son, Jalen.

**The Honorable
Tupac A. Hunter**

Senator, 5th District
Michigan Senate

John A. James

Chairman
James Group International

John A. James is chairman and chief executive officer of James Group International (JGI) in Detroit. JGI offers international supply chain services including consolidation, deconsolidation, sub-assembly, inventory management, warehousing, distribution and transportation. His first business venture was O-J Transport, which he founded with his uncle, Calvin Outlaw, in 1971.

James' pioneering efforts in the transportation industry include taking his case for transportation authority to the U.S. Supreme Court in 1975. *O-J Transport v. United States* contributed greatly to the inclusion of African Americans in national transportation policy. He was the first African American in the United States to be issued broad operating authority to transport automotive parts and other commodities in interstate and foreign commerce. O-J Transport evolved into the group of five companies that comprise JGI.

A native of Starkville, Mississippi, James received a Bachelor of Science degree in sociology from Mississippi Valley State University in 1964. He is a former commissioned officer of the Corps of Engineers.

James is married to the former Sharon Nicks, also of Starkville, Mississippi, and they have three children, John, Lorron and Keri.

**The Honorable
Sylvia A. James**

Chief Judge
22nd District Court

Past Judicial Council chair of the National Bar Association (NBA), Sylvia James was the first female judge and first African-American woman elected citywide in the history of Inkster. A University of Michigan graduate, she obtained a law degree from the University of Wisconsin School of Law.

During her tenure, James has instituted three highly successful programs, Save African American Boys, the Community Service Program and the Annual Law Day Program and Essay Contest. She served as president of the Wolverine Bar Association, regional director of the NBA and on the Public Safety and Justice Committee of New Detroit. A gubernatorial appointee to the State Board of Ethics, she served on the board of directors of SCLC (Detroit). James is a life member of Delta Sigma Theta Sorority, Inc.

James has received numerous awards, including The Raymond Pace Alexander Distinguished Jurist and Humanitarian Award from the Judicial Council of the National Bar Association. In 2000 she penned the foreword in the inaugural edition of *Black Judges in America®*.

James' most significant accomplishment is her daughter, Alexxiss S. Jackson, a National Merit Scholar.

A native Detroiter, the Honorable Patricia L. Jefferson is a graduate of the Wayne State University School of Law. Jefferson practiced as a civil trial attorney, specializing in automobile insurance law, medical malpractice and construction site accidents. She later entered into private practice with her husband, Melvin D. Jefferson Jr., specializing in criminal defense.

Elected to the 36th District Court in 1996, Jefferson was instrumental in implementing Detroit's first Drug Treatment Court, becoming the court's first judge. She is currently serving her second term on the bench.

Jefferson served as vice president and board member of the Michigan Association of Drug Court Professionals, and as past president of the Association of Black Judges of Michigan. Appointed by the mayor, she currently serves on the City of Detroit Health Department's substance abuse advisory council.

Jefferson has received numerous awards for her work on the bench and in the community, including special congressional recognition, the governor's Certificate of Tribute, the Spirit of Detroit Award and the National Coalition of 100 Black Women Achievement Award.

**The Honorable
Patricia L. Jefferson**

Judge
36th District Court

The Honorable Shelia R. Johnson is chief judge pro tempore of the 46th District Court, which serves Southfield, Lathrup Village, Beverly Hills, Bingham Farms, Franklin, and Southfield Township, Michigan. She is the first African-American judge in the 46th District Court and the first African-American female district judge in Oakland County, Michigan. Johnson spearheaded the establishment of a Court in Schools Program, where court is held at various schools with the goal of deterring youth from criminal behavior and inspiring future career choices.

Johnson is a graduate of Dartmouth College and the University of Michigan Law School, where she was the first African-American president of the Law School Student Senate and the commencement speaker. She served as a law clerk to a federal judge, and thereafter as an attorney in private practice.

Johnson has received numerous community awards. Currently, she serves as president-elect of the Association of Black Judges of Michigan, and as a board member and district director of the National Association of Women Judges.

Johnson enjoys weightlifting, waterskiing and the arts.

**The Honorable
Shelia R. Johnson**

Chief Judge Pro Tempore
46th District Court of Michigan

Diana C. Jones

Vice President, Community Affairs
Blue Cross Blue Shield of Michigan

Diana C. Jones is vice president of community affairs for Blue Cross Blue Shield of Michigan. She is responsible for corporate social responsibility and philanthropy.

She joined the company in 1974, and has held positions as a senior community relations representative, coordinator of case management and manager of GM managed care.

Diana holds a juris doctorate degree from the University of Detroit Mercy School of Law, and master's and bachelor's degrees from Wayne State University. Diana has received advance certification in corporate community relations and social responsibility at Boston College, and serves on the Community Involvement Leadership Roundtable.

Her board memberships include Black Family Development Inc., the Michigan Nonprofit Association, the Central Michigan University President's Advisory Council, the Visiting Nurses Association, Elder Law of Michigan Inc. and Detroit Long Term Care Connection. A trustee of the Downtown Detroit Partnership, she was appointed to the Certificate of Needs Commission and recently to the Governor's Task Force on Elder Abuse.

Born in Detroit, Diana is a member of the Renaissance Chapter of The Links Inc., and enjoys golfing, reading and travel.

Theresa C. Jones

President & Owner
Northwestern Dodge, Inc.

Theresa Jones is president and owner of Northwestern Dodge, Inc. In this position, she oversees the daily management and major decisions for the automobile dealership. She has 70 employees in departments including new cars, used cars, service, parts and the body shop. She is the only African-American female Dodge dealer in Michigan.

Theresa was named the first woman president of the Daimler Chrysler Minority Dealer Association in 1994. She serves on their board of directors Council of Presidents. She has received numerous awards with the association.

Theresa received a Bachelor of Arts degree from St. Mary's College in Leavenworth, Kansas, and a master's degree from Wayne State University. She is in the process of defending for a Doctor of Philosophy degree.

A native of Kansas City, Kansas, Theresa is the widow of Jesse Jones since 1990, and the proud mother of three children, Michelle, Jason and Joseph.

In 2002, at 31, the Honorable Kwame M. Kilpatrick became the youngest mayor of any major U.S. city. Now in his second term as mayor of Detroit, he has revitalized America's 11th-largest city.

As mayor, Kilpatrick has successfully handled an oil spill, a blackout and a sluggish economy. He led Detroit to the largest residential, commercial and economic boom in 50 years. In 2006 Detroit was named the top city in Michigan's southeast region in terms of new development.

Prior to his election as mayor, Kilpatrick was the first African American and the youngest person elected as the leader of any party in the history of the Michigan legislature. As a state representative, he helped to design the Clean Michigan Initiative.

A lifelong resident of Detroit, Kilpatrick graduated from Cass Technical High School. He earned a Bachelor of Science degree in political science from Florida A&M University, and a law degree from the Detroit College of Law at Michigan State University.

He and his wife, Carlita, have twin 10-year-old boys, Jelani and Jalil, and a 4-year-old son, Jonas.

**The Honorable
Kwame M. Kilpatrick**

Mayor
City of Detroit

The Honorable Brenda L. Lawrence is the first African American and the first woman mayor of Southfield, a city with a resident population of 78,300, a budget of $118 million and 833 city employees. She is committed to diversity, fiscal responsibility, education, and keeping a clean and safe city. She has also served in a variety of leadership capacities with the United States Post Office in Detroit.

Since becoming mayor in 2001, Lawrence has initiated the Mayor's Walk community health program; the Mayor's Roundtable, a citizen-driven forum; Southfield Reads; Flower Day; and the annual citywide blood and bone marrow drives. The recipient of numerous awards and recognitions for her accomplishments, she serves on advisory boards for the U.S. Conference of Mayors, the Michigan Association of Mayors and the American Heart Association's Go Red For Women. Lawrence also serves on the board of governors for the Renaissance/Skyline Club.

She and her husband, McArthur Lawrence, are the parents of Michael and Michelle, and have a granddaughter, Asya.

**The Honorable
Brenda L. Lawrence**

Mayor
City of Southfield

Joe W. Laymon

Group Vice President
Corporate Human Resources &
Labor Affairs
Ford Motor Company

Joe W. Laymon is group vice president of human resources and labor affairs at Ford Motor Company. In this position, which he has held since October of 2003, he directly oversees Ford's global activities, policies, and programs for salaried and hourly employees. Laymon, the company's first African-American group vice president, is one of the highest-ranking African Americans in the automotive industry.

Laymon has dedicated his career to being an employee advocate. His extensive human resources background includes labor affairs, leadership development, and recruiting and retention.

Prior to joining Ford in 2000, Laymon worked for the U.S. State Department's Agency for International Development. He spent 17 years at Xerox Corporation and then four years at Kodak Company, where he held human resources leadership positions.

Laymon serves on the board of directors for Volvo Cars, and is an active board member for the HR Policy Association. He is also committed to seeking affordable health care for the underserved and increasing literacy for migrant workers.

Laymon holds a bachelor's degree from Jackson State University and a master's degree from the University of Wisconsin.

Elaine Lewis

Vice President, Public Affairs &
Strategic Planning
Detroit Tigers, Inc.

As vice president of public affairs and strategic planning for the Detroit Tigers, Elaine Lewis is the highest-ranking African American and woman in Tigers business operations. She is fully committed to community service and the empowerment of youth.

Elaine plays a pivotal role in developing programs that encourage Detroit's youth to embrace the game of baseball. Under her leadership, the Tigers Fields of Champions program has renovated numerous inner-city fields, including the Willie Horton Baseball and Softball Diamonds.

Elaine's accomplishments include the establishment of the Detroit Tigers Foundation, Negro Leagues Weekend Community Events, the Community Ticket Fundraising Program and the Detroit Tigers Speakers Bureau. She also oversees the Tigers' Diverse Business Partners Program, one of the most successful in Major League Baseball.

Elaine earned a bachelor's degree from Wayne State University and a master's degree from Central Michigan University. A member of Delta Sigma Theta Sorority, Inc., she serves on the boards of Ilitch Charities for Children, the Michigan Sports Hall of Fame, the University of Detroit Jesuit High School and CATCH.

Elaine resides in northwest Detroit with her husband, Freman.

B orn in Detroit, the Honorable Leonia J. Lloyd taught at Cass Technical High School in 1971. She received a Bachelor of Science degree in education and a juris doctorate degree from Wayne State University. She was elected to the 36th District Court in 1992, and became a Drug Treatment Court judge in 2002.

Lloyd was a partner in the law firm of Lloyd and Lloyd with her late sister, the Honorable Leona L. Lloyd. The country's first twin judges to sit on the same bench at the same time, they were affectionately dubbed "twins for justice." In memory of her sister, Lloyd has endowed two scholarship funds that assist undergraduate students in the field of education and law.

Currently, Lloyd is the presiding Drug Treatment Court judge, which includes Project Fresh Start, a program designed to help women in the sex trade remain drug-free, restore self respect, acquire housing and employment, and become productive citizens. This program was the second-place winner in the National Association of Drug Court Professionals for 2006-2007.

Lloyd is married to DeMarcus Holland.

**The Honorable
Leonia J. Lloyd**

Judge
36th District Court

B arbara J. Mahone is executive director, human resources for global product development. She is responsible for developing and implementing human resource strategies covering leadership development, succession planning, performance management, compensation/reward systems, organization development and change management.

Barbara was recognized as one of *Crain's Detroit Business'* Most Influential Women, and one of *Ebony's* Women at the Top in Corporate America. She also received the Mary McLeod Bethune Award. Additionally, the library at the Pimlico Elementary School in Baltimore, Maryland, was renamed the Barbara J. Mahone Multi-Cultural Learning Center, honoring Barbara's commitment and dedication to youth education. She is a lifetime member of the NAACP and the National Black MBA Association, where she previously served as national president.

Barbara earned a bachelor's degree from The Ohio State University and a Master of Business Administration degree from the University of Michigan. She also completed the Harvard University Program for Management Development.

A member of the board of directors for William Beaumont Hospital, she previously served on the boards of Charter One Bank, Blue Cross and Blue Shield of Michigan and the Detroit Urban League.

Barbara J. Mahone

Executive Director,
Human Resources
General Motors Corporation

The he Honorable Miriam B. Martin-Clark is a judge of the 36th District Court in Detroit, where she has served since 1997. As a judge on the second-busiest court in the nation, Martin-Clark has general jurisdiction of criminal and civil cases ranging from felony preliminary exams to civil matters, including landlord tenant summary proceedings.

Martin-Clark is a graduate of both Howard University, where she earned a Bachelor of Arts degree in English literature, and Wayne State University, where she earned a post degree in education and a juris doctorate degree.

Martin-Clark is the former assistant general counsel of Wayne State University. A native of Detroit, she lives there with her husband, Dr. Frank M. Clark, a physician. She is an active member of several community organizations, and a recipient of numerous awards and citations. She is also the proud mother of two adult children, Frank II, a lawyer, and Christina, a physician.

The Honorable
Miriam B. Martin-Clark

Judge
36th District Court

George eorge Mathews is currently the president of WGPR Inc. and supreme president of the International Free and Accepted Modern Masons, a black Masonic organization with 350,000 members.

A native of Montgomery, Alabama, Mathews is a graduate of Buffalo State College with a degree in accounting. He served in the U.S. Navy and began his career at Union Carbide Corporation as a benefit plans administrator, retiring after 32 years of service.

Mathews is a board member of the Rotary Club of Niagara, a chairman of the Commission of Civil Service, and a planning board chairman of the City of Niagara Falls. He is involved with the Casino Gambling Commissioner Study Group, the Urban Renewal Agency of Niagara Falls, the Niagara Political Action Committee, the Black Achievers Committee, and the Human Rights Commission. A member of the NAACP, Mathews also serves the United Way of Niagara, the Salvation Army, the Boys and Girls Club of Niagara, and the Industrial Management Club. Mathews is the recipient of the honored Top Hat Award from WHLD radio.

Mathews is married to Alline, and father to Patricia.

George Mathews

President & General Manager
WGPR Inc.

Governor Jennifer Granholm appointed the Honorable B. Pennie Millender to the 36th District Court in December of 2003. She was elected to serve a full term in November of 2004.

Prior to her appointment, Millender served as a magistrate in the 36th District Court for five years. She earned a bachelor's degree in psychology from Southern University in Baton Rouge, Louisiana; a Master of Arts degree in vocational rehabilitation counseling from Wayne State University; and a juris doctorate degree from Detroit College of Law.

While studying law, Millender received several awards, including the American Jurisprudence Book Award. She held internships with the Honorable Claudia House Morcom (Wayne County Circuit Court) and the Honorable Dennis W. Archer (Michigan Supreme Court).

The former president of the Association of Black Judges of Michigan, Millender is a member of the Wolverine Bar Association and a life member of the NAACP. She has received numerous awards and honors.

Millender credits her parents, the late Robert and Louise Millender, with influencing her commitment to public service, and the pursuit of justice and equality for all Americans.

**The Honorable
B. Pennie Millender**

Judge
36th District Court

The Honorable Cylenthia LaToye Miller serves on the third-busiest district court in the nation. She presides over cases from all of the court's dockets, including real estate, traffic and ordinance, and general civil and criminal cases.

First vice president of the National Bar Association (NBA) Women Lawyers Division, Cylenthia is a trustee of the Charles H. Wright Museum of African American History. She is also a past president of the Wolverine Bar Association (WBA) and the Women Lawyers Association of Michigan.

Her awards include the NBA President's Award (2000 and 2006), WBA Shining Star (2005) and Member of the Year (2001), the State Bar of Michigan's Citizen Lawyer (2005), Wolverine Student Bar Association Distinguished Alumni (2003), and *Michigan Lawyers Weekly*'s Top 5 Up & Coming Lawyers (2001).

Cylenthia earned a bachelor's degree from Wayne State University and a juris doctor degree, cum laude, from Michigan State University – Detroit College of Law, becoming the first African-American woman class president in its history.

She enjoys all music, swimming, movies and reading. She believes that "What you make of yourself is your gift to God."

**The Honorable
Cylenthia LaToye Miller**

Judge
36th District Court

The Honorable
Denise Langford Morris

Judge
6th Judicial Circuit Court

The Honorable Denise Langford Morris is the first African-American Oakland Circuit Court judge. She received a juris doctorate degree from the University of Detroit Mercy School of Law. She has extensive trial experience as a private practitioner, an assistant Oakland County prosecutor and an assistant U.S. attorney for the Eastern District of Michigan.

Morris has been the recipient of many awards, including the State Bar of Michigan 2007 Champion of Justice Award, the 2007 City of Detroit Distinguished Service Award, the 2006 National Bar Association Chair's Award and the 2006 National Bar Association Presidential Award. Likewise, she received the 2006 Pontiac Chamber of Commerce Appreciation Award, the 2005 Salute to Justice Judicial Award, the 2005 BALSA Lifetime Achievement Award and the 2005 Judge William Waterman Courage in Leadership NAACP Award. Additionally, she received the honor of African American Pioneer in 2007 from Comcast and McDonalds, and the 2006 University of Detroit Mercy BALSA scholarship was named after her.

Morris strongly believes in giving back and "that to whom much is given, much is required."

The Honorable
John A. Murphy

Judge
3rd Judicial Circuit Court

The Honorable John A. Murphy was first elected to the Court of Common Pleas on November 7, 1978. He also served with distinction on the 36th District Court until his election to the 3rd Judicial Circuit in 1986.

A graduate of Southeastern High School, Murphy received an undergraduate degree from the University of Michigan. He received a law degree from Wayne State University Law School.

Murphy is a member of numerous professional and civic organizations. These include the American Trial Lawyers Association, the American Judges Association, the Wolverine Bar Association, the Association of Black Judges of Michigan and Optimist International.

Murphy is married to the former Patricia Ann Van Dyke, and is the father of one son, John Brandon. His family resides in a happy home in Plymouth Township.

Appointed president and chief executive officer of the Detroit Riverfront Conservancy in September of 2003, Faye Alexander Nelson is responsible for overseeing the planning, design, construction, operations and programming of the Detroit International Riverfront, including the RiverWalk and adjacent parks, plazas and pavilions. Previously, she was vice president of governmental affairs for Wayne State University, where she led the development of the university's research and technology park. From 1981 to 1996, she was senior corporate attorney, then director of government affairs for Kmart.

Committed to working for progress in her hometown of Detroit, Nelson serves on the board of directors for Compuware Corporation, the Michigan Economic Growth Authority, the University of Detroit Mercy and TechTown. She is also a member of the American Bar Association and the State Bar of Michigan. Additionally, she is a life member of the Judicial Conference of the Sixth Circuit, Leadership Detroit XIII, the Detroit Athletic Club and the Detroit Economic Club.

Nelson has a Bachelor of Arts degree in political science from Mercy College of Detroit, and a juris doctorate degree from the University of Detroit.

Faye Alexander Nelson

President &
Chief Executive Officer
Detroit Riverfront Conservancy

Rodney O'Neal is president and chief operating officer of Delphi Corporation, a leading maker of automotive and transportation electronics and systems. He is a member of the Delphi strategy board, the company's top policy-making group.

O'Neal has also held numerous positions at General Motors (GM), including a number of engineering and manufacturing positions in Dayton, Portugal and Canada. In 1997 he was elected a GM vice president. In 1998 he was elected a Delphi vice president, and in 2003 he was named president of the dynamics, propulsion, thermal and interior sector.

O'Neal earned a bachelor's degree from Kettering University and a master's degree from Stanford University. He is a member of the Executive Leadership Council and sits on the board of directors for the Goodyear Tire and Rubber Company. He is a former member of the board of directors for INROADS, Inc., the Michigan Manufacturers Association and the Woodward Governor Company, as well as the advisory board for Focus: HOPE.

Rodney O'Neal

President &
Chief Operating Officer
Delphi Corporation

Linda V. Parker

Director
Michigan Department of Civil Rights

Linda V. Parker is director of the Michigan Department of Civil Rights (MDCR). In this position, she has been an outspoken advocate for diversity as both a moral and economic imperative, while focusing priorities at MDCR on housing discrimination, segregation and promoting equality for all. Before her appointment by Governor Jennifer M. Granholm to her current position, she served as first executive assistant U.S. attorney for the Eastern District of Michigan from 1994 to 2000.

Parker is the recipient of the 2005 Damon J. Keith Community Spirit Award, and was one of six recipients of the Anti-Defamation League's 2006 Women of Achievement Award. In 2007 she was named Professional Woman of the Year by the Detroit Club National Association of Negro Business and Professional Women's Clubs, Inc.

A native Detroiter and attorney, Parker is a University of Michigan graduate with a juris doctorate degree from the National Law Center at George Washington University in Washington, D.C.

Glenn R. Plummer

Chairman &
Chief Executive Officer
Christian Television Network

Glenn R. Plummer founded the Christian Television Network (CTN) in 1982, and has gone on to own and operate three local independent stations. He is well known as the host of a daily, live one-hour television program, *CTN Live!* Passionate and confrontational, Plummer is admired for his courage and leadership in dealing with controversial issues from a foundation of biblical principles. Recently ending his three-and-a-half-year term, he was the first African American to serve as chair and chief executive officer of the National Religious Broadcasters (NRB) in their 63-year history.

Several years ago, Plummer had a vision for Israel and black America, but 2004 proved to be pivotal in unfolding his new role of leadership in this area. Thus, the Fellowship of Israel and Black America was launched in February of 2006 as a partnership with the International Fellowship of Christians and Jews.

Plummer is senior pastor of Ambassadors for Christ Church. He sits on the board of directors of the NRB and the board of advisors of El Al Israel Airlines.

Kevin D. Poston is president and chief executive officer of Professional Sports Planning, Inc. (PSP), a sports management company with offices in metropolitan Detroit, Michigan, and Houston, Texas. PSP has represented some of the top professional football and basketball players in the world. Since PSP's inception in 1989, the firm has negotiated contracts for its clients in excess of $1 billion.

Kevin negotiated the first maximum contract for a second round selection when he did so for Michael Redd of the Milwaukee Bucks in 2005. In 2006 PSP negotiated more than $190 million in NFL free agent contracts. As PSP's marketing director, Kevin worked with Nike to create the successful Lil' Penny campaign, where Anfernee Hardaway, then of the Orlando Magic, became marketing's most popular professional athlete in 1996, surpassing Michael Jordan.

Kevin graduated from Fisk University in 1981 with a Bachelor of Science degree in business administration. He received a juris doctorate degree from Texas Southern University in 1985.

Kevin lives with his wife, Kathy, and his two sons, Garrison and Myles. His oldest child, daughter Alexx, is attending college.

Kevin D. Poston

President &
Chief Executive Officer
Professional Sports Planning, Inc.

The Honorable Mark Randon serves as a judge of the 36th District Court in Detroit, one of the largest and busiest district courts in the nation. In this position, he presides over a wide variety of civil and criminal cases that occur in Detroit.

Appointed by the governor in 2001 at age 32, Randon holds the distinction of being the youngest judge appointed to the bench in Michigan since the constitutional requirements were changed. In 2002 the citizens of Detroit elected him to a six-year term, which he is currently serving.

Randon has authored several articles that have appeared in newspapers and legal journals. He has received many awards for his community service, including *Crain's Detroit Business*' 40 Under 40. In 2005 he established an educational program for young offenders through Wayne County Community College.

Randon is a graduate of Cass Technical High School and Michigan State University. He received a law degree from the University of Michigan in 1992. He has been married for 11 years to Dr. Lisa Marie Randon, and together they have two children.

The Honorable
Mark A. Randon

Judge
36th District Court

Pamela E. Rodgers

Owner
Rodgers Chevrolet

After receiving a Master of Business Administration degree from Duke University in 1983, Pamela Rodgers returned to her hometown of Detroit, where she joined Ford Motor Company as a financial analyst.

Rodgers launched her career in automotive sales working as a sales person at several dealerships, where she gained invaluable experience in all aspects of dealership operations. She applied and was admitted to Ford's Minority Dealer Development Program in 1988, making her one of only a handful of women granted this opportunity.

In early 1993 she took over the Flat Rock dealership in Detroit, managing to increase sales to $18 million. In 1995 it became No. 1 in service satisfaction for the Detroit area. Unfortunately, General Motors closed the Flat Rock facility, so Rodgers purchased the neighboring dealership in Woodhaven, and named it Rodgers Chevrolet, which she has operated since 1996.

Rodgers Chevrolet has grown from 40 units per month to 210 units. In 1996 the dealership generated revenues of $37 million. By 2001, sales were more than $80 million and continue to average more than $75 million.

Nettie H. Seabrooks

Chief Operating Officer
Detroit Institute of Arts

Nettie H. Seabrooks was named the Detroit Institute of Arts (DIA) chief operating officer on September 19, 2002, after having joined the museum in February of 2002 as senior associate to the director.

Prior to joining the DIA, Seabrooks was the chief operating officer and chief of staff for Detroit Mayor Dennis W. Archer. Appointed to this position on January 1, 1998, she had served as Mayor Archer's deputy mayor and chief administrative officer during his first four-year term of office. At the time of her appointment by Mayor Archer in 1994, she was director of government relations for General Motors (GM) Corporation's North American Operations, and had been with GM for 31 years.

Seabrooks has a Bachelor of Science degree in chemistry from Marygrove College, a Master of Arts degree in library science from the University of Michigan, a Master of Arts degree in art history from Wayne State University, and honorary Doctor of Humane Letters degrees from Marygrove College and the University of Detroit Mercy.

S hirley R. Stancato is president and chief executive officer of New Detroit, a race relations coalition. Previously, her career spanned 30 years at what is now Chase Bank, where she rose to the position of senior vice president.

Under Stancato's leadership, New Detroit conducts a series of initiatives to further its mission of improving race relations, and fostering economic and social equity. They include a leadership summit on race, a summer youth business camp, financial literacy programs in schools, multicultural leadership education, helping small nonprofits build their organizational capacity, and leading the revitalization of southeastern Michigan as a founding member of One D: Transforming Regional Detroit.

A lifelong Detroiter, Stancato earned bachelor's and master's degrees from Wayne State University. She serves on numerous boards, including the Coleman A. Young Foundation, the Detroit Symphony Orchestra, the JPMorgan Chase National Community Advisory Board and the United Way for Southeastern Michigan.

Stancato has received many awards and recognitions, including the National Association of Community Leadership's Distinguished Leadership Award, the Anti-Defamation League's Woman of Achievement Award and a Regional Power Broker Award by *Crain's Detroit Business.*

Shirley R. Stancato

President &
Chief Executive Officer
New Detroit, Inc.

B orn in Detroit, Marjorie Ann Staten is a graduate of the University of Detroit Mercy and the University of Detroit School of Law. For nine years, she worked at the country's largest minority-owned law firm, Lewis & Munday, P.C.

Staten serves as executive director of the General Motors Minority Dealers Association (GMMDA). In the past six years, she has helped the GMMDA to increase membership, and develop and implement benefits, programs and initiatives. Staten was a key player in a major research project to develop the first private investment fund with a group of minority investors.

Staten is involved with numerous civic and professional organizations. She serves on the boards of the National Association of Minority Automobile Dealers and the Student Mentor Partners Program. A member of the State Bar of Michigan and the Wolverine Bar Association, she was awarded the WAAI's 2004 Spirit of Leadership Award and was honored as one of the 25 Influential Black Women in Business by *The Network Journal.*

An active member of St. Mary's of Redford Church, Staten is the mother of one son, Martin.

Marjorie Ann Staten

Executive Director
General Motors Minority
Dealers Association

Herbert J. Strather

Chairman
Hitsville Venture, LLC

Herbert J. Strather is the chairman of Hitsville Venture, LLC and the president and chief executive officer of Strather & Associates. As a real estate entrepreneur for more than 30 years, Strather has cultivated more than $1 billion in real estate assets.

Strather's current projects include a majority partner position in the development of Woodbridge Estates, a $120 million residential community consisting of senior living, apartments and 100 new single-family townhomes and condos. Another project includes a majority partnership position in the acquisition, renovation and repositioning of the historic Hotel St. Regis Detroit.

Strather serves on a myriad of boards, including the Progressive National Baptist Convention (chairman), Optimist International (established and endowed the Optimist Youth Foundation of Detroit – $1 million personal commitment, resulting in more than 2,500 scholarships to Detroit area youth), the Benjamin E. Mays Male Academy (member), and Hartford Memorial Baptist Church (member, board of trustees).

Strather has written numerous columns on real estate investment, including a ten-week series on wealth creation in the *Michigan Chronicle*, and a book, *Getting Rich is Easy, a Guide to Real Estate*.

The Honorable Craig S. Strong

Judge
3rd Judicial Circuit of Michigan

In 1978 the Honorable Craig S. Strong was appointed referee in the Traffic and Ordinance Division of Detroit Recorders Court. Being the youngest to serve in this capacity, he was elected judge of Detroit Recorders Court. An officer of the Wolverine Bar Association, Strong became its youngest president. He later became one of the founding members of the Association of Black Judges of Michigan, and served as president.

Strong has served on the National Bar Association board of governors, and was chair of the Judicial Council. A retired commander in the U.S. Navy Reserve, he was the only African-American judge presiding over special courts-martial during his tour in the Navy-Marine Corps Trial Judiciary. Strong was part of the National Bar Association's delegation to South Africa, where he met with representatives from the African National Congress, and sat on the Supreme Court of South Africa.

A 33rd degree Prince Hall Mason, Strong is a lifetime member of the NAACP, and a member of the Charles H. Wright Museum of African American History, Alpha Phi Alpha Fraternity, Inc. and the Navy Reserve Officer Association.

O'Neil D. Swanson is the founder and president of Swanson Funeral Home in Detroit. He has served as the director of the National Funeral Directors and Morticians Association, and is a board trustee of the National Foundation of Funeral Services.

A graduate of Central State University in Ohio, Swanson attended the Cincinnati College of Mortuary Science. He established The Swanson Foundation to support education and civic life, providing scholarships for minority students and support for higher education. Swanson is the recipient of honorary doctorate degrees from Central State University, Shaw College and the Urban Bible Institute.

Swanson has been an active member of numerous organizations, including Alpha Phi Alpha Fraternity, Inc., the People's Community Civic League, the Booker T. Washington Business Association, the Detroit Better Business Bureau, Boy Scouts of America, the Michigan Department of Commerce and many more.

A lifetime member of the NAACP, Swanson was awarded the Freedom and Justice Award, honoring his civic leadership and lifetime commitment to the NAACP in Detroit. He is also a veteran of the U.S. Army and belongs to Mt. Zion Baptist Church.

O'Neil D. Swanson

Founder & President
Swanson Funeral Home

The Honorable Deborah A. Thomas is the middle child of three daughters born into a working-class family. At the age of three, she contracted polio. She recalls the loving attention and encouragement from her father during the challenges of her early years. Following her father's death, when she was ten years old, it was her mother, extended family and church that guided her to become the person she is today.

Thomas is a lifetime resident of Detroit, and was educated in the Detroit Public Schools. A graduate of Cass Technical High School, she attended Western Michigan University, where she earned a bachelor's degree in education and sociology. She also has a master's degree in criminal justice and a law degree.

Thomas' favorite pastime is community volunteer service. She is a member of the Order of the Elks, the Mary McLeod Bethune Association, the A. Phillip Randolph Institute and many other organizations. She believes that working with youth is an especially important use of time.

**The Honorable
Deborah A. Thomas**

Judge
3rd Judicial Circuit Court

The Honorable Samuel "Buzz" Thomas III

Senator, 4th District
Michigan State Senate

The Honorable Buzz Thomas has been called "A Rising Star" by *The Detroit News* and *The Hotline*, one of Michigan's five "Key Technology Leaders" by the *Detroit Free Press*, and an "Under-40 Political 'Buzz' Saw" by the *Michigan FrontPage*. He was also recognized as one of four "Up-And-Coming Leaders" by *Savoy* magazine. Thomas (D-Detroit) is known not only as a political force, but also as a dynamic legislative leader.

One hundred and four years after Michigan's first African American, William Web Ferguson, was elected to the state legislature, his great-grandnephew, Thomas, was elected to the Michigan House of Representatives. In 2002 Thomas was unanimously voted as the Michigan House Democratic leader.

Thomas is a leader in the fields of energy and technology, health policy and urban development. He is also an avid supporter of the arts and culture community.

Thomas continues his activism by donating his state salary adjustments to several community, civic and cultural organizations. He serves on several community boards, including the Diabetes Association of Michigan, Independent Policy Group, Matthew NcNeely Neighborhood Foundation and Plowshares Theater.

Carolynn Walton

Vice President & Treasurer
Blue Cross Blue Shield of
Michigan

Carolynn Walton, CPA, is vice president and treasurer for Blue Cross Blue Shield of Michigan (BCBSM). In this role, she is responsible for managing the company's investment portfolios, employee benefit plans and financing options for BCBSM and its subsidiaries. Walton is also responsible for risk management and business continuity planning functions. Previously, she served as director of treasury services.

Walton received a Master of Business Administration degree from Western Michigan University and a bachelor's degree from the University of Michigan Ross School of Business.

She is a member of the American Institute of Certified Public Accountants, the Michigan Association of Certified Public Accountants and the National Association of Black Accountants. She also serves on the Michigan Chamber of Commerce board of directors, the Financial Executive International Detroit board of directors and the Michigan Women's Foundation Investment Committee.

A West Bloomfield resident, Walton is married to John Andrews, and they have successfully raised two children, Crystal D. Andrews of Chicago and John L. Andrews of New York City.

The Honorable Mary D. Waters is serving her third term as the state representative for Michigan's 4th District, and her second term as the Democratic floor leader in the Michigan House of Representatives.

Mary has served on several committees and task force groups, working to improve the quality of life for citizens in her community. Her recent activities include working on the transition team for Detroit Public Schools and promoting literacy programs in Michigan. She also works diligently to ensure services for seniors and low-income residents. She annually sponsors Operation Dental Flush, a program that provides free teeth cleanings.

Mary's numerous memberships include the Detroit Branch NAACP, Spanish Speaking Democrats, the Trade Union Leadership Council, the National Political Congress of Black Women and Women's Action for New Directions (WAND).

A true advocate for the rights of all people, Mary is dedicated to representing the needs and concerns of her constituency.

The Honorable Mary D. Waters

Representative, District 4
Michigan House of
Representatives

When you peruse Heaster Wheeler's background, his commitment to community is pristine. His activism in the political, civil rights and the social justice advocacy process goes back to junior high school, when he was a member of the Black Student Union.

Currently, Wheeler serves as the executive director of the Detroit Branch National Association for the Advancement of Colored People (NAACP). In this appointed position since October of 1999, he has tackled major issues, including regressive juvenile justice laws, driving while black, employment discrimination, the takeover of Detroit Public Schools, voting rights, and protecting and preserving affirmative action.

Prior to being appointed executive director, Wheeler served as a lobbyist for Ameritech and Detroit Public Schools, and as legislative assistant to then Representative Carolyn Cheeks Kilpatrick. He also served as deputy director of communications for then Speaker of the House Curtis Hertel.

Family is important to Wheeler, and he is married to Jennifer and has three children, Khari, Jeneva and Jeremiah. He also has four grandchildren, Kaylin, Khari II, Kennedy and Kristopher. He is a member of Fellowship Chapel Church in Detroit.

Heaster L. Wheeler

Executive Director
Detroit Branch NAACP

Vickie Winans

Recording Artist

The name Winans and gospel music are synonymous, and Vickie Winans definitely lives up to her name after 20 years of singing the good news of Jesus Christ. The captivating vocals of this multitalented artist pique the emotions and uplift the spirit. Vickie lends a high-powered, energetic, yet smooth and inspirational style, as showcased in all her Grammy-nominated, Stellar Award and NAACP Award-winning albums. She was just 8 years old when she sang her first solo in church. From then on, the biggest challenge for Aaron and Mattie Bowman was keeping a tight rein on their seventh child.

One of the industry's most beloved and respected artists, Vickie is in firm control of her career. She manages herself and is president of Viviane, Inc., her Detroit-based management company, where she books and performs approximately 230 shows a year.

Vickie says her favorite job is being the proud mother of her two sons, hit producer and singer Mario "Skeeter" Winans, and Marvin "Coconut" Winans. She also loves being "Nannie" to her 10-year-old grandson, Mario Winans II, and 7-year-old granddaughter, Skyler Destiny Winans.

Kimberlydawn Wisdom, M.D.

Surgeon General
State of Michigan

Dr. Kimberlydawn Wisdom is a board-certified emergency medicine physician, who has practiced for 20 years at the Henry Ford Health System. Wisdom founded and directed the Institute of Multicultural Health at Henry Ford and a national award-winning community-based health screening initiative entitled AIMHI (African American Initiative for Male Health Improvement). AIMHI focused on improving the health of those disproportionately affected by poor health outcomes: African-American men.

In February of 2003, Governor Jennifer M. Granholm took an important step toward revitalizing public health in Michigan by appointing Wisdom as Michigan's, and the nation's, first state-level surgeon general. In that role, Wisdom has focused on physical inactivity, unhealthy eating habits, childhood lead poisoning, tobacco use, chronic disease, infant mortality, unintended pregnancy and health disparities, among other areas of concern.

While retaining her role as Michigan surgeon general, in early 2007 Wisdom returned to the Henry Ford Health System as vice president of community health education and wellness, and is leading efforts to improve the health of the metropolitan Detroit community.

interest

limelight

Southern Hospitality Restaurant Group

CORPORATE SPOTLIGHT

attention

prominence

highlight

celebrate

headline

focus

recognition

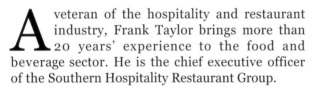

Frank A. Taylor

Chief Executive Officer
Southern Hospitality Restaurant Group

Robert Porcher III

President
Southern Hospitality Restaurant Group

A veteran of the hospitality and restaurant industry, Frank Taylor brings more than 20 years' experience to the food and beverage sector. He is the chief executive officer of the Southern Hospitality Restaurant Group.

Taylor oversees Seldom Blues, Detroit's only upscale jazz restaurant and supper club. Seldom Blues was named Restaurant of the Year 2006 by the *Detroit Free Press*, Best Overall Restaurant by *Hour Detroit* magazine, Most Sophisticated Venue by *Style* magazine, as well as Detroit's Breakfast House & Grill for Best Place for Breakfast and Motown Soul Food Café. The company also handles food service operations for One Ford Place, the corporate office center for the Henry Ford Health System. Most recently, Taylor received the 2007 Thurgood Marshall Award of Excellence.

Prior to forming the SHRG, Taylor served as director of food and beverage at Marriott in Pontiac, Michigan, and the Troy Marriott, the Doubletree Hotel in Pittsburgh and the Sheraton Imperial Hotel in Research Triangle Park, North Carolina. Notably, he also assisted with the conception of several well-recognized, fine dining establishments, including the Pittsburgh Fish Market and the Seldom Blues Cafe in Cary, North Carolina.

Robert Porcher III, the All-Pro Detroit Lions defensive end, played in the NFL for 13 seasons.

Porcher has proven to be a force off the field as well. Since his retirement from the NFL, he has developed into a skilled businessman with an impressive portfolio of business ventures in Detroit.

In 2002 Porcher established the Detroit Football Classic. The Detroit Football Classic is an annual historically black college football game played at Ford Field. The inaugural game in 2003 featured Florida A&M and Alabama State universities in front of a sellout crowd, and catapulted into the top three attended black college classics in the country.

Porcher broadened his business interests in 2004, as partner of Seldom Blues Restaurant & Jazz Supper Club. He is president of Southern Hospitality Restaurant Group, which owns and operates restaurants in Detroit, including Seldom Blues, Detroit's Breakfast House & Grill and Motown Soul Food Café (formerly Grand City Grille).

Porcher recently accomplished one of his long-term goals as he graduated and received certification from the National Automobile Dealers Academy Program in March of 2007.

Jerry Nottage

Corporate Executive Concept Chef
Southern Hospitality Restaurant Group

Joan H. Craig

Corporate Director, Business &
Organizational Development
Southern Hospitality Restaurant Group

Executive Chef Jerry Nottage is a seasoned master chef with more than 25 years of experience in the culinary world. His surprising and artful use of ingredients has earned him a reputation as one of the most imaginative and talented chefs on the American culinary scene.

As executive concept chef of Southern Hospitality Restaurant Group, Nottage has led culinary teams for Seldom Blues Restaurant & Jazz Supper Club, Motown Soul Food Café, Detroit's Breakfast House & Grill, The Woodward Restaurant and Sweet Georgia Brown.

Nottage has been named Best of the Best Chef by *Hour Detroit* magazine and Best Chef by *Metro Times*. His culinary influences resulted in Seldom Blues being named Restaurant of the Year 2006 by the *Detroit Free Press*, Best Overall Restaurant by *Hour Detroit* magazine, Most Sophisticated Venue by *Style* magazine, as well as Detroit's Breakfast House & Grill for Best Place for Breakfast.

Recognized nationally for his culinary prowess, Nottage has prepared dishes for international dignitaries and celebrities, including the Queen of England, the Duchess of York, Stevie Wonder, Vivica A. Fox, Sidney Poitier and Audrey Hepburn.

A native of Ohio, Joan Craig brings more than 20 years of business management, marketing and organizational development skills to the Southern Hospitality Restaurant Group. Prior to her joining the team in 2002, Craig was senior director of customer marketing for the Handleman Company based in Troy, Michigan. She was responsible for marketing and customer service programs for Kmart, Wal-Mart, Meijer and Best Buy.

As director of business and organizational development for Southern Hospitality Restaurant Group, Craig is the operations liaison for Seldom Blues Jazz Restaurant & Supper Club. Seldom Blues was named Restaurant of the Year 2006 by the *Detroit Free Press*, Best Overall Restaurant by *Hour Detroit* magazine, as well as Detroit's Breakfast House & Grill for Best Place for Breakfast. She is also operations liaison for Motown Soul Food Café (formerly Grand City Grille); One Ford Place, the corporate office center for Henry Ford Health Systems; The Woodward Restaurant; and Sweet Georgia Brown.

Craig is also dedicated to serving the metro Detroit community, and has been actively involved in numerous church and community service projects over the years.

Detroit's *Premier*

FINE DINING AND JAZZ SUPPER CLUB

SERVING CONTEMPORARY CUISINE WITH AN INTERNATIONAL FLAIR

SELDOM BLUES HAS RECEIVED MANY PRESTIGIOUS AWARDS, INCLUDING

◇ HOUR Detroit "2006 Best Restaurant General Excellence"

◇ Detroit Free Press "2006 Restaurant of the Year"

◇ Style Magazine "2006 Most Sophisticated Venue"

◇ Named one of America's Best Bars by Esquire Magazine

◇ Wine Spectator Award, 2005, 2006 and 2007

SELDOM BLUES
PLAY HERE

Hours: Mon. – Thurs: 11:30 a.m. to 10 p.m. | Fri.: 11:30 a.m. – 12 a.m.
Sat.: 5 p.m. – 12 a.m. | Sunday Brunch: 11:30 a.m. – 4 p.m.
313.567.7301 | 400 Renaissance Center, Detroit, Michigan | www.seldomblues.com
A Southern Hospitality Restaurant Group Property

interest

limelight

CORPORATE SPOTLIGHT

attention

prominence

highlight

celebrate

headline

focus

recognition

Chrysler LLC

Chrysler LLC is one of the world's largest manufacturers of passenger vehicles and light-duty trucks. More than 78,000 employees work for Chrysler in nearly every state and province in the United States, Canada and Mexico, and in offices and facilities in more than 125 countries around the world. We produce approximately two dozen Chrysler, Dodge and Jeep passenger vehicles and have 14 assembly, 10 powertrain, three stamping and four component plants in North America.

Headquartered in Auburn Hills, Michigan, Chrysler LLC is the center of all administrative, engineering and design operations, while other major engineering and research facilities are located in Detroit and Windsor, Ontario. Two vehicle proving grounds for testing — one in Chelsea, Michigan, and the other in Wittman, Arizona — and an advanced vehicle design center in Carlsbad, California, also support our organization.

Our subsidiaries include Chrysler Motors LLC, Chrysler Canada Inc. and Chrysler de Mexico S.A de C.V., as well as other international automotive affiliates. These companies manufacture, assemble and sell cars and trucks under the names Chrysler, Dodge and Jeep. We also provide our customers with parts and accessories marketed under the Mopar® brand name.

At Chrysler LLC, diversity is a bottom-line imperative. An inclusive workforce is what drives the smart solutions and innovative products needed to win in the highly competitive global marketplace. The Chrysler Foundation annually contributes millions of dollars to local, regional and national organizations serving ethnic communities. Our minority supplier development represents 13.5 percent of our total purchasing, an increase of $150 million from the previous year. And minorities comprise nearly 30 percent of our workforce, which allows us to integrate our diversity philosophy into all aspects of our business.

For more information, visit us at **chryslerllc.com**

Chrysler Financial

Chrysler Financial was founded in 1964 as Chrysler Credit Corporation. During our four decades of service to dealers and consumers of Chrysler, Dodge and Jeep vehicles, we've built a reputation for providing a complete line of world-class automotive financial products and services that are second to none. From leasing vehicles to financing retail and commercial sales, financing and managing passenger and commercial fleets, and offering financial support and insurance to dealers, Chrysler Financial is committed to providing the widest variety of financial services to our customers.

Headquartered in Farmington Hills, Michigan, Chrysler Financial strives to be a responsible member of our industry and community. We have developed a unique culture that is founded upon the highest business and ethical standards. We are committed to an inclusive environment, respectful of the differing lifestyles, backgrounds, perspectives, skills and talents of all of our employees.

75 billion dollars strong, and counting, Chrysler Financial supports a global portfolio in countries including the United States, Canada, Mexico, Puerto Rico and Venezuela. More than 4,400 Chrysler, Dodge and Jeep dealers have chosen us as their primary source for vehicle wholesale and retail financing. In the U.S. alone, nearly 3 million drivers enjoy the benefits of leasing or financing with Chrysler Financial.

4,200 employees and five core values make us what we are today. Our associates focus solely on satisfying the needs of our customers, and to that end, we provide the latest tools and support technology. To help us become a more dynamic and responsive company, we empower our employees by encouraging them to offer up their unique vision, ideas and experience. And our drive toward excellence is built upon a simple foundation of five core values: Financial and Social Responsibility, Inspired and Empowered Employees, Customer Focus, Commitment to Excellence and Integrity, Openness and Respect.

For more information, visit us at **corp.chryslerfinancial.com**

Tonya M. Blander

Senior Manager
Troy Customer Contact Center
Chrysler Financial

Monica E. Emerson

Executive Director
Corporate Diversity Office
Chrysler LLC

Tonya M. Blander is senior manager of the Troy Customer Contact Center for Chrysler Financial. She is responsible for managing the overall customer service, collection and center operation activities for a $13 billion portfolio. Her responsibilities include the development of more than 400 employees supporting Chrysler Financial.

In December of 1995, Tonya joined Chrysler Financial as a customer service representative. During her career, she has held numerous positions including zone relation manager for Chrysler Financial and region manager for Mercedes-Benz Financial. As a dealer relation manager, she was bestowed the distinguished honor of the Portland Zone Dealer Relations Manager Award.

Tonya frequently represents Chrysler Financial during various leadership events including Hip-Hop Summits on Financial Empowerment, the National Black MBA Conferences and the Great Place to Work Conferences. In 1994 she received a Bachelor of Arts degree in psychology from the University of South Carolina, where she pledged Delta Sigma Pi. Tonya is completing a Master of Business Administration degree at City University.

She resides in Rochester Hills, Michigan, with her daughter, Britńi. In her spare time, Tonya enjoys cycling and photography.

Monica E. Emerson is executive director of the Corporate Diversity Office. She is responsible for the overall design, development and deployment of Chrysler's corporate diversity strategies aligned to business objectives. She is also responsible for EEO compliance and governance, and work/life policies and programs.

Emerson is a nationally respected corporate strategist on diversity and inclusion in the workplace. Her efforts inside Chrysler have resulted in the company being recognized as an industry leader. She has received numerous external awards for her accomplishments, including the Women of Color in Technology and Business Lifetime Achievement Award.

Emerson is active in the community and affiliated with organizations such as Catalyst, the National Coalition of 100 Black Women, The Executive Leadership Council and Focus: HOPE. She was appointed by Governor Jennifer M. Granholm to the Oakland University board of trustees on May 15, 2007.

Emerson, a native Detroiter, received a Bachelor of Arts degree from Oakland University and a Master of Arts degree from Wayne State University.

CORPORATE SPOTLIGHT

Chrysler Financial

Donald E. Goodwin

Vice President, Global Service
Chrysler LLC

Kim Harris Jones

Vice President & Chief Controller
Chrysler LLC

Donald "Don" E. Goodwin was appointed Chrysler LLC's vice president of global service in February of 2007. In this capacity, Don oversees service program management and strategy, global service marketing, dealer technical operations, warranty operations and the customer assistance center. He is also responsible for the development of process improvement efforts for Chrysler, Jeep and Dodge service worldwide.

Don came to global service from the scientific labs and proving grounds, in which he managed DaimlerChrysler materials and fasteners engineering, engineering development laboratories, prototype build, and proving grounds and testing for Chrysler LLC's brands. In addition, he was responsible for all engineering activities at then DaimlerChrysler Canada, Inc. and DaimlerChrysler de Mexico.

Don serves on the boards of the Chrysler African American Network, the Engineering Society of Detroit and the Rackham Engineering Foundation. He is vice chair of the board of trustees at New Calvary Baptist Church.

A native Detroiter, Don graduated from Cass Technical High School. He received a Bachelor of Science degree in mechanical engineering and a master's degree in management from the University of Michigan.

Kim Harris Jones was appointed vice president and chief controller of Chrysler LLC in August of 2007. She is responsible for corporate financial activities, including business planning, short and medium term financial forecasting, manufacturing finance and financial reporting. The corporate economist also reports to her.

Prior to this position, Jones, the first African-American female vice president at Chrysler, served as vice president of product, procurement cost management finance for the Chrysler Group.

Jones is a member and former president of the Boys and Girls Republic Youth Home board, a lifetime member of the National Black MBA Association and a member of The Executive Leadership Council. In 2007 she was named one of Metro Detroit's Most Influential Women by *Crain's Detroit Business*, and received the Peter C. Thorpe Leadership Award. She was named the African American Executive of the Year by OnWheels, Incorporated in 2006, and to *Automotive News*' list of 100 Leading Women in the North American Auto Industry in 2005.

Jones received a Bachelor of Business Administration degree in accounting and an MBA in finance from the University of Michigan.

Talvis P. Love

Vice President of Information
Technology Management &
Chief Information Officer
Chrysler Financial

Machelle A. McAdory

Vice President
Human Resources &
Administrative Services
Chrysler Financial

Talvis P. Love is vice president of information technology management (ITM) and chief information officer for Chrysler Financial. Talvis began his career with Chrysler Financial as an ITM senior manager for dealer and point-of-sale systems and a liaison to the Chrysler Financial brand in 2005.

Currently, Talvis is responsible for directing the development of information technology (IT) systems as aligned to the Chrysler Financial strategic requirements. He also oversees IT systems operations to support Chrysler Financial at optimal cost and manage IT development and implementation to ensure data protection, security and privacy for Chrysler Financial customers.

Talvis began his IT career in 1990 with Mobil Oil Corporation and has held various IT and sales and marketing positions within Oracle Corporation, Monsanto and Ford Motor Company. He holds a Bachelor of Science degree in information systems management from the University of Maryland and completed graduate studies at The University of Chicago Graduate School of Business. He is a 2008 candidate in the Executive MBA Program at Michigan State University. Talvis resides in Novi, Michigan, with his wife, Kimberly, and three children.

Machelle A. McAdory is vice president of human resources and administrative services for Chrysler Financial. Prior to this position, she was senior manager of human resources and global procurement and supply at Chrysler. Machelle joined Chrysler in 1987 as a placement and development coordinator in Auburn Hills, Michigan. She has held several human resources management and employee relations positions.

Her work-related responsibilities include all aspects of human resources strategic planning and implementation, including organizational effectiveness, employee relations, diversity, employment, compensation and benefits, leadership and professional development, and facilities services.

Machelle is a board of directors vice chair for the American Red Cross of Southeastern Michigan. In addition, she is a member of the Chrysler African American Network, the National Black MBA Association, the Society of Human Resources Management and the National Association of Female Executives.

Machelle received a Bachelor of Science degree in industrial administration at GMI Engineering and Management Institute, and a Master of Business Administration from the University of Michigan. She lives with her husband, Randall, and their three children in Rochester Hills, Michigan.

Chrysler Financial

Karla E. Middlebrooks

Vice President
Finance & Controlling Americas
DaimlerChrysler Financial Services Americas

David L. Nelson

Vice President & Treasurer
Chrysler Financial

Karla E. Middlebrooks is vice president of financial reporting and corporate controlling for DaimlerChrysler Financial Services Americas. In her previous position, she was director of capital investment financial control. In August of 1984, Karla joined DaimlerChrysler as a financial analyst. She has also served in various areas of financial and controlling management, including competitive analysis, marketing cost analysis, Mopar Parts, product finance, and procurement and supply.

As vice president in financial reporting, she is responsible for directing all accounting and financial reporting for DaimlerChrysler Financial Services Americas.

Karla participates as a member of the Detroit Chapter of The Links Inc. She was also the 2001 recipient of the National Eagle Leadership Institute Award.

She received a Master of Business Administration degree from Harvard Graduate School of Business in 1984, and a Bachelor of Industrial Engineering degree from Northwestern University in 1980.

A native of Detroit, Karla resides in West Bloomfield with her husband, Bill, and two sons, Arthur and Andrew.

David L. Nelson is vice president and treasurer for Chrysler Financial. David began his career as a financial analyst in 1990. He was promoted to several management positions within Chrysler and gained experience in all areas of finance, treasury and investor relations.

Currently, David is responsible for all treasury functions including capital markets funding, cash management, asset-liability and pension management, interest rate risk management and development of financing alternatives optimizing the company's capital structure. He maintains relationships with rating agencies, banks and institutional investors through communication of the company's business model, strategy, operational and financial objectives.

David volunteers on the board of directors for Michigan State University Multicultural Business Programs and the Detroit Area Pre-College Engineering Program. He is also a member of the National Black MBA Association and the National Association of Securities Professionals.

David holds a Bachelor of Arts degree in finance from Michigan State University, a Master of Business Administration degree in finance and a master's degree in economics from the University of Detroit Mercy. He resides in Novi, Michigan, with wife Karyn and three children.

interest

limelight

CORPORATE SPOTLIGHT

attention

prominence

highlight

celebrate

headline

focus

recognition

Michael G. Bickers

Executive Vice President &
Market Executive
National City

Joyce Conley

Senior Vice President
Michigan Public Funds
National City

Michael Bickers is executive vice president and market executive for the Detroit market. In this position, he oversees 123 branches in National City's nearly 1,400-branch network. He is a Detroit native and joined National City's predecessor bank, First of America, in 1986 as a commercial credit analyst.

Michael is active in the Detroit community, including participation in the Detroit Black Chamber of Commerce, the Booker T. Washington Business Association, the Local Initiatives Support Corporation (Urban Housing Development), and the Detroit Economic Club.

Michael has actively served as a panelist in forums such as the 2005 Urban and Automotive Industry Symposium and the 2006 Economic Strategies for Rebuilding New Orleans. Internally, he is a member of National City's Local Charitable Contributions Committee, and a member of the National City Community Development Corporation's advisory board.

Michael's education includes the Graduate School of Retail Banking at the University of Virginia.

Joyce Conley is senior vice president and manager of the Public Funds Group for National City Bank in Troy, Michigan. She specializes in providing an array of financial services to municipalities and public school districts. She started her career in banking in 1981, and has a wide variety of experience and expertise in the field of treasury management.

Joyce is an active member in various organizations, including the Detroit Treasury Management Association. She is also an executive board member of the Urban Financial Services Coalition. Her professional memberships include Wayne County treasurer, Oakland County treasurer, Macomb County treasurer, the Michigan Government Finance Officers Association, the Michigan Municipal Treasurers Association, the Detroit Economic Club and Inforum.

Joyce received a bachelor's degree from Loyola University in Chicago. She is a certified treasury professional.

A native of Chicago, Illinois, Joyce is the proud mother of two, daughter Kenya and son Trevor.

Josephine Henyard

Vice President &
Branch District Sales Executive
National City

Ivan A. Johnson

Vice President &
Real Estate Manager
National City

Josephine Henyard is a branch district sales executive for National City Bank. She joined National City's predecessor bank in Detroit in 1971 as a part-time teller. During her career, she has managed branch offices, and was responsible for training more than 200 platform staff during the conversion of First of America to National City.

Josephine has received numerous awards for generating revenue growth and customer excellence. She is responsible for customer service and sales growth at the Detroit, Dearborn, Hamtramck and Oak Park branch offices.

For her community work, Josephine was recognized by the Detroit City Council, the Dearborn Heights Chamber of Commerce, and was a YWCA Minority Achiever. Other community activities include board of directorships for Oak Grove Day Care and Kindergarten, McAuley Commons, the LUMA Business Association, University Commons and United For Progress CDC.

Josephine earned a master's degree in organizational management and a business information systems degree from the University of Phoenix, with a banking certificate from The Robert Perry School of Banking at Central Michigan University.

Josephine and her husband, Ronald, spend time with children Ryan and Stephanie.

Ivan A. Johnson joined National City more than 25 years ago. Through the years, he has worked in the International Department and the commercial real estate area, which broadened his expertise and management skills. For the past 15 years, he has managed the Michigan Trust Real Estate portfolio, which exceeds $100 million and is comprised of residential, commercial and agricultural real estate.

Ivan is skilled in lease negotiations, sales and purchases of all real estate properties. In addition to Michigan, Ivan also manages real estate in several other states and Canada.

He received a bachelor's degree from the University of Detroit, and has continued his education by obtaining a real estate license for the state of Michigan and a valuation specialist designation for real estate appraising. He is pursuing a real estate broker designation for the state of Michigan.

Ivan is a member of the Real Estate Trust Investment Committee at National City, and the Birmingham, Bloomfield, Rochester, South Oakland Association of Realtors®. He is also secretary of the board of directors for Allen Academy, a K-12 school located in Detroit.

National City® CORPORATE SPOTLIGHT National City®

Renee Kent

Assistant Vice President
Community Development
National City

J. Greg Mickens

Vice President
National City

Renee Kent is assistant vice president and manager of National City Community Development Corporation's Greater Detroit Region. In this position, she manages tax credit and equity investing activities for National City throughout the southeast region of Michigan.

Renee is proud to be one of 65 individuals selected to participate in the Leadership Detroit Class of XXIX. She was part of the community development team that received a Local Excel Award, National City's highest honor, for generating revenue growth. Additionally, she received a National City Champion Award for exemplifying customer champion management principles.

Renee stays active in the community through membership in community nonprofit organizations. She serves on the board of Grandmont Rosedale Development Corporation, and is a loan committee member for other government and corporate lending initiatives.

Renee earned a bachelor's degree in accounting from Eastern Michigan University. Married to Willie Kent, she is the proud mother of three children, Darryn, Alana and Mariah. They reside in Detroit.

Greg Mickens is a vice president in National City's Upper Middle Market Commercial Group, which serves larger corporate customers. He is a lending officer responsible for an existing portfolio, as well as business development for the bank.

Greg has been a banker in the Detroit metro area for 24 years, and has experience in corporate banking, small business lending, commercial real estate and capital markets. Until recently, he was a member of the Lower Woodward Housing Fund Loan Committee and the Detroit LISC's Local Advisory Committee.

Greg earned a bachelor's degree in economics at Michigan State University, and a master's degree in business administration at the University of Michigan. Prior to that, he served as a cast director and tour coordinator for the international educational organization Up With People, during tours of the United States, Puerto Rico, Venezuela and Mexico.

A native of Port Huron, Michigan, Greg is the husband of Ann M. Mickens, and the very proud father of a son and daughter, Quinn and Taylor.

Shaun Wilson is vice president, marketing manager for National City in southeast Michigan. In this position, he oversees and implements all integrated marketing efforts for the bank throughout the southeast Michigan market. Prior to joining National City, Wilson was managing partner of Wilson PR, a joint-venture strategic public relations and marketing firm that represented top Detroit-area companies and institutions, including National City Bank, The Bing Group, Global Automotive Alliance, Bartech Group, Piston Group and Detroit Branch NAACP, among numerous others.

He also held the position of vice president at John Bailey & Associates, Inc. Public Relations (JB&A). At JB&A, Wilson was a member of the executive leadership team, responsible for overseeing daily operations, strategic planning and management policies for the firm.

Wilson holds a bachelor's degree in public relations from Wayne State University. He is a member of the Public Relations Society of America, and a past board member of the Detroit Chapter – National Association of Black Journalists. Wilson was also named to *Crain's Detroit Business'* 40 Under 40 in 2001. He served eight years in the U.S. Marines.

Shaun Wilson

Vice President, Marketing Manager
National City

National City®

There are certain things you can depend on — no matter what.

For 68 years, Blue Cross Blue Shield of Michigan has been there — a nonprofit company, accepting everyone, regardless of medical history — providing more access to Michigan hospitals and doctors than anyone.

As your needs change — as life changes — you can depend on Blue Cross Blue Shield of Michigan to be there ... no matter what.

bcbsm.com

  Blue Cross Blue Shield of Michigan

interest

limelight

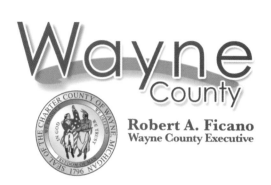

GOVERNMENT SPOTLIGHT

attention

prominence

highlight

celebrate

headline

focus

recognition

Sharon Banks

Communications Director for the
Wayne County Executive

Mulugetta Birru, Ph.D.

Director, Economic Development
Department
Wayne County

Since 2003 Sharon Banks has served as the communications director for Wayne County Executive Robert A. Ficano.

As a senior advisor, Banks develops messaging strategies for the county executive's office and 11 county departments. She has led the county's communications efforts for Super Bowl XL, the Major League Baseball All-Star Game, and various community and economic development projects. She has participated in three business trade missions to China, and an airport trade mission to Amsterdam, Netherlands, and Frankfort, Germany, in 2007.

Prior to joining the Ficano administration, Banks operated the Banks Marketing Group, a marketing communications agency that she formed in 1998 with a Fortune 500 client roster. She also served in sales and marketing positions with the IBM Corp., Hewlett Packard, the Ford Motor Co. and the AM General Corp.

A graduate of Wayne State University, Banks is the marketing chair of Gleaners Community Food Bank of Southeast Michigan. She also serves on various boards and committees.

Banks has received several awards for community service and professional achievements. She has two children and one grandchild.

Dr. Mulugetta Birru is director of Wayne County's Economic Development Department and chief executive officer (CEO) of the Greater Wayne County Economic Development Corporation. He oversees a 1,200-acre development adjacent to Detroit Metropolitan Airport and the development of a new Airport City project. He supports the development of Detroit and 42 other communities in the county.

Birru previously served as executive director of the Urban Redevelopment Authority in Pittsburgh, and the Allegheny County Department of Economic Development.

Birru has approximately 30 years of experience in development banking, manufacturing and economic development in the U.S. and overseas. In his native Ethiopia, he was CEO of the National Chemicals Corp., deputy CEO of the Ethiopian Beverages Corp., and senior vice president of the Agricultural and Industrial Development Bank of Ethiopia.

He holds a Doctor of Philosophy degree in public and international affairs from the University of Pittsburgh, an MBA in finance and a master's degree in economics from Syracuse University, and a BBA in accounting from Addis Ababa University. He was an adjunct professor at Carnegie Mellon University.

Birru is married with three daughters.

James P. Buford

Director, Homeland Security &
Emergency Management
Wayne County

James A. Jackson Jr.

Director, Public Services
Wayne County

James Buford is director of homeland security and emergency management for Wayne County, Michigan. He is responsible for coordination with 34 communities in Wayne County for emergency planning. The department oversees $17 million in homeland security grants for protection of critical infrastructure, first responder equipment and training.

James has dedicated his professional life to law enforcement. Prior to his appointment as director, he had been a member of the Wayne County Sheriff's Department for 21 years. The last five years were spent as commander of the Sheriff's Road Patrol. James has received two departmental citations, three unit citations and the Community Service Citation.

James received a Bachelor of Science degree in criminal justice from Wayne State University in 1981. He received a Master of Liberal Studies degree from Eastern Michigan University in 2002.

A native of Detroit and Highland Park, Michigan, James is the father of Jujuan, Jonathan, Jennifer and Kristin, and has five grandchildren.

James A. Jackson Jr. is director of public services for Wayne County, overseeing a budget of $166 million, and the morale, safety and welfare of 820 personnel. He is responsible for more than 1,581 miles of roads, maintenance of more than 1,500 traffic signals and intersections, maintenance and replacement of more than 800 pieces of equipment and 100,000 acres of county parks land.

Prior to coming to Wayne County, Jackson served as director of public works for the City of Detroit, as well as director of streets and sanitation for the City of Grand Rapids.

Jackson is a former officer of the U.S. Marines, having served honorably for 11 years. He holds a Bachelor of Science degree in the field of mathematics from Knoxville College, and a Master of Public Administration degree in general government from Columbus State University.

He is a member of the National Forum for Black Public Administrators, the International City/County Managers Association, Omega Psi Phi Fraternity, Inc. and the American Public Works Association.

Married with five children, Jackson is a member of Hart Memorial Baptist Church.

GOVERNMENT SPOTLIGHT

Edith Killins

Director, Department of
Health & Human Services
Wayne County

Bella I. Marshall

Chief Operating Officer
Wayne County

As director of the Wayne County Department of Health and Human Services, Edith J. Killins oversees a vast array of programs, including public and mental health, Head Start and the medical examiner's office, in the 11th most populated county in America.

Prior to joining the county management staff, Killins served as director of human resources for the state Department of Community Health for six years. During her 23 years with the state, she worked in the corrections and mental health departments, and the state Employment Security Commission.

Killins received an executive MBA in health care management from Oakland University and a bachelor's degree in psychology from Wayne State University.

Killins serves on the board of directors for the Greater Detroit Area Health Council, and is a member of the board of trustees for Wayne County Health Choice. Additionally, she serves on the Detroit Executive Leadership Council of the National Kidney Foundation. Killins is also a member of Alpha Kappa Alpha Sorority, Inc. and the Greater Love Tabernacle COGIC in Detroit.

She has one son who is a senior in college.

Bella Marshall is chief operating officer for Wayne County. As a member of the chief executive officer's executive staff, she is responsible for advising on and often implementing operational initiatives and special projects, such as the Regional Justice Complex.

Bella was formerly area office director for the Michigan State Housing Development Authority. She was also the first female chief financial officer of the City of Detroit, and the chief operating officer of Barden International. She has been featured in *Newsweek*, and has been named One of the Most Powerful People and One of the Most Powerful Women in Detroit by *Crain's Detroit Business*.

Bella serves on the boards of Wayne County Stadium, the Wayne County-Detroit CDE, Inc. and the Land Bank. A graduate of The University of Michigan Law School and an attorney, her recognitions include the Metropolitan Detroit Area Boys Scouts, Wayne State University's Distinguished Alumni and Distinguished Black Alumni, and the Thurgood Marshall Award of Excellence.

A frequent speaker on diversity, finance and politics, she is married to Don Barden. They have one child and reside in Detroit.

Benny N. Napoleon

Assistant County Executive
Wayne County

Rev. Larry L. Simmons Sr.

Chief Information Officer &
Director, Strategic Planning
Wayne County

Benny N. Napoleon, the former Detroit police chief, is an assistant Wayne County executive.

Napoleon joined the Detroit Police Department in 1975, and rose through the ranks until he was appointed chief of police in 1998. He retired from the department in 2001. His career highlights include supervising the investigation of the assault on international figure-skating champion Nancy Kerrigan, and the investigation that led to the apprehension of ten escapees from the Ryan Correctional Facility in Detroit. Napoleon also implemented a plan that reduced violent crime by an unprecedented 30 percent during his tenure as chief of police.

Napoleon earned a Bachelor of Arts degree from Mercy College of Detroit, and a juris doctor degree from the Detroit College of Law. He is a graduate of the FBI National Academy and an area chair for criminal justice for the University of Phoenix, Detroit campus.

Napoleon has a long history of community service, including coaching and mentoring children, and serving as chair of the Michigan Civil Rights Commission.

He is single with one daughter, who is a sophomore in college.

The Reverend Larry L. Simmons Sr. is a 60-year-old, lifelong Detroiter. A graduate of Detroit Public Schools, he graduated from Wayne State University in computer science. He has five sons and five grandchildren.

Simmons has merged two disparate careers successfully as Wayne County chief information officer and director of strategic planning, and pastor of Baber Memorial A.M.E. Church.

As chief information officer for the 11th-largest county in the United States, Simmons occupies a rare position for African Americans in his highly technical role as leader of the Department of Technology.

Simmons serves on the Southeast Michigan Council of Government executive board, the Metropolitan Affairs Coalition board, the Detroit River Front Conservancy board and the executive committee of the Michigan Democratic Party. He also chairs the Community Development Board for Wayne County, and serves as vice chair of the Greater Wayne County Economic Development Corporation.

Previously, Simmons served as political director for Mayor Coleman A. Young; a panelist for *Mort Crims Free 4 All*, an Emmy-winning local public affairs show; and president of the AME Ministerial Alliance.

GOVERNMENT SPOTLIGHT

Carla Elissa Sledge

Chief Financial Officer
Wayne County

Edward M. Thomas

Corporation Counsel
Wayne County

Carla Elissa Sledge is chief financial officer for Wayne County, overseeing an annual budget of $2.4 billion and directing the Department of Management and Budget.

She has served as chief financial officer and chief deputy financial officer since 1995, leading the county to several awards for excellence in financial reporting. Sledge oversees a wide array of county services, including purchasing, assessment and equalization, budgeting, accounting and four satellite offices.

Prior to joining the county, Sledge was an audit manager at the Detroit office of Deloitte. She has a Bachelor of Science degree in accounting from Wayne State University, and Bachelor of Music Education and Master of Arts degrees from Eastern Michigan University.

Sledge is the immediate past president of the national Government Finance Officers Association. She is a member of several accounting and professional boards, and has won numerous awards for leadership and integrity in finance.

In 2001 Sledge was recognized as one of Detroit's 30 Most Influential Women by a metro Detroit-area organization. She lives in metro Detroit with her family.

Edward M. Thomas, currently serving as corporation counsel for Wayne County, is a retired Wayne County judge who served for 15 years on the Circuit Court bench. Prior to serving on the Circuit Court, he was a member of the Recorder's Court bench for 11 years.

Thomas presided in more than 1,400 trials of criminal and civil cases during his 26-year judicial career. In 1991 trial attorneys ranked him in the top ten out of 204 Michigan state and federal judges. He has also served as a visiting judge on the Michigan Court of Appeals.

Thomas has chaired the board of directors for the Detroit/Wayne County Criminal Advocacy Program. He has also served on the Wayne County Circuit Court Executive Committee, the Bench and Bar Liaison Committee, and the Supreme Court Mediation Rule Committee.

Outside the courtroom Thomas has been an active volunteer with numerous community organizations, and his personal and professional contributions have been highly recognized.

A lifelong Detroiter, he is married to a retired Detroit Public Schools teacher.

distinguished

representative

Government

DETROIT'S

GOVERNMENT LEADERS

commanding

progressive

inspired

leader

influential

excellence

important

Christine Beatty

Chief of Staff
Office of the Mayor
City of Detroit

Creating the NEXT Detroit requires capable leadership that knows how to manage people, build coalitions and put the citizens of Detroit first. As chief of staff, Christine Beatty has a solid "can do" reputation. With direct oversight of human resources, the Detroit Building Authority, Office of the Mayor, Neighborhood City Halls and Senior Citizens Department, Beatty has served in this important cabinet post since 2002.

Named one of Michigan's Most Influential Women by *Crain's Detroit Business*, Beatty's relentless commitment has produced solid results for the Kilpatrick administration. From successfully negotiating open labor contracts to playing a key role in creating the Detroit Wayne County Health Authority, Beatty has helped to bring about several victories for the City of Detroit.

For more than ten years, Beatty's commitment to public service has benefited Detroit, first serving as legislative aide for former State Representative Kwame Kilpatrick. While Kilpatrick was House Democratic leader, she was his district director in Detroit. Prior to working in state government, she worked in the social services field, where she gained experience that has helped her contribute to public policy in Detroit.

Charles Beckham

Chief Operating Officer
Director,
General Services Department
City of Detroit

Charles Beckham has been called to serve the City of Detroit more than once in the past 35 years. Beginning in 1974 as part of the Coleman A. Young administration, he served for ten years. He held numerous positions, including vice president of the public lighting commission, president of the water board, director of the Water and Sewerage Department and executive assistant to the mayor.

As part of the NEXT Detroit leadership team under Mayor Kilpatrick, Beckham brings tremendous experience and past success to the newly created Department of General Services. As chief operating officer, his talents for organization will be greatly utilized in shaping a modern government for Detroit.

His non-governmental achievements include founding BEnterprises in 1984, a technical management consulting firm in Detroit.

A graduate of the University of Michigan, Beckham is president of the African American Alumni Council for the university. He has served on numerous boards and is a lifelong supporter of families, economic access and business in the African-American community.

The Honorable Alisha R. Bell is the youngest African-American woman to serve as a county commissioner in the nation. Bell was elected to the Wayne County Commission in November of 2002. She is the chair of the Committee on Health and Human Services and the Special Committee on Women in Government and Business. She is also a member of the Committee on Economic Development and the Committee on Ways and Means.

As an active member of the community, Bell serves on the board of Planned Parenthood of Southeast Michigan, the National Council on Alcohol and Drug Dependence, the Salvation Army Southeastern advisory board, the Women's Informal Network and the Detroit Recovery Project. Moreover, she is a proud member of Delta Sigma Theta Sorority, Inc.

A graduate of Cass Technical High School, Bell received a bachelor's degree in business administration from Florida A&M University, and a master's degree in education from the University of Nevada at Las Vegas.

Bell is a native Detroiter and grew up in the 8th District of Wayne County. Alisha was married in November of 2004 to Kranston Young.

The Honorable Alisha R. Bell

Commissioner, District 8
Wayne County Commission

Mary Blackmon serves as president of the City of Detroit's Board of Water Commissioners. The board's responsibilities include approving rates and overseeing the provision of service of one of the nation's largest systems.

Mary has an outstanding record of public service. She was elected citywide to the Detroit Board of Education in 1978. In 1981 she became the first African-American female to serve on the Wayne County RESA Board of Education, and is the board's immediate past president. She also serves on the board of directors of the National Black Caucus of School Board Members.

Having earned numerous service awards, Mary is a member of the Detroit Branch NAACP Fight For Freedom Fund Dinner's Executive Committee, and chairs the branch's annual art/essay contest. Additionally, she has been a member of the Southeast Michigan Council of Governments since 1988, and will assume the chairmanship in June of 2008.

Mary is the national music director for the Shrines of the Black Madonna. She is also the proud wife of George and the mother of their two sons, Chaka and Dedan.

Mary E. Blackmon

President
Detroit Board of Water Commissioners

Marion A. Brown

Deputy Chief of Staff
14th District of Michigan
U.S. House of Representatives

Marion A. Brown is deputy chief of staff in the Detroit office of U.S. Representative John Conyers Jr., chairman of the House Committee on the Judiciary. Prior to her current position as a senior-level congressional staffer, she was executive director of the Chrysler Minority Dealers Association.

Before entering the political arena, Marion worked successfully for ten years as a corporate executive. Additionally, she is a co-developer of a multimillion-dollar housing project in Detroit.

Having a keen interest in global affairs, Marion is passionate about connecting the people of the continent of Africa to the African Diaspora. Furthermore, she is an advocate for voter protection and education, protecting human and civil rights, prisoner reform and reentry, public education and urban community development.

Marion enjoys dancing and aerobic exercises. She is a member of Straight Gate International Church in Detroit.

A Chicago native, Marion received a bachelor's degree from Bradley University in Peoria, Illinois. She is the mother of four, and two of her children are graduates of historically black colleges and universities (HBCUs).

Jeanean M. Bryant

Chief of Staff, District 8
Wayne County Commission

Jeanean M. Bryant is chief of staff for Wayne County Commissioner Alisha Bell, District 8. Her compelling graduate thesis research on lead poisoning helped Commissioner Bell introduce Wayne County's Public Lead Poisoning Ordinance.

Jeanean is a member of and holds executive positions with the Detroit Branch NAACP, the National Congress of Black Women, Inc., the 14th Congressional District, the National Conference on Adult Literacy and Education, the Detroit Alumnae Chapter of Delta Sigma Theta Sorority, Inc. and many other organizations. She also advocated to raise Michigan's minimum wage and to preserve affirmative action in Michigan as part of One United Michigan.

In 2006 Jeanean became the first African-American woman to serve as the Michigan Young Democrats' statewide chair for the Michigan Coordinated Campaign. That same year, she received the Rosa Parks Leadership Award, and was profiled as one of the *Michigan Chronicle*'s Young History Makers. She was also named the 2007 Michigan Young Democrat of the Year.

Jeanean holds a Bachelor of Science degree in psychology from Wayne State University and a master's degree in human resources from Central Michigan University.

The Honorable Kenneth V. Cockrel Jr. has served on the Detroit City Council since 1998. A former journalist, Wayne County commissioner and community activist, Cockrel made history as the youngest person ever elected to this body in 1997. He was re-elected in 2001 and elevated to the position of president pro tem. Additionally, he was elected to his third term in November of 2005 and elevated to the position of president after receiving more votes than any other City Council candidate.

A cum laude graduate of Wayne State University with a Bachelor of Arts degree in print journalism, Cockrel is a former reporter for the *Detroit Free Press*, *The Grand Rapids Press* and *The Cincinnati Enquirer*. He is a graduate of the inaugural class of the Michigan Political Leadership Program at Michigan State University as well as the program for state and local government officials at Harvard University's John F. Kennedy School of Government.

Cockrel and his wife, Kimberly, have two sons, Kenneth III and Kyle, as well as three daughters, Kennedy, Kendal and Kayla.

The Honorable
Kenneth V. Cockrel Jr.

Council Member
Detroit City Council

As director and health officer of the Wayne County Department of Public Health, Loretta V. Davis is responsible for planning, implementation and evaluation of public health programs designed to prevent disease and promote health. She was previously director of health, wellness and disease control with the Michigan Department of Community Health.

In her 20 years in health and human services, program development and community organizing, Davis has translated her passion for public and minority health to focus on the critical fields of sexually-transmitted disease, HIV/AIDS, teenage pregnancy prevention and reproductive health care. In 2002 she was chosen by the National Alliance of State and Territorial AIDS Directors (NASTAD) to help plan and mobilize Ethiopia's response to the AIDS epidemic. Davis also served as past chair of NASTAD. She is the recipient of the Harriet Tubman Award for Outstanding Service on Behalf of Women and the Spirit of Detroit Award for her leadership in HIV/AIDS education.

Davis holds a bachelor's degree in sociology from the University of Michigan and a master's degree in health administration from Central Michigan University.

Loretta V. Davis

Director & Health Officer
Wayne County Department of
Public Health

The Honorable Warren C. Evans

Sheriff
Wayne County

As Wayne County sheriff, the Honorable Warren C. Evans oversees the second-largest law enforcement agency in Michigan, including a staff of 1,300, three jails that house more than 2,600 inmates and a $100 million budget.

Throughout the past 35 years, Evans has worked in virtually every area of law enforcement in Wayne County. He has held every rank in the sheriff's office, worked as a chief assistant prosecutor, and run the county's adult and juvenile community corrections programs.

Since becoming sheriff in 2003, Evans has collaborated with area law enforcement agencies to reduce crime. One of his partnerships, the F.A.S.T. team, has taken more than 12,000 fugitive felons off the streets. Other units he has created to find missing children, rehabilitate drug-addicted prostitutes, track down drunken drivers who skip out on their court dates, and perform unannounced checks on the homes of parolees, have all garnered national awards for their excellence and innovation.

Evans is a lifelong Detroiter, and has two daughters and three granddaughters. An accomplished horseman, he also rides and trains horses for the department's Mounted Unit.

George Jackson Jr.

Chief Development Officer
City of Detroit

The NEXT Detroit requires strong and aggressive economic development leadership that will do what is necessary to create a global destination through increased economic and development activity. In January of 2006, Mayor Kilpatrick named George Jackson Jr. as the city's chief development officer to continue the economic progress Detroit has made during the past several years.

As chief development officer, Jackson will be responsible for coordinating all economic development activity within the city. With an extensive professional background and deep-rooted ties to the community, Jackson is uniquely qualified to serve in this critical cabinet position.

In 2002 Jackson was elected president and chief executive officer of the Detroit Economic Growth Corporation. In this role, Jackson led efforts to transform Detroit by completing monumental revitalization projects such as the Lower Woodward Improvement Program, which redefined the city's decades-old central business district. Playing such an integral role in Detroit's economic momentum for the past five years, Jackson is sure to help continue the transformation of Detroit, neighborhood by neighborhood.

The Honorable Brenda Jones is a member of the Detroit City Council. There, she is committed to improving the safety of neighborhoods and schools, as well as preserving the character of residential neighborhoods, creating affordable living and exhibition space, and fostering an atmosphere of responsible development.

Jones is the former president of Communications Workers of America, Local Union 4004. She also serves as secretary for the CWA International Union Minority Caucus. She is a trustee of the Detroit chapter of the Michigan Minority Networking Women and a trustee of Friends of Black Men in Unions.

Jones is a precinct delegate of the City of Detroit and vice president of the Detroit chapter of the A. Philip Randolph Institute. She is a member of the Coalition of Black Trade Unionists, the Trade Union Leadership Council and the NAACP. She is the NEB delegate of the Coalition of Labor Union Women.

A graduate of Wayne State University's Labor School, Jones is a native of Detroit.

The Honorable Brenda Jones

Council Member
Detroit City Council

The Honorable Sylvia Jordan currently serves as the president of the Southfield City Council and was elected to council in 1997. She and her husband are founders of Family Victory Fellowship Church, located in Southfield.

Appointed to the National League of Cities as a nationwide panelist, Sylvia has received the Leadership Award from the National League of Cities and the Michigan Municipal League for her leadership. She has also received the distinguished Leadership Award from the International Third World Leadership Association and many awards for her community service and achievements.

Sylvia annually conducts a Women's Empowering Conference in South Africa. Local and international missions are one of her passions coupled with taking tangible resources to the areas traveled. Her foundation secures and mobilizes resources for local and overseas distribution.

A graduate of Cass Technical High School, Jordan holds a bachelor's degree in urban studies from Michigan State University and performed graduate studies at Oakland University.

The acclaimed pastor, author, entrepreneur and public speaker is married to Pastor Larry T. Jordan and the proud mother of two young adult children.

The Honorable Sylvia Jordan

President
Southfield City Council

Daedra A. Von Mike McGhee

Director/Special Advisor
Southeast Michigan
Office of the Governor

Daedra A. Von Mike McGhee is director/special advisor for business and civic affairs in the Office of the Governor. She is responsible for the establishment of aggressive executive outreach efforts with leadership of business, civic and professional organizations. Daedra engages leaders in constructive dialogue on state programs, initiatives, policies and procedures essential to the success of emerging organizations. She then facilitates implementation of the resulting creative strategies designed for positive transformation of Michigan's emerging businesses and civic communities.

Daedra has received numerous honors for leadership and commitment to community transformation. These include the National Association of Women Business Owners, the Michigan Women's Business Council and the Center for Empowerment and Economic Development, the National Association of Black Auto Suppliers, the African Women Economic Consortium, and the Women's Justice Center/My Sister's Place.

Daedra earned a Bachelor of Arts degree in interdisciplinary studies from Wayne State University. She also received a fellowship to the prestigious Center for Creative Leadership in Brussels, Belgium, and LaJolla, California. Her goal is to complete a master's-Doctor of Philosophy degree in international peace and conflict studies.

Derrick Miller

Chief Information Officer
City of Detroit

In 2001 Derrick Miller was appointed deputy chief of staff under the first African-American democratic leader in the Michigan House of Representatives, Kwame M. Kilpatrick. In this role, Derrick was responsible for developing the Democratic caucus agenda, and he worked closely with members of each branch of government.

In 2002 Kilpatrick was elected mayor of Detroit and appointed Derrick the chief administrative officer. There, Derrick served as senior advisor to the mayor, provided strategic oversight of key large-scale initiatives and coordinated the enterprise-wide processes for the City of Detroit.

Derrick was appointed chief information officer in 2006. He leads the city's information technology systems, and is currently working on plans to make Detroit a completely wireless community for 2008.

Derrick serves as co-chair for the Detroit East Riverfront Development Conservancy, vice chair for the Wayne State University Research and Tech Park board, and co-chair for the Detroit Area Regional Transportation Authority. He serves on the boards of the Detroit 300, the Detroit Economic Development Corporation, the Greater Downtown Partnership Committee, NEXT Detroit and NextEnergy.

Creating the NEXT Detroit requires capable leadership that can work closely with the legislative branch of city government to improve the overall quality of life for the citizens of Detroit. As the Mayor's Office liaison to City Council, Kandia Milton has helped to forge a more cooperative relationship between the executive and legislative branches of city government to implement progressive policy that will help create the NEXT Detroit.

For more than two years, Milton has worked daily with the Detroit City Council and their staff on several initiatives and policies to help improve the city. He has worked tirelessly to help pass initiatives, such as the Lower Eastside Development Plan, the creation of the Department of Administrative Hearings, and four important capital improvement bonds worth millions in infrastructural enhancements in neighborhoods across Detroit.

Joining the Kilpatrick administration in 2002, Milton has developed a strong grasp on the inner workings of city government, an invaluable asset in his continued efforts to move the administration's various policies and initiatives to enhance Detroit, neighborhood by neighborhood.

Kandia Milton

Mayor's Office Liaison
City Council
City of Detroit

The Honorable Martha Reeves serves on the Detroit City Council.

Elijah Joshua Reeves and wife Ruby moved from Eufaula, Alabama, in 1942 with their three children, Benny, Thomas and Martha, the youngest at 11-months-old. Mother Ruby sang to them, especially at bedtime, and Father Elijah sang and played a blues guitar. Pastor Elijah Joshua Reeves Sr. ministered at the family's church, Metropolitan A.M.E., where Martha's singing skills and approval of the elders was acknowledged, and the hope of stardom was recognized.

For Martha, elementary school and high school were the first stages of entertainment. The 1959 class performed a successful concert upon graduation from Northeastern High. She was featured singing Bach's aria "Hallelujah" before 4,500 spectators and won rave reviews.

Martha actively joined girls' groups, and recorded a single on Checkmate Records with the Del-Phis until age 21. In 1962 Motown Records contracted Martha & the Vandellas after an invite by William "Mickey" Stevenson, A&R director. Traveling and celebrating hit records, such as "Dancing in the Street" and "Love is Like a Heatwave," she entered into politics.

The Honorable Martha Reeves

Council Member
Detroit City Council

Pamela Scales

Budget Director
City of Detroit

Creating the NEXT Detroit will require sound knowledge of the city's fiscal and budgetary functions. Having served as the deputy budget director, Pamela Scales has more than 20 years of service with the City of Detroit. She brings extensive experience in dealing with the specific challenges of managing the city's budget to her post as budget director.

During her tenure as deputy budget director, the City of Detroit has been awarded nine Distinguished Budget awards from the Government Finance Officers Association. A faculty member with the University of Phoenix, Scales teaches graduate and undergraduate finance courses. Her invaluable knowledge of the inner workings of budgetary functions, coupled with her commitment to the citizens of Detroit and demonstrated service will help strengthen fiscal operations as they create the NEXT Detroit.

Roger Short

Chief Financial Officer
City of Detroit

Creating the NEXT Detroit requires strong and experienced fiscal stewardship. As the director of the city's Budget Department and former city auditor general, Mayor Kilpatrick appointed Roger Short as chief financial officer to lead the effort to improve the city's financial condition. As a part of the mayor's cabinet team, Short is responsible for overseeing the daily financial matters of the city. His portfolio includes the Finance, Budget and Purchasing departments.

As a certified public accountant with more than 21 years of accounting and financial management expertise within city government, in addition to seven years in the public accounting sector, Short is uniquely qualified to help develop the necessary strategies to deal with the city's financial challenges, and ultimately help put Detroit on solid financial ground.

Donyale Stephen-Atara is deputy director of human resources for Wayne County. She began her career with the City of Detroit Office of the Ombudsman, and has the distinction of being the youngest person appointed to the deputy city ombudsperson position.

Stephen-Atara is a graduate of Cass Technical High School, Eastern Michigan University and Wayne State University. She possesses a Bachelor of Science degree and a Master of Public Administration degree.

Stephen-Atara is chair of the Greater Detroit Chapter of the National Congress of Black Women, an organization founded by the late Honorable Shirley Chisholm to focus on the empowerment of African-American women. She has many current and previous affiliations with civic and professional organizations. In 2004 she was featured in the "Emerging Leaders" supplement of the *Michigan Chronicle*.

Stephen-Atara and her husband, Kwaku Atara, live in Detroit and have two adult sons.

Donyale Miechele Stephen-Atara
Deputy Director, Human Resources
Wayne County

Kim Trent is one of Detroit's most outspoken political activists, using her talents as a communicator to forward a progressive agenda. A former newspaper reporter and Congressional press secretary, Trent now serves as Detroit regional manager for U.S. Senator Debbie Stabenow. Trent is Stabenow's link to Detroit's political, business and grassroots leadership.

Trent is a graduate of Leadership Detroit and has completed fellowships with the American Political Science Association and the Michigan Political Leadership Program. She holds bachelor's and master's degrees from Wayne State University.

She serves on many boards, including the Rosa Parks Scholarship Foundation, the Detroit Institute of Arts' Friends of African and African-American Art, and the Michigan State Council of Delta Sigma Theta Sorority, Inc. Her social activism has garnered her many awards, including the State Bar of Michigan's Liberty Bell Award, the Michigan Democratic Party's Martin Luther King Freedom Award, the YWCA of Western Wayne County's Woman of Achievement Award, the Michigan Women's Political Caucus' Millie Award, and the Detroit Chapter of NOW's Harriet Tubman Award.

Trent and her husband, Kenneth Coleman, live in downtown Detroit.

Kim Trent
Detroit Regional Manager
U.S. Senator Debbie Stabenow

Lucius Vassar

Chief Administrative Officer
City of Detroit

The NEXT Detroit will require strong legislative and advocacy leadership. As Detroit's chief administrative officer, Lucius A. Vassar brings an extensive background in legislative and relationship management to this important cabinet post. As chief administrative officer, he is responsible for managing all intergovernmental and international affairs, as well as local policy making that impacts the city. In addition, he is responsible for building and managing strategic partnerships with the city's corporate, civic and philanthropic communities.

Vassar joined the Kilpatrick administration in 2002 as director of corporate and civic affairs, where he worked daily with the business and civic community. In that role, he led the effort to retain a $1 billion company in Detroit, keeping the city as its headquarters for years to come. Having previously served in both the public and private sectors, Vassar offers a well-balanced approach to bring a new result-driven culture to city government. Addressing key issues such as property taxes and business retention, his advocacy and commitment to Detroit are sure to continue to bring about a positive transformation.

Jewel Ware

Chairwoman
Wayne County Commission

Jewel Ware has been a Wayne County commissioner since 1995, and became chair of the Wayne County Commission in 2003. As chair, she provides fiscal and legislative oversight of Wayne County's $2.4 billion annual budget. She was the first African-American female to be elected chair of the commission.

A social worker by trade, Ware is a forceful advocate for the underserved of Detroit and Wayne County. In Wayne County, she has worked to develop new programs to better serve senior citizens, underprivileged children, the mentally ill and the developmentally disabled. During her tenure, Wayne County has developed novel health care programs that serve the working poor.

Ware received bachelor's and master's degrees from the University of Detroit. She is a member of numerous civic and community organizations, including Mack Alive, the NAACP, the National Black Caucus on Aging, the Coalition of Labor Union Women, the Pittman Memorial Housing Development, HOPE (Helping Our Prisoners Elevate), the Warren-Conner Development Coalition, and Genesis Lutheran Church. Ware is also chair and founder of the Mattie Ware Community Fund.

The Honorable Keith D. Williams was elected Wayne County Commissioner of the 6th District in June of 2003. He is currently chairman of the Committee on Public Services, and serves on the Committee on Economic Development and the Committee on Ways and Means.

Williams is the owner of Williams Opportunity Investment Properties and Williams Development Group LLC.

He is a member of the Michigan Democratic Party, Crispus Attucks Lodge (Mason), past precinct delegate of the 14th Congressional District, Prospect Baptist Church, and a longtime supporter of Fellowship Chapel.

A product of the Detroit Public Schools, Williams earned a degree from Eastern Michigan University.

Born to the late Fredrick Williams, a community activist, and Lelia Williams, he was reared with compassion and concern for his friends and neighbors. His best friend is his loving wife, Cathy Garrett, who serves as Wayne County clerk. He is the father of Marlin Maxwell, a graduate of Central Michigan. Williams enjoys golfing, reading and interacting with people. One of his greatest joys is watching his son grow into a team player.

The Honorable Keith D. Williams

Commissioner, District 6
Wayne County Commission

City Clerk Janice M. Winfrey is a public administrator and educator who has been serving Detroiters for more than a decade.

A committed public servant, Winfrey views public office as the most effective way to affect public policy and ensure efficiency and accountability in local government. Since being elected, she has earned certification as an accredited clerk by the State of Michigan. She has successfully implemented two new voting systems, and set a precedence in the election community by being one of the first among the 11 major cities in the United States to release 100 percent election results on election day.

A native Detroiter, Winfrey graduated from Eastern Michigan University. She is a member of the Detroit Federation of Teachers, the Association of Wayne County Clerks, the Michigan Municipal Clerks Association, and the International Association of Clerks, Recorders, Election Officials and Treasurers. She is also a member of the NAACP and Alpha Kappa Alpha Sorority, Inc.

Winfrey resides with her husband of 20 years and their three children in northwest Detroit. They are members of Greater Grace Temple of the Apostolic Faith.

The Honorable Janice M. Winfrey

City Clerk
City of Detroit

explorer

industrialist

DETROIT'S
ENTREPRENEURS

pioneer

capitalist

tycoon

proprietor

catalyst

magnate

trailblazer

Ty Adams

Chief Executive Officer
Heaven Enterprises

Ty Adams, chief executive officer and founder of Heaven Enterprises, is a sex and relationship expert, best-selling author and life coach. She is the voice of counsel to thousands around the world through her nominated online daily radio broadcast.

Ty is highly recognized as the creative pen behind the bestselling book *Single, Saved, and Having Sex*. Reaching bestseller's status in its inception, this literary work has landed her on numerous television and radio programs, including TBN's *Praise the Lord, The 700 Club*. The book was also earmarked as an *Essence* magazine bestseller and Amazon.com's Top 100.

Affectionately known as Dr. Ty, she skillfully navigates through multimedia, books, television and theater to help fashion and design healthy lifestyles. Whether speaking or writing, Ty is a prominent influence in unlocking the hidden potential in both men and women alike. "Helping Life Live" is the motto and mission of this dynamic orator.

Ty's bold, ram's horn approach to sex and relationships makes her one of the most sought-after speakers in the country, distinguishing her as a leading "SEXpert" in America.

Xzun (Malik) Bellefant

Owner & Consultant
Xzun Business Consultants LLC

Xzun Bellefant is the owner of Xzun Business Consultants LLC (XBC), which provides business and nonprofit consulting services to industry leaders and small businesses. XBC prides itself on the fact that the company's consulting services are guided by evidence-based practices that increases the sustainability of its clients.

Bellefant's involvement has been instrumental in implementing several initiatives in Detroit, including the Youth Opportunity Movement, Mentors of Faith, the Juvenile Michigan Reentry Initiative, the Michigan Prisoner ReEntry Initiative and the Work Force Mentoring Program. He has also been awarded with the Pioneers for Peace Award for his fight against gun violence.

Bellefant earned a Bachelor of Arts degree in English from Tennessee State University, and holds a Master of Business Administration degree from the University of Phoenix. He is a certified serious and violent offender reentry initiative trainer and a certified survival skills trainer.

A native of Nashville, Tennessee, Bellefant is supported by his fiancée, Joycelene, and children, Talika, Jasmine, Xaviar, Demarco and Malinda.

Kimberly Benjamin started Be Blessed Career Consulting Inc. and HR Strategies Plus LLC to be resources to people needing assistance in career planning and new business development. She has more than 16 years of human resource experience working for Fortune 500 Companies such as General Motors, Ford Motor Company, ITT Industries, Wal-Mart, Toys "R" Us and Cornerstone Schools. She is currently a career and job search professor at Concordia University.

Kimberly is also the author of the *How to Be Highly Favored and Empowered to Prosper in Your Job Search* book and workbook, and the producer of *Has God Given You a Business Idea? Workshop*, a 13-part DVD series and television show.

She received a bachelor's degree in merchandise management from Eastern Michigan University in 1992, and a master's degree in labor relations and human resource management from Wayne State University in 1997.

Kimberly is a certified professional in human resources, a State of Michigan personnel agent, and a member of the Society of Human Resource Management (SHRM) and the Human Resource Association of Greater Detroit (HRAGD) organizations.

Kimberly A. Benjamin

President &
Chief Executive Officer
Be Blessed Career Consulting Inc.

Kimberly A. Black is president and chief executive officer of Black Diamond Entertainment Group. Specializing in advertising, marketing, promotions, media production and special events, she has more than two decades of communications experience. She and Black Diamond Entertainment are committed to maintaining their standard of promotional excellence by leading the market in creativity and originality.

Black Diamond Entertainment and its staff have always been on the cutting edge of national special events, advertising, marketing and public relations. Black has worked and produced many promotional events in the local, regional and national markets. A few of these include Dr. Bobby Jones, Dr. Creflo Dollar, T.D. Jakes Productions, Sound of Gospel Record Label, The O'Jays, Puff Daddy, Lil' Kim, Slum Village, Eve, Ruff Riders, The "Pjazz" Jazz Series, *The Contender* television series, and Emanuel Steward and The Kronk Boxing Team.

Black also serves as president and chief executive officer of Diamond Acres, a nonprofit youth outreach, which provides life skills, literacy, boxing and other recreational activities for youth.

Kimberly A. Black

Founder, President &
Chief Executive Officer
Black Diamond
Entertainment Group

Dr. Sabrina D. Black

Chief Executive Officer &
Clinical Director
Abundant Life Counseling Center

An author, counselor, mentor, and life coach, Dr. Sabrina D. Black is the clinical director of Abundant Life, which emphasizes spiritual values. She is an international speaker who empowers people around the world. Sabrina's dynamic message of life's struggles, temptations and triumphs challenges others to deal with the real issues of daily living. She connects with audiences that are multicultural, cross-generational and of various denominations. She is a much sought-after consultant for schools, churches and organizations.

Sabrina is host of the nationally syndicated broadcast *IT'S RELATIONAL with Dr. Sabrina D. Black*, which airs Wednesdays at 8 a.m., CST.

President of the National Biblical Counselors Association, she is a member of the American Association of Christian Counselors, Writers Resources and Accountability for Publishing (WRAP), American Christian Writers and Delta Sigma Theta Sorority, Inc.

Additionally, Sabrina is a columnist for *Precious Times Magazine*, and has authored the books *Can Two Walk Together?*, *Prone to Wander*, *Counseling in African American Communities* and *HELP! For Your Leadership*.

Laurita Bledsoe

President
Bledsoe Enterprises LLC

Laurita Bledsoe is chief executive officer and founder of Seen Your Express and Just for You Boutique, which are components of Bledsoe Enterprises LLC. Seen Your Express adheres to all non-medical needs of seniors.

Laurita is the monthly event coordinator for Ladies of Destiny and Purpose. She is responsible for planning events, used as a networking resource for women in various businesses, services and ministries.

She is the inventor of the talking potty training chair, which is included in the Charles Wright Museum of African American History, Black (traveling) Museum, *Who's Who in America*, and the *Detroit Almanac 300 Years of Life in the Motor City.*

Laurita has received numerous awards and certificates as well as degrees with honors from the International School of Ministry, Christian Leadership University and Highland Park Community College.

A native Detroiter and retiree from the U.S. Postal Service, Laurita is blessed to have three gifted and beautiful children, Miranda, Curtis and Kia. She is a published writer, praise and worship leader at Harvest Christian International Church, and minister. Yearly, she enjoys performing the role of Harriet Tubman.

Willie E. Brake is president and chief executive officer of All About Technology, Inc., a company that provides high-quality computer sales, service, training and upgrades for residential and business customers. Willie is also executive director of the Center for Creative Arts, Inc. and a faculty member at the University of Phoenix. Additionally, he serves as a speaker for various organizations.

Prior to the creation of All About Technology, Willie spent more than 12 years in positions of increased responsibility in the automobile, consulting, education and manufacturing industries in locations around the world.

An award-winning hometown hero and international freedom fighter, Willie is a member of various civic, community and philanthropic organizations. These include Alpha Phi Alpha Fraternity, Inc., the United Way and Service Corps of Retired Executives (SCORE).

Willie earned a bachelor's degree from Wayne State University and a Master of Business Administration degree specializing in technology management from the University of Phoenix.

A native of Detroit, Willie is the proud father of one daughter, Olivia Madison.

Willie E. Brake

President &
Chief Executive Officer
All About Technology, Inc.

The Reverend Dr. Velva D. Burley graduated from Detroit Central High School, and received a bachelor's degree from Michigan State University. She received a Master of Science degree from the University of Detroit Mercy, and a Master of Divinity degree and a Doctor of Ministry degree from Ashland Theological Seminary.

Burley is president of anSpire, LLC, a training and development company. She is also one of the co-founders of anSpire Ministries. She is a member of Delta Sigma Theta Sorority, Inc. and The Lydia Circle, and is treasurer for Ashland Theological Seminary Alumni Association. Additionally, Burley is an adjunct professor at Ashland Theological Seminary and the Heritage Center for Religious Studies, as well as co-author of the book *Talitha Cumi: Daughters Arise.* She is an ordained minister serving at Third New Hope Baptist Church.

Burley is the proud mother of a beautiful boy, James Ronald, who is affectionately known as "big boy James." Her favorite scripture is Philippians 4:13, "I can do all things through Christ who strengthens me."

Rev. Dr. Velva D. Burley

President
anSpire, LLC

Kevin J. Butts

President
ER Credit Education Solutions

President of ER Credit Education Solutions, Kevin J. Butts is a leading credit expert. The forever passionate Butts has conducted presentations, panel discussions or training for financial institutions; high schools; colleges; corporations; churches; the Michigan State Housing Development Authority; the Detroit Entrepreneurship Institute; the Michigan Small Business & Technology Development Center; Midnight Golf; New Detroit, Inc.; Greektown Casino; UAW/Ford; Youth In Transition; the Don Bosco Hall; the Judge Greg Mathis Empowerment Expo; the Emerging Minority Business Leader-Governors Office; The Next Vision Foundation; the International Detroit Black Expo; Herb Strather Real Estate Academy; the United Way of Southeastern Michigan; the U.S. Conference of Mayors; InCharge Education Foundation; Chase Credit Card Services; the Federal Reserve Bank of Chicago/Money Smart; the NAACP National Conference; Credit Professionals International; and the Michigan Civil Rights Commission.

A certified professional credit executive, Kevin is from Southfield by way of River Rouge. He graduated from the University of Alabama at Birmingham. Additionally, he is a human services committee member of COTS, and a board member for the Optimist Club of Southfield. Kevin is the husband of Sheila D. Butts.

LaQuanah Crawford

Owner
L³ Lips Lids Lavish

LaQuanah Crawford, owner of L³ Lips Lids Lavish (L³), has been making faces beautiful for more than 15 years. L³ specializes in professional makeup artistry for weddings, fashion shows, video and photo shoots, individual or group consultations, and tutorials. After three years of teaching in Detroit Public Schools, LaQuanah was blessed with a layoff, which gave her time to transform her God-given talent into a minority-owned business. With minimal start-up capital, she created L³ and reached out to professional and personal contacts to secure clients. Since then she has worked countless fashion shoots, shows and weddings in the Detroit area, and her work has been featured in *The Michigan Citizen* Newspaper.

In addition to her professional pursuits, LaQuanah is committed to making a difference in the Detroit community. As a mentor to underprivileged and troubled teenagers, she serves as a role model influencing positive change. She participates in several annual fundraising walks, including Making Strides Against Breast Cancer Awareness and Aids Partnership of Michigan. With a triple threat of talent, intelligence and community involvement, LaQuanah will surely leave her mark on Detroit and beyond.

Gwendolyn Esco Davis is president and chief executive officer of The Hascom Group, LLC, a management consultancy. With more than two decades of operational and management experience, she has developed a keen eye for how businesses become bloated with inefficiencies, cross-purposes and clouded missions, as well as how they can retool for a sleeker, smoother, and strategically focused organization change and transformation. She also coaches business owners to set priorities to create balance.

Gwendolyn serves on several boards, including the Matrix Theatre Company and Preservation Wayne, and volunteers with the Detroit Executive Service Core. Additionally, she was featured in *Who's Who in Professional and Executive Women 1987* and *Who's Who in Black Detroit® The Inaugural Edition.*

An alumna of the 2006 Leadership Detroit-Regional Chamber, Gwendolyn has been instrumental with organization turnarounds in for-profits and nonprofits of nearly a dozen organizations in the past year. She also has a column in *Detroit Black Monthly.*

Gwendolyn holds a bachelor's degree in business and math. A Detroit native, she is married to Alex Davis and the proud mother of three daughters and three grandsons.

Gwendolyn Esco Davis

President &
Chief Executive Officer
The Hascom Group, LLC

Kevin Davis is a managing partner for Crush Media Group, LLC, a Detroit-based company specializing in photography, videography, graphic design and promotions. He is in charge of the day-to-day operations and strategic planning for Crush. His photography skills are in high demand for many special events and performances in and around the Midwest region for many local and national celebrities.

Kevin is a member of Phi Beta Sigma Fraternity, Inc. – Alpha Alpha Beta Sigma Detroit Alumni Chapter, the National Black Public Relations Society and the National Pan-Hellenic Council Foundation. Likewise, he is a member of the Redford High School Alumni Association, the Eastern Michigan Black Alumni and the Michigan Democratic Party. He is also a Prince Hall Mason.

Kevin attended Detroit Redford High School and Eastern Michigan University. He majored in communication technology with a concentration in organizational communication.

Kevin is the proud father of two sons, Kian and Kameron Davis. In his spare time, he enjoys photography and networking.

Kevin L. Davis

Managing Partner
Crush Media Group, LLC

Valarie Davis

Artist & Owner
Valaria's Studio Art Gallery, Inc.

Valarie Davis is an artist and the owner of Valaria's Studio Art Gallery in Detroit. She recently released a series of *African American Heritage Tiles* to educate youth about African-American history. Each tile includes a brief bio of the historical person on the back. Valarie also created a mosaic series titled *Brothers and Sisters*. Her mosaics depict African Americans in positive activities in an effort to dispel negative stereotypes of black people living in urban America.

Valarie's tiles, mosaics and pottery are carried by the gift stores at the DuSable Museum of African American History in Chicago and the Charles H. Wright Museum of African American History in Detroit. The Detroit Institute of Arts' gift store will carry selected works by Valarie starting this November. She has a ceramic display at the Michigan Design Center in Troy. Additionally, she has been a featured guest artist several times on WJBK–TV Fox 2 in Detroit.

Valarie holds a Bachelor of Fine Arts degree from the Center for Creative Studies, and has studied art abroad at the Studio Arts International in Florence, Italy.

Reginald J. Dockery

Chief Executive Officer
Created Wealthy Entrepreneurs LLC

"Making it happen instead of watching it happen" is the theme statement for this 29-year-old entrepreneur. Reginald Dockery has successfully launched several business ventures. At Created Wealthy Entrepreneurs LLC, he and his wife, Ebony, lead teams that provide services, which include business and marketing plan development, business publications and resource assistance consultation. This company was formed to help young aspiring entrepreneurs develop their business ideas and teach financial empowerment.

Reginald is an executive level visionary with ten years in the executive level business development industry. His verifiable track record for the successful completion of multimillion-dollar projects by coordinating and developing partnerships and building strong marketing plans has earned honor.

Reginald does extensive speaking and business training where he has been recognized by several organizations, including the NAACP Detroit Chapter, the United Way and the ASCAP. As a licensed and ordained minister, he believes in excellence or nothing. Reginald is a Detroit native where he resides with his wife, Ebony, and his son, Reginald II. He always says, "You will never change your life until you change your choices!"

Sharon DuMas-Pugh is founder and president of Full & Fabulous Inc. International, a nonprofit organization celebrating 25 years of promoting health, beauty, and self-esteem in plus-sized women and teens. As an industry pioneer, she received the Key to the City from Mayor Coleman Alexander Young in 1986.

In March of 2004, Michigan Governor Jennifer Granholm named DuMas-Pugh a Hometown Health Hero for her more than 20 years of service, philanthropy and continued efforts to increase the health and wellness of her community.

In February of 2006, DuMas-Pugh was successful at presenting the importance of her concept of health, beauty, and self-esteem for plus-sized women and teens to the Detroit Super Bowl XL Host Committee. As a result, she became one of 20 programs selected as an official sanctioned event from a group of more than 2,000 businesses.

DuMas-Pugh received a Bachelor of Arts degree in business and leadership studies from Windsor University in 1999. She is the proud mother of one son, Harold Lamont, and one granddaughter, Latasha.

Sharon DuMas-Pugh

Founder & President
Full & Fabulous Inc. International

Mary Edwards is founder of Widows With Wisdom. Prior to becoming a widow, she helped her late husband establish a million-dollar ministry dedicated to revitalizing a community on the eastside of Detroit called Ravendale. For this work, they received the 107th Point of Light Award from former President George H.W. Bush.

Mary has received numerous awards throughout the past 33 years for impacting the lives of thousands of women, writers and widows. In 2002 she was honored by the Women's Informal Network (WIN) as being One of the Most Influential African American Women in Metropolitan Detroit. Mary recently completed her autobiography, *Born Grown*, which is a candid account of 30 years of ministry and 30 years of a scandalous life before that. She is the only Detroiter included in the first *Chicken Soup for the African American Soul* book.

Born in Canada, Mary migrated to the U.S. at an early age and began motherhood at the age of 13. She is an international author, speaker, book coach and editor, as well as a grandmother and great-grandmother.

Mary Edwards

Founder
Widows With Wisdom

Victoria B. Edwards

Chief Executive Officer
vbEdwards Consulting

Victoria B. Edwards is chief executive officer of vbEdwards Consulting, a Detroit-based project management firm providing administrative and corporate development solutions to community, faith-based and nonprofit organizations.

Victoria has established and coordinated corporate participation programs in local community events at Fortune 500 companies throughout Michigan and Ohio. She has served on task forces that passed laws to strengthen the effect of PPOs, and a coalition that preserved $45 million for hospitals serving low-income patients. While serving on various committees for the Charles H. Wright Museum and the Adopt A Child Christmas Program, Victoria chairs committees and annual events for the Pilgrim Village Association, the Detroit Association of Women's Clubs, The Mission and the women's ministry of her church.

She is a graduate of Renaissance High School, and holds Bachelor of Arts degrees in business and history from Marygrove College.

In all that she does, Victoria's strength comes from her Lord and Savior, Jesus Christ. She attends Northwest Church of God in Detroit, where she serves on the Pastor's Anniversary Committee and the Nurses Guild, and is president of the Sisterhood.

Sandra Epps

Founder & Executive Director
Sandy's Land

Sandra Epps is founder of Sandy's Land, a publishing house and children's entertainment service whose mission is to empower young people. An award-winning artist, she has created various products and apparel with the signature theme of hope, love and faith.

Epps is a survivor of Systemic Lupus Erythematosus (SLE), an auto-immune disease. She was inspired to write her first children's book, *Imani Has The Most Exciting Dream!*, to help children deal with a parent's serious illness.

Epps has been featured in *Heart & Soul* magazine, *The Detroit News*, *The Michigan Citizen*, the *Detroit Free Press*, *African American Family Magazine* and *K.E.Y.S. Kids TV Show*. She received the Distinguished Service Award from Detroit City Council in June of 2007, the Phenomenal Women's Award from the Toledo City Council in November of 2003 and the Women of Action Award from the Million Man Alumni Detroit Chapter in May of 2004.

A native Detroiter, Epps holds a bachelor's degree in fiber arts from Wayne State University.

Hajj E. Flemings is the author and founder of The Brand YU Life: "Re-thinking who you are through personal brand management." The Brand YU Life, LLC specializes in personal and corporate brand management, consulting, training and seminars. He has been featured in radio, television and print, impacting lives with his message of branding. Hajj travels nationally enabling individuals to live their dreams. His branded customers include the General Motors Minority Dealers Association, the Ford/NAACP Youth Summit, BlackEnterprise.com, DAPCEP and the University of Detroit.

Hajj is a managing partner of Broken Chains Design Group. His clientele includes Skechers, George Fraser, universities and churches with his work featured in *GQ*, *Men's Health*, *Details* and *Slam* magazines.

A collegiate athlete turned adjunct lecturer for his alma mater, Michigan Technological University, Hajj wrote the personal brand management curriculum. He has a Bachelor of Science degree in mechanical engineering from Michigan Technological University and a Master of Business Administration degree from Lawrence Technological University. A FraserNet top achiever, he serves on the International Detroit Black Expo board of directors.

He is married to his lovely wife, Kasandra.

Hajj E. Flemings
Author, Speaker & Founder
The Brand YU Life, LLC

Jordan Fox, a native Detroiter and portrait photographer, graduated from Michigan State University with a Bachelor of Arts degree in humanities. The late Jim Wilson, renowned Detroit and Motown era photographer, served as his mentor.

Fox worked as a freelance photographer for the *Michigan Chronicle*, *The Oakland Press* and *Metro Exposure* magazine. It was during this period that he photographed many Detroit luminaries, including political aspirant Freeman Hendrix, jazz musician Marcus Belgrave, U.S. Congresswoman Carolyn Cheeks Kilpatrick and Mayor Kwame M. Kilpatrick. Later, Fox furthered his professional experience with an internship at Bak Photography, a studio specializing in wedding photography.

Fox opened Metro Image Studio (MIS), the largest, black-owned downtown Detroit photography studio in 2000. MIS combines film and digital technology to create unique and enduring images for family portraits, senior graduates, model portfolios, weddings and special events. Recently, MIS served as the official event photographer for the Honorable Erma Henderson's 90th Birthday Celebration.

Fox continues giving back to the community through ongoing efforts with mentoring workshops and internships for aspiring students interested in learning the business and art of photography.

Jordan Fox
Owner & Photographer
Metro Image Studio

Marc W. Hardy

Founder &
Chief Executive Officer
SMART Management Group, LLC

Ken "Blanks" Harrell

Founder & Chief Executive Officer
The Detroit Black Dollar, LLC

arc W. Hardy is a licensed certified public accountant in the state of Michigan, and has an extensive background in the areas of corporate financial and business management. He is founder and chief executive officer of SMART Management Group, LLC, which supplies its clients with professional accounting, fiscal and operational management, general business and administrative-related consultation, resources and support services.

Marc is a graduate of Morehouse College in Atlanta, Georgia. He is a member of the American Institute of Certified Public Accountants, the Michigan Association of Certified Public Accountants and the National Association of Black Accountants.

Active in his community, Marc serves in leadership with many organizations, including African American Magazine Inc., Big Brothers Big Sisters of Metropolitan Detroit, the Booker T. Washington Business Association, the Detroit Regional Chamber's Leadership Detroit, Greater Grace Temple and Omega Psi Phi Fraternity, Inc. He also serves with The Rhonda Walker Foundation Inc. and the YMCA of Metropolitan Detroit, and has been appointed to serve on various boards and commissions for the City of Southfield by its mayor and city council.

Ken "Blanks" Harrell is the visionary behind The Detroit Black Dollar, LLC. In this position, he manages a dynamic team of highly experienced professionals who have a passion for developing and marketing black-owned businesses.

Blanks is a highly accomplished entrepreneur and investor. He has acquired equity stakes in several growing companies in Detroit's community, including Alabama Style Chicken and Soul Food restaurants, HBz Premier Comedy Agency, LLC and a Web site. Additionally, he runs a weekly sales and marketing training program for college students and working adults.

A native of Detroit's East Side, Blanks serves as the lead project coordinator of the International Detroit Black Expo, Inc.'s 2008 Buy Black Weekend. He is also the account executive at WGPR "The Rhythm" 107.5 FM.

A graduate of Renaissance High School, Blanks earned two Bachelor of Arts degrees from Northwood University. He is also a member of Omega Psi Phi Fraternity, Inc.

DETROIT'S ENTREPRENEURS

Walter Harvill is an entrepreneur and barber in the city of Detroit. He has occupied the same location on Concord for the last 30 years. Many of his clients have been faithful and diligent for weekly visits throughout the years.

Walt's Style Center & Barber Shop serves as the community base for the neighborhood. Many notable clients will comment on the atmosphere and climate that is experienced during weekly visits. Harvill can be sighted throughout the week servicing neighborhood seniors, nursing homes and other organizations with his Walt's on Wheels Mobile Barber Shop.

Harvill has been a community supporter of the Berry Parent Teacher Association, the East Side Community and the Mack Area Community Association for more than 25 years.

He is married to Dr. Deborah Hunter-Harvill, and has six adult children.

Walter Harvill

Owner
Walt's Style Center &
Barber Shop

For more than ten years, Kimberly Hill served as a senior legislative assistant in the district office of Congressman John Conyers Jr., chairman of the House Judiciary Committee. In this position, she spearheaded several policy seminars and meetings on affordable housing and economic development issues related to the City of Detroit with Detroit city officials, the academic community, neighborhood leaders and the business community. These efforts spurred economic development, including bringing Staples and BORDERS® retail stores to the downtown Detroit area.

Recently, Kimberly left Congressman Conyers office, and launched Future Insight Consulting (FIC), LLC, which will work to strengthen relationships among the urban Christian community and elected officials, political candidates and state parties. FIC will serve as an issue advocate for the Christian community on Capitol Hill, as well as assist in securing federal funds for various community development initiatives.

A native of Milwaukee, Wisconsin, Kimberly earned a Bachelor of Science degree, with additional concentrations in journalism and public relations, from the University of Wisconsin Milwaukee. She also earned a Master of Educational Administration degree from Temple University.

Kimberly Hill

President & Chief Strategist
Future Insight Consulting, LLC

Carolyn J. Hopkins

President
De'Spa Elite &
De'Elegance Floral Designs

Carolyn J. Hopkins is president of De'Spa Elite, Inc. and De'Elegance Floral Designs in Detroit. As president of these two businesses, she oversees daily operations, interacts with customers on a daily basis to ensure good customer relations, and is responsible for securing major accounts and events. She is also the owner of Lifestyle Solutions, which focuses on educating African Americans on changing their lifestyles to live longer, healthier lives and becoming more knowledgeable about health benefits.

Carolyn was featured in *Women's HealthStyle Magazine* as an outstanding female entrepreneur in Detroit. She served on the Michigan Minority Business Development Council's (MMBDC) board.

Carolyn's entrepreneur experience extends from various business-related careers, and a number of college and business-related programs. She is closely affiliated with organizations such as the SBA, the MMBDC, the Booker T. Washington Business Association, the National Association of Women Business Owners, and the Women's Economic Club.

A Tennessee native, Carolyn is the wife of Larry Hopkins, the mother of Frenchie LaMont Hopkins, and the grandmother of Layla Simone Hopkins, 2. Her hobbies include decorating, floral designing, walking, working out and cooking.

Sylvia Hubbard

Author & Literary Leader
Motown Writers
Network/HubBooks

Sylvia Hubbard is founder of Motown Writers Network, one of Michigan's largest literary writing and reading organizations. As an independent published author of ten novels, she has garnered millions of readers around the world through powerful Internet marketing techniques. She was voted by Romance Book Cafe as a Favorite Author, and in 2005 her psychological-suspense novel, *Stone's Revenge*, was voted Best African-American Mystery by Mojolist.

Sylvia created Motown Writers Network because there was a need for a stronger literary community in Michigan. Through her hard work and dedication, she was awarded the Spirit of Detroit Award and the State of Michigan Governor's Emerging Minority Business Leader Award, and was honored as the Triumphant SPIRIT Award Winner by Sigma Gamma Rho Sorority, Inc.

Sylvia has a degree in marketing and management from Tampa University, and has a certificate in broadcasting from Specs Howard. She also teaches how to electronically publish and market on the Internet throughout the United States and Canada.

A Detroit native and proud graduate of Cody High School, Sylvia is a divorced single mother of three young children.

Julia Hunter is owner of G Publishing LLC, an independent, small press publishing company located in Detroit. She started the company in 2003 to publish a self-help book for a friend. Since that time, she has published more than 70 titles, and her authors span six states.

In addition to owning and operating a publishing company, Julia is a marketing educator at one of the premier high schools in Detroit. She has earned countless awards for being an outstanding educator as well as several awards for being an outstanding businesswoman. These awards include WDIV/*Newsweek* Teacher of the Year, Michigan Marketing Educator of the Year, The Jim Boyce Foundation Recognition Award, A Great Woman of the 21st Century, and Manchester Who's Who. She was also listed in the inaugural edition of *Who's Who In Black Detroit*®.

Julia holds a master's degree in business education from Eastern Michigan University, and is very passionate about teaching and publishing. She also enjoys watching Tigers baseball.

Julia Hunter

Owner & Publisher
G Publishing LLC

Amin Irving is co-founder of Ginosko Development Company (GDC). He is responsible for the overall performance and operation of all the divisions of the GDC family of companies. He also oversees the selection of various projects, municipality processing, and debt and equity financing. Amin waited three years before taking over operations, and in his first year, revenues increased more than 1,000 percent from 2005 to 2006, and net income increased more than 800 percent.

Amin's previous experience includes investment banking in Manhattan, where he effectively and efficiently operated $450 million in developmental projects. His decision to return to Michigan afforded him the opportunity to discover more than $4 million in annual savings for a nonprofit HMO, which played an integral role in saving the company.

Amin graduated from the University of Michigan Business School in Ann Arbor, majoring in finance and real estate. He was the recipient of the University of Michigan Achievement Award.

He is the proud husband of Tiffaney Irving.

Amin Irving

President
Ginosko Development Company

Sabrina A. Jackson

Founder & President
Sabrina Jackson Enterprises

Sabrina Jackson is founder and president of Sabrina Jackson Enterprises, a Detroit-based consulting firm that provides corporate training and motivational speaking to a variety of clients throughout the United States and abroad. Sabrina has built her reputation as a speaker/trainer in front of some of the most discerning audiences. Her personable manner and professionalism – over a 20-year career – have captivated the spirit of her audiences and led them to discover new truths inside themselves. Various affiliations and a client roster that includes McDonald's Corporation, Detroit Public Schools and Data Kinetics of Ottawa, Canada, have reached the same conclusion: "This Woman is Awesome!"

A proud graduate of Cass Technical High School in 1984, Sabrina received a Bachelor of Science degree from Eastern Michigan University in 1988 and a Master of Social Work degree from Wayne State University in 1989. She has been honored to receive the 1998 Michigan Children's Alliance Hugh Whipple "Rising Star" Award.

Sabrina is certified in several national and international training models. One of the most requested is True Colors. Lastly, she is the proud mother of scholar/athlete Marcel.

Brenda A. Jenkins

Founder &
Chief Executive Officer
ARIEL Connections

Brenda Jenkins is founder and chief executive officer of ARIEL Connections in metro Detroit. In this position, she manages the business consulting, speaking and writing of self-help resources to empower others to move to the next level. Brenda is a national speaker that gets right to the heart of the issue. She has the ability to see the expected outcome of tasks and works to put plans in place to reach that end. She is well versed in problem solving, organizational and interpersonal tasks.

A member of the National Speakers Association (NSA), Brenda serves as a board member of the NSA – Michigan Chapter. She is also active with Parent Advocacy, and is a member of the American Association of Christian Counselors (AACC), the National Biblical Counseling Association (NBCA) and the American Society of Quality (ASQ).

Brenda is the author of five books, including her latest release, *He is Not Left Behind... He is with Me! A handbook to encourage parents, while offering tips for raising children.*

Claudy E. Jones is president and chief executive officer of Odyssey Enterprises Inc. (OEI) and Lighthouse Direct Buy Showroom (LHDBS), a wholesale greeting card company and a Christian product retailer. As president of OEI and LHDBS, he is committed to operating his businesses with Christian excellence and applying biblical principles at every level.

In addition to owning and operating OEI and LHDBS for the past 15 years, Claudy accepted his calling to preach and teach the gospel. He was licensed and ordained by his pastor, Bishop Keith A. Butler of Word of Faith International Christian Center (WFICC). He and his wife, Mrs. Jack E. Jones, serve as volunteer instructors and coordinators of volunteers at WFICC's Kingdom Business Institute.

Claudy is a current board member for two evangelistic ministries located in Detroit and Atlanta. He is also a current member, past board member and chaplain of the Booker T. Washington Business Association of Detroit. He is a past board member of the Metropolitan Detroit Jail Ministries.

Claudy and his wife have two children.

Claudy E. Jones

President &
Chief Executive Officer
Odyssey Enterprises Inc.
Lighthouse Direct Buy Showroom

Odell Jones III is president of JOMAR Building Company, a leading institutional, industrial and commercial builder headquartered in Detroit. He has more than 32 years' experience in building design and construction.

Jones employs and mentors a staff of 20 people. Under his leadership, JOMAR Building Company has grown through a commitment to deliver superior construction services on time, within budget and to specified levels of quality.

Among his many professional and community affiliations, Jones is a trustee of the Michigan Opera Theatre and Eastern Michigan University. He is also chairman of the A. Philip Randolph Career and Technical Center's Tie Advisory Committee, and immediate past chairman of the Greater Detroit Chapter of Associated General Contractors, the region's leading organization for construction contractors and industry-related companies dedicated to skill, responsibility and integrity.

Jones is a lifelong Detroit resident and a responsible corporate citizen committed to protecting the environment and improving the quality of life where he lives and works. With 15 years of entrepreneurial success, he takes pride in providing every client with unparalleled construction services, and is dedicated to the pursuit of excellence.

Odell Jones III

President
JOMAR Building Company, Inc.

DETROIT'S ENTREPRENEURS

Jacob B. Keli

President & Chief Executive Officer
Kaskel Construction Company, Inc.

Jacob Keli is a true success story of perseverance. As a young student, he moved to America penniless from his home country in Tanzania, East Africa. Overcoming many obstacles, he earned bachelor's degrees in economics and international relations from Wayne State University, and master's degrees in international economics and political science from the University of Detroit Mercy.

Utilizing his education, Jacob went on to work for various corporations in metro Detroit, including serving as assistant vice president of civic and community affairs for NBD Bank.

Today, with 20 years' experience in finance, accounting, banking, economic development, public relations, international trade and corporate management, Jacob is the president and chief executive officer of Kaskel Construction Company, Inc., based in Detroit.

Some of his memberships and accomplishments include the political science honor society Pi Sigma Alpha, the Detroit Lions Club and the International Rotary Club of Metropolitan Detroit. Jacob also served as president emeritus for the Detroit Lions Professional Retired Football Players Charity, and received the President's Commission on White House Fellowships Regional Award and the Paul Harris Rotarian Award for his humanitarian achievements.

Matthew Sam Kuofie, Ph.D.

Chief Executive Officer
Global Strategic Management Inc.

Dr. Matthew Sam Kuofie is chief executive officer of Global Strategic Management Inc. (GSMI). GSMI helps governments, businesses and individuals apply the best practices in business and information technology by leveraging global management resources through transformational leadership insight. Kuofie is leading GSMI to improve the Detroit economy by propelling businesses to increase market share in the Africa market, revenue and profit. GSMI is organizing the First Annual USA-Africa International Business Conference, which will be held in Detroit on November 29-30, 2007. Additionally, Kuofie teaches business and information technology at universities, including the University of Michigan.

A native of Cape Coast, Ghana, Kuofie was referred to as "One of the greatest sons of Africa" in the *Ghanaian Journal*, August 9, 2007. Due to his outstanding international accomplishments, he was installed as His Royal Highness Chief Enyi Oma I of Abia State, Nigeria, on October 26, 2006.

Kuofie holds a Doctor of Philosophy degree in systems engineering, a Master of Business Administration degree, a Master of Science degree in computer science and a Bachelor of Science degree in statistics and mathematics.

Karee Laing is chief executive officer of the Write Business Solution. She manages the daily operations of the company while also overseeing the Small Business Development Training Institute. She assists entrepreneurs, business owners and nonprofit organizations with business development, strategic planning and marketing.

Additionally, Karee is founder of McKardel Property Investments Group, a real estate development company that provides housing solutions for low- to middle-income families. She is a member of the Boys & Girls Clubs, and volunteers her time with the United Way and the United Negro College Fund. She has received several honors, including the *Cambridge Who's Who Among Business Executives and Professionals*, and the Capital University Business Leader Award.

Karee received a Bachelor of Arts degree from Wayne State University and a Master of Business Administration degree from the University of Phoenix Graduate School. She was also awarded a juris doctorate degree from Capital University Law School, and inducted into the Order of the Barristers.

Karee Laing
Chief Executive Officer
Write Business Solution, LLC

Ellis Liddell is president and chief executive officer of ELE Wealth Management, LLC, a client-based asset management company with its corporate office in Southfield. He is a wealth manager, insurance expert and retirement planning specialist. He is also the author of the book *Wealth Management: Merging Faith with Finance*.

Liddell's financial advice and commentary have been featured on radio and television programs, and in newspapers in the Detroit and Dallas areas. A regular guest on News Talk 1200 WCHB AM's *Inside Detroit* morning show, he serves as a consultant on financial issues for WXYZ Channel 7 Action News. He has conducted financial seminars and workshops for thousands around the country, and has been the keynote speaker at the prestigious Investors Capital Convention in Boston.

In 2006 Liddell became the first African American to be ranked the No. 1 financial advisor by Investors Capital Corporation. His brand of financial planning is uniquely rooted in sound financial and biblical principles. He presents complex financial information in layman's terms, giving clients and seminar participants a wealth of knowledge, some homespun humor and common sense.

Ellis Liddell
President &
Chief Executive Officer
ELE Wealth Management, LLC

Naomi Long Madgett

Founder, Publisher & Editor
Lotus Press, Inc.

Naomi Long Madgett founded Lotus Press, Inc. in 1972, where she continues as publisher and editor. Working alone except for one volunteer, she consults with authors on editing problems, prepares manuscripts for the printer, handles book orders and correspondence, and reports and keeps records. In 1993 the press established an annual, national award, the Naomi Long Madgett Poetry Award for an outstanding manuscript by an African American. The winner of the award receives $500 in cash, and Lotus Press publishes the book. Madgett received an American Book Award for her work as publisher and editor.

Poet Laureate of Detroit since 2001, Madgett is author of nine collections of her own poetry, and most recently, her award-winning autobiography, *Pilgrim Journey.* Her poetry, for which she has won numerous awards, appears in more than 190 anthologies and textbooks.

Madgett holds degrees from Virginia State, Wayne State and Greenwich universities. She is professor emerita of English at Eastern Michigan University.

Darci E. McConnell

President & Chief Executive Officer
McConnell Communications, Inc.

Darci E. McConnell is president and chief executive officer of McConnell Communications, Inc., a full-service public relations firm. The company provides public relations, crisis management, media training and marketing services.

An established communicator who made a seamless transition from investigative reporter to trusted publicist, Darci has provided consulting services to a diverse group of clients in just three short years. Those clients include Michigan Governor Jennifer M. Granholm, Service Employees International Union Healthcare Michigan, casino magnate Don H. Barden and St. John Health.

Darci sits on the board of the Detroit Community Initiative and the Detroit City Chess Club. She is also a member of the Public Relations Society of America and the past president of the Detroit Chapter of the National Association of Black Journalists. She holds a Bachelor of Arts degree in English and communication from the University of Michigan, and recently served as an adjunct professor of journalism at Wayne State University's School of Communication and Fine Arts.

Sharon L. McWhorter, president of American Resource Training System, Inc., is an alumna of Cass Technical High School. She is a highly intense individual with a talent for identifying problems and developing effective solutions.

McWhorter has more than 26 years of experience in the areas of business management, innovation, credit awareness, customer care and strategic planning. She is highly respected as a course developer, strategist, relationship specialist, violence/conflict and change management facilitator, and lecturer.

Active in community affairs, McWhorter serves as chair of the Detroit Empowerment Zone Development Corporation, and is a gubernatorial appointee to the Collections Practices board. She sits on the board of directors for Matrix Human Services, ZIAD Health Services and the Inventors Council of Michigan. An NANBPW member, McWhorter has also been involved with the Museum of African American History, the Detroit Public Schools transition team and the Wayne County chapter of MADD. She is a contributing writer for *OurPC Magazine*.

A graduate of Wayne State University, McWhorter has two patents and certifications in sound board engineering and international training.

Sharon L. McWhorter

President
American Resource Training
System, Inc.

Kevin Meredith is president of Paradise Travel & Events in the Metro Detroit area. He organized the business in 2002 and recently celebrated a five-year anniversary. His responsibilities are to increase customer base and productivity with travel partners, annually. He also oversees staff, trains, motivates and positions clients in a win-win situation.

Kevin has completed several training classes and earned certificates from Cancun, Sandals, the CLIA and Las Vegas. He has attended familiarization trips to Cancun, Jamaica, the Bahamas and Toronto.

Kevin attended Henry Ford Community College in Dearborn, Michigan. He has worked in the travel business to 20 years, serving as vice president of his father's agency.

He works with his wife, Leah Meredith, at their agency. They are the blessed parents of two children, Justin and Madison Meredith.

Kevin Meredith

President
Paradise Travel & Events

Danielle M. Morgan

Chief Executive Officer
The Insurance Agency with Grace,
LLC

D anielle Morgan is chief executive officer of The Insurance Agency with Grace, LLC. As a representative for this new and upcoming agency, her position involves providing competitive insurance rates, building business relationships and providing excellent service to her clients.

Danielle has been in the insurance business for eleven years, winning multiple awards for high sales, group coordinating and new group opening. She has won National Leaders Conference trips and performed as the number two new agent in the nation for one of the companies she currently represents.

Danielle received a Bachelor of Arts degree in finance from Michigan State University and a Master of Arts degree in business administration from the University of Phoenix. She has received her life, health, Series 63, property and casualty licenses from the state of Michigan.

A Detroit native, Danielle is the proud mother of two sons. She devotes her time to her sorority, Eta Phi Beta Sorority, Inc. (Delta Chi chapter), the International Detroit Black Expo, Inc., the Michigan Business Professional Association, and her church, Greater Grace Temple.

Monica Morgan

Photojournalist

I nternational photojournalist Monica Morgan lives life through the lens.

Monica's work has appeared internationally via Associated Press Worldwide, Wireimage.com and *Newsweek-Japan*. Her credits include CNBC, *People, New York Post, Fortune, Ebony, Jet, O*, AOL, ESPN.com, *Entertainment Weekly, US Weekly Magazine*, and *The New York Daily News*. Additional credits include *Black Enterprise, Essence, TV Guide, GQ, Vanity Fair, The Detroit News, Detroit Free Press, Michigan Chronicle*, MTV, VH1, *Saturday Night Live,* and *ELLEgirl*.

Monica has documented lifestyles in Dakar, Senegal; Banjul, Gambia; Lome, Togo; Cottonou, Benin; Abuja, Nigeria; Dafur, Sudan; Kumasi, Ghana; and cities in Israel. She captured the inaugural activities of Dominica's late Prime Minister Rosie Douglass, and the memorial services for Israel's former First Lady, Leah Rabin. She covered children with AIDS in Tanzania, Uganda and Kenya. Additionally, Monica served as personal/official photographer to civil rights icon Rosa Parks.

Although she claims to be shy, Monica has the undeniable ability to communicate with people from all walks of life. Her strength comes in getting close enough to subjects to make them comfortable enough to allow their true essence on film.

Marlin Page is chief executive officer of Knowledge Brokers Technology Solutions, a technology consulting and staffing firm. She is responsible for ensuring that the company exceeds its client's technical, staffing and strategic business requirements.

Marlin received a bachelor's degree from Wayne State University (WSU) and a master's degree from the University of Detroit Mercy. She also earned certification as an organizational development specialist through DePaul University. Marlin mastered mainframe and client server programming through a corporate professional development program, and began Doctor of Philosophy degree studies at WSU. She went on to become a corporate executive and deputy chief information officer for the City of Detroit.

Marlin was selected as an alternate speaker for the late civil rights activist, Coretta Scott King, for a statewide diversity celebration. She was also selected to serve as honorary chair for the Black Data Processing Association's national conference. She has been featured in numerous publications, and is nationally recognized as a strategic business consultant.

A Detroit native, Marlin is the wife of Robert L. Page, Esq. and the proud mother of one daughter, Morgan.

Marlin G. Page
Chief Executive Officer
Knowledge Brokers
Technology Solutions

A native of Camden, New Jersey, Randi Payton, president and chief executive officer of OnWheels, Incorporated, founded the nation's only multimedia automotive communications company for African-American, Latino and Asian consumers.

African Americans OnWheels (AAOW) is a bi-monthly magazine that currently boasts a circulation of 750,000. AAOW was the first minority-owned media to distribute nationally in minority newspapers and mainstream dailies.

Latinos OnWheels (LOW) launched in 2001 with a quarterly circulation of 500,000 in 37 Latino newspapers nationally. LOW was re-launched in June of 2006, along with *Asians OnWheels* at a circulation of 137,000. Both publications will serve second and third generation minorities who primarily read and speak English, and buy more new vehicles, which is something the industry did not understand several years ago.

Payton has also established the Urban Wheel Awards, now in its tenth year. The event has become the automotive industry's most significant diversity event. He also founded the Edward Davis Education Foundation, named for the first African American to receive a new car franchise in the U.S. The foundation has granted more than $200,000 in scholarships.

Randi Payton
President &
Chief Executive Officer
OnWheels, Incorporated

DETROIT'S ENTREPRENEURS

Cydni Penn

President & Owner
Cydni Charise Creations

Cydni Penn is the proprietor of Cydni Charise Creations, based in Detroit. As head consultant and designer, she provides the services of wedding coordinating, decoration, interior design, event planning, consulting, employee training and holiday decoration. Cydni has planned, coordinated, consulted and decorated for corporate events, weddings, fashion shows and private parties in Maryland, Florida, Washington, D.C., Georgia and the Detroit metro area.

Cydni has multiple talents, including painting, drawing, fashion design and dance choreography using her 20 years of dance. She founded a nonprofit teen girl competition dance group named the Shining Stars. As head choreographer, Cydni and her team earned national awards and recognitions, and were even invited to dance at the Orange Bowl in Miami, Florida. She is actively working and volunteering in several community, political and social organizations, including the UNCF, CBC, NAACP and DWIS.

Cydni earned a bachelor's degree in fashion buying merchandising and design from Clark Atlanta University, and is pursuing an MBA degree with a concentration in marketing.

A native Detroiter, Cydni is the daughter of Dr. Maggie Penn and the late Luther Penn.

Orena Perry

Chief Executive Officer
The Acquisitionist

In 2005 Orena Perry formed a company called The Acquisitionist. The name originated because Orena found herself acquiring the needs of individuals and companies alike. In the summer of 2005, The Acquisitionist helped organize Jazz on the Blvd. Jazz on the Blvd. provides an intimate, breezy and mellow vibe, in a serene and relaxing atmosphere. It includes live entertainment, free food and drink specials each Thursday at the historic Hotel St. Regis.

Now in 2007, she is at it again assisting the president of the International Detroit Black Expo, Inc. during Buy Black Weekend. She will soon partner with VStyle to create a new company called Brazen, and will launch their first event, Rhythmic Fete.

Orena is a single, loving mother of five beautiful children. Eyes have not seen and ears have not heard what this phenomenal woman will do next. She says, "We can all make a difference, and it will begin with me."

The *Detroit Free Press* called Pam Perry "a marketing whiz on an almost immortal mission." Known as the "connector and PR coach," Perry knows how to pull the right people together for the right project at the right time and garner the right publicity. Her public relations (PR) and advertising career spans two decades.

A local Emmy Award-winning professional, Perry has worked the entire gamut of media, including print, radio and television. Additionally, her career includes nonprofit and PR agencies.

One of the nation's foremost experts in the African-American Christian market, Perry is the chief visionary of Ministry Marketing Solutions, Inc., the PR and marketing consulting firm launched in 2000. Some author clients include Bishop T.D. Jakes, Dr. Suzan Johnson Cook, Dr. Fred Price and Pastor Bill Winston.

Her passion is Christian books and assisting writers in becoming authors through the American Christian Writers Association; she is president and founder of the Detroit chapter. Perry also hosts teleconferences on various PR and marketing topics with self-published authors, and provides PR counsel to ministries nationwide.

She is married to Marc Perry.

Pam Perry
Chief Visionary
Ministry Marketing Solutions, Inc.

James K. Ralph Jr. is president of James Ralph Agency, Inc., a full-service insurance agency. The agency specializes in commercial insurance and employee benefits.

A board member of the Oak Park Business and Education Alliance, Ralph is a member of the Oakland County Business Roundtable, president of the Southern Oakland County NAACP and chairman of the board of Southfield Downtown Development Authority. He also serves on the Blue Cross Blue Shield Agent Advisory Council, as treasurer of the National African-American Insurance Association, Michigan Chapter, and as board member of the Michigan Minority Business Development Council.

Ralph's past community involvement includes serving as chairman of the Southfield Chamber of Commerce, president of the Council of Minority Business Organizations and president of the Oakland County Business Consortium. He also served as chairman of Southfield Adult Education and treasurer of Southfield Public Schools Community Foundation, and was involved with the Life Underwriters Association and the 46th District Court Substance Abuse Task Force.

Additionally, Ralph was named 2002 Volunteer of the Year and 2006 Business Person of the Year by the Southfield Chamber of Commerce.

James K. Ralph Jr.
President
James Ralph Agency, Inc.

Brenda Reeves

Chief Executive Officer
Reeves Business Solutions

Brenda Reeves has established herself as one of Michigan's leading businesswomen. She began her mission in business support 15 years ago, and has experienced astounding growth in her business endeavors through Reeves Business Solutions. As chief executive officer, she focuses on developing new business opportunities, business coaching, and leading her multifaceted managers and directors.

Although she is a businesswoman, Reeves is also sincerely passionate about helping others develop their businesses by utilizing her extensive resources in the business world. She has been successful in spreading her education and business savvy to encourage and motivate many budding entrepreneurs to take a chance at business and "step outside the box." Her approach in assisting both new business owners and established business owners is one that seeks to build strong business relationships that will last and ultimately increase the prosperity of all.

Additionally, for the past ten years, Reeves has been co-owner of B & D Novelty, also based in Michigan. She encompasses an astounding ability to effectively spearhead a host of projects simultaneously, which is the basis of her constant achievements.

Lawrence R. Roberson

President
Wealth Management Group, Inc.

Lawrence R. Roberson is president of Wealth Management Group, Inc. (WMG). WMG provides a myriad of financial planning and money management services. Roberson has more than 31 years of experience in finance. He served in several managerial positions at Ford Motor Company. After 13 years, he started his own firm in 1985. His transition from Ford to an entrepreneur was featured on the front page of *The Wall Street Journal*.

Roberson graduated from Alabama A&M University with a Bachelor of Science degree in mathematics. He received a Master of Business Administration degree from Indiana University, and was one of the first African Americans to obtain the CFP (certified financial planner) designation in Michigan. He is also a past president of the Detroit Chapter of the National Black MBA Association.

Roberson was born in Birmingham, Alabama. In the 1960s, he participated in the civil rights struggle of the South. Most notable was a bombing that took place on December 24th. Though no one was killed, Roberson's home, Bethel Baptist Church and many other homes were damaged.

Craig Sanders is an author, speaker, business consultant and personal development coach. He is the author of *Keys to Manifesting Your Destiny: A Roadmap for Turning Your Setbacks Into Accelerated Comebacks*, and has a wealth of experience in sales, administration, public speaking, public relations, management and consulting.

Craig, known as "The Comeback Specialist," is the founder of Craig Sanders Unlimited, LLC, a small business and personal development company. He works with entrepreneurs, small business owners, professionals, churches and others to provide strategies on turning setbacks into accelerated comebacks in life and business. As a result of his coaching and motivational skills, many have experienced personal transformation and business turnarounds, and are able to hit the ground running using his concepts to get them closer to their desired goals. According to international speaker and professional recording artist Dr. Marvin L. Sapp, Craig is "probably one of the most prolific motivational and inspiration speakers of our time."

Craig and his lovely wife, Charisse, have been happily married since 1994.

Craig L. Sanders

Founder, Author,
Speaker & Coach
Craig Sanders Unlimited, LLC

Ada Smith is owner and principal consultant of JAS Events, a full-service events planning company. In this position, she is responsible for coordinating events, and also heads up fundraising initiatives for several clients. Ada facilitates workshops, meetings and conferences for both local and national organizations. She also spearheaded a new summer festival for the city of Highland Park called the Market on Manchester.

Prior to forming JAS Events, Ada served as director of chapter development and community relations for the Detroit Black Alliance for Educational Options.

Ada received a bachelor's degree in psychology from Xavier University of Louisiana, where she also earned a master's degree in counseling. In 2005 she was one of the youngest graduates of the Detroit Regional Chamber of Commerce's Leadership Detroit program. She served on The Skillman Foundation Good Schools Task Force.

A native of Detroit, Ada is a member of Perfecting Church and a graduate of Cass Technical High School, where she is vice president of the alumni association.

Ada Smith

Owner & Principal Consultant
JAS Events

Beverly Smith

Photographer

Originally from Lake Charles, Louisiana, Beverly Smith relocated to Detroit, Michigan, with her family in 1968. She has provided photographic services for schools, churches, organizations and businesses for 20 years.

Smith has also photographed for many businesses, including Ernst & Young LLC, Strategic Staffing Solutions, Deloitte & Touche, PricewaterhouseCoopers, Mobil Oil Corporation, the City of Detroit, Pepsi Bottling Group and Greektown Casino. She has photographed the U.S. Border Patrol of Laredo, Texas, and the Livonia and Garden City Police departments.

Smith is co-chair of the Detroit City Council's Keep Detroit Beautiful Task Force, board member of Keep Michigan Beautiful and a member of the Women's Informal Network. Additionally, she is the publisher of two Detroit-based newspapers: the *Detroit Black Pages Business News and Directory* and the *Minority Auto Dealers Customer Buying Guide*. The monthly newspapers promote and market African-American and other minority-owned businesses in the Detroit metropolitan area. *Minority Auto Dealers Customer Buying Guide* and its Web site is an automotive newspaper and Web site promoting minority auto dealers.

Jeana Tall

Founder & Chief Executive Officer
International Community
Services of Detroit

Jeana Tall is founder and chief executive officer of the International Community Services of Detroit, or ICSD. The ICSD is a solutions-oriented consulting company that engages nonprofit and profit entities to provide training, resources and information technology support. Her specialty training areas include board development, logic modeling, strategic planning, management solutions, and pipeline and fund development. She has been working with immigrant and indigent populations in Michigan for more than ten years, bringing 15 years of corporate administration experience to the nonprofit arena.

A lecturer on topics that cover race relations, diversity, urban studies and cross-cultural dynamics, Tall is currently conducting immersion workshops on grant writing and professional writing. She is also a published poet and author.

Her lifelong learning pursuits include a Microsoft certified professional (MCP) program from Davenport University, a Bachelor of Arts degree in sociology from the University of Detroit Mercy and a master's degree in interdisciplinary studies – nonprofit sector from Wayne State University. Additionally, Tall is completing a master's degree in teaching – adult education and instruction from the University of Phoenix.

Gwendolyn Thomas is president of Promotions Unlimited 2000, Inc., a promotional model and talent agency. Promotions Unlimited opened in Chicago in 1988 and moved to Detroit in 1990. This year marks the company's 19th anniversary. Today, it services Fortune 500 companies across the globe.

The company's clients have included AlliedDomecq, AT&T, Anheuser-Busch, Belle Tire, BET, Blue Cross, Coca-Cola, Colgate, CompUSA, Cub Foods, Chrysler, Ford, General Mills, General Motors, Glory Foods, Greektown and MGM Casinos, and Harley-Davidson. They also include Johnson Controls, HBO, Heinz, Kmart, Kraft, L'Oreal, Mattel, Mercedes-Benz, Miller Brewing, NAACP, NWA, OfficeMax, P&G, Pepsi, Publix, Reebok, Seagram, and Wayne and Oakland Counties.

An events and marketing guru, Thomas has worked on the BE Tennis and Golf Challenge, and has hosted events for AJ Jamal, Mary J. Blige (30) and Yolanda Adams (10). She has worked with the NAACP Image Awards, the Mercedes-Benz Gala Opening, and national Chrysler and Ford events.

Thomas holds an MBA and a bachelor's degree. A resident of West Bloomfield, she is a single mom with one son, Cameron, who attends Morehouse College.

Gwendolyn Thomas

President
Promotions Unlimited 2000, Inc.

Larry Thomas Jr. is owner and director of operations for The Inner Link, a graphic and Web design company. Established more than three years ago, The Inner Link has continued to expand its services to an ever-growing client base that includes the City of Detroit, Jenkins Construction, AdvaSure Insurance Agency and various faith-based organizations.

Thomas serves under the leadership of pastors Steven and Valorie Bennett of House of Prayer and Praise Ministries as the head of their men's ministry, The Foundation. He also serves on the executive committee for the University Commons as the marketing and promotions chair.

Born and raised in Detroit, Thomas is a graduate of Cass Tech High School. He is husband to the lovely Terese Thomas and father to the incredible Larry Xavier Thomas. His future plans include developing a nonprofit organization to help strengthen the mind, body and soul of individuals within the community, increasing his speaking endeavors and completing his first book.

Larry Thomas Jr.

Owner & Director, Operations
The Inner Link

Tyra C. Thomas

Health & Wellness
Program Director
LIFESHAPE Corporate
Fitness Solutions LLC

Speaker and educator Tyra Thomas is wellness program director for LIFESHAPE Corporate Fitness Solutions LLC. LIFESHAPE serves the corporate sector with wellness and work-life balance programs. As director, Tyra is masterful at designing programs that reposition the client business for growth to No. 1 status in their respective market. She empowers businesses through her extensive knowledge of healthy living and a unique ability to "kindle fire" in people to be their best.

A champion in fighting for the health and healing of people, Tyra is executive producer of the forthcoming television series, "Healthy Living 101™," feature fitness columnist for the *Detroit Black News*, and community advocate and teacher, known for her charismatic word on health and living powerfully.

An eight-year veteran of the fitness industry, Tyra is certified by the American Council on Exercise, the nation's top fitness certifying body, with additional certification in group exercise and yoga. She has worked with industry leaders, Bally Total Fitness and Fitness USA, and is currently completing exercise science studies at Wayne State University.

Tyra is the proud mother of one son, Tori Anthony Thomas.

Velonda Thompson, Ph.D.

President
Be-Fit Inc.

Dr. Velonda Thompson is president of Be-Fit Inc., a nutrition education and health promotion organization that has provided a variety of corporate, small business and individualized health promotion services in the Detroit metropolitan area since 1989. Additional services include local and national conference lecture and workshop presentations.

As a nutritionist, Thompson is the author of an educational cookbook entitled *Pass the Sweet Potatoes, Please!* She is also an adjunct professor for Schoolcraft College. Additionally, she has spent numerous years in the nonprofit sector facilitating physical fitness, nutrition education and health promotion activities for youth 6 years of age and older.

Thompson received a Bachelor of Science degree from Wayne State University, and Walsh College awarded her a master's degree in management. In 2001 she was awarded a doctoral degree in nutrition and health promotion from the Union Institute & University in Cincinnati, Ohio.

A native of Washington, D.C., Thompson has called Detroit home since 1983. She can be found walking, running or biking from West Eight Mile Road to Belle Isle.

David G. Watkins is president and chief executive officer of Oxygen Photography LLC, a privately owned photography business venture specializing in providing industry-leading digital imaging and reproductions. For more than five years, Oxygen Photography LLC has become a catalyst for cutting-edge photojournalism and creative composition. Watkins and Oxygen Photography LLC provide a variety of services, including charity fundraisers, political events, product advertising, portraits and wedding photography.

As a freelance photojournalist, Watkins has graced the cover of several newspapers, including the *Michigan Chronicle* and *The Michigan FrontPage*, *The Indianapolis Recorder* and *The Washington Informer*. As a jazz columnist, he created "Jazz in Review," a mainstream jazz forum devoted to bringing behind-the-scenes interviews from recent and vintage jazz artists from all over the world.

Watkins earned Associate of Business Administration and Bachelor of Business Administration degrees from Davenport University in Dearborn, Michigan, and is currently working towards a Master of Business Administration degree from Walsh College of Novi, Michigan. He is employed as the manager of marketing and communications for the Detroit Rescue Mission Ministries.

David G. Watkins

President &
Chief Executive Officer
Oxygen Photography, LLC

Bartel Welch is chief executive officer of FMWebmasters, LLC. In 1997 he established one of the most elite and well-known minority-owned print, Web and design corporations in Metro Detroit. As owner and chief executive officer, he is responsible for establishing policies, contracts and offers, as well as supervising all print and designs, giving FMW a true distinction from others with high quality work at low cost, fast turnaround and world-class customer service.

Welch is featured in an array of local and national publications, including FOX 2 News, *Michigan FrontPage*, *Michigan Chronicle*, *Detroit Free Press* and *rolling out*. He was honored as a Cambridge Who's Who 2007, and previously received a Webby Web Award in 2002. Bartel is also a member of the International Detroit Black Expo, the NAACP and Kappa Alpha Psi Fraternity, Inc.

Bartel graduated summa cum laude and received a Bachelor of Science degree in chemistry from Xavier University in Louisiana in 2001.

A native of Detroit, Michigan, Bartel is the husband of Raquel Welch and the proud father of two children, Seth and Alaya.

Bartel Welch

Owner & Chief Executive Officer
FMWebmasters, LLC

Marvin Winans Jr.

Founder, President &
Chief Executive Officer
M2 Entertainment

S howing the world how to live the "complete" lifestyle through his music, Marvin Winans Jr. is undoubtedly ready for pop success and public attention. As the last name denotes, he is no stranger to a mainstream audience.

Born to gospel greats Marvin L. Winans Sr. and Vickie Winans on December 28, 1979, Marvin began capturing the hearts of audiences at the early age of 5.

At the age of 18, he began to blaze his own trail as a member of the Grammy-nominated group Winans Phase 2 with their debut album, *We Got Next*.

Marvin has worked alongside the best producers in the music industry, such as Cedric Caldwell, Warryn Campbell, Rodney and Fred Jerkins, and Noel "Detail" Fisher. He is also known for his work with gospel artists Vickie Winans, Fred Hammond and Mary Mary.

This singer/producer/songwriter is founder, president and chief executive officer of M2 Entertainment. Marvin is continuing the legacy set before him as he prepares to release his debut solo album on M2 Entertainment, *Image of a Man*.

Lee A. Yancy III

Founder & Chief Executive Officer
Moving Screen Marketing

L ee A. Yancy III is founder and chief executive officer of Moving Screen Marketing, a unique and innovative marketing venue that is revolutionizing the advertising industry. Moving Screen Marketing has captured markets in the Midwest and Northeastern areas of the United States. His national clientele list includes Sean John, Clinique and Macy's, to name a few.

Born and raised in Detroit, Lee earned a Bachelor of Science degree in business economics at Florida A&M. Since returning home, he has been an avid community activist, serving on many organizational boards, including Third Eye, Incorporated (of which he was a founding member and vice president), the Empowerment Zone and the Second Tuesday RainbowPUSH Coalition. Additionally, he is a member of Prince Hall Affiliated Masons and the United Supreme Council.

Married to Dr. Amanda F. Yancy, Lee's pastimes include golfing and biking.

proficient

excel

DETROIT'S

CORPORATE BRASS

outshine

surpass

transcend

enhance

surmount

master

triumph

James Adams

Director of Food and Beverage
Greektown Casino

Pamela G. Alexander

Director, Community Development
Ford Motor Company Fund

James Adams is director of food and beverage at Greektown Casino. His responsibilities include directing the operation of activities, including banquets, employee dining, the VIP Pantheon Lounge and Greektown Casino's two restaurants, the upscale Alley Grille Steakhouse and the casual dining Grapevine Café.

James completed a successful career in the U.S. Air Force, specializing in computer operations, guidance system engineering on the Titan ICBM, weapons systems deficiency analysis and club operations. He received service awards, including the Air Force Meritorious Service Medal, the Club Operation Director Award and the Outstanding Achiever Award.

The second phase of his career began in Phoenix, Arizona, nine years ago, when James began working in the casino industry. He managed the food and beverage department for the largest casino enterprise in Arizona, consisting of three casinos.

James received a Bachelor of Science degree in management from Park University in Missouri, and an associate degree in hotel restaurant management from the CCAF.

James recently relocated to Michigan from Phoenix, Arizona. He is the proud father of one daughter and two sons.

Pamela Alexander is director of community development and fund operations for Ford Motor Company Fund. In this position, she is responsible for Ford Fund's community development and outreach initiatives with key communities and organizations throughout the U.S. She also oversees the business operations of Ford Motor Company Fund. In 2005 Ford Fund dedicated almost $80 million to educational initiatives, cultural sponsorships and performing arts programs across the nation.

Pamela joined Ford in 1990 and began her career in the controller's office. Prior to her appointment to the Ford Fund, she held a variety of positions in Ford Motor Company's governmental affairs office. Her experience includes policy development, legislative and community interaction, and managing the company's PAC and grassroots activities.

A native Michigander, Pamela holds a bachelor's degree from Georgetown University and a master's degree from Columbia University.

Pamela has dedicated her time to serve on various nonprofit boards, and has been featured in *Ebony* magazine's "Speaking of People" column and *African Americans on Wheels* as one of the auto industry's most influential African-American women.

Jené Allen

Director, Organization &
Talent Effectiveness
Human Resources
Trinity Health

Jocelyn K. Allen

Vice President, Communications
OnStar

Jené Allen has been with Trinity Health since July of 1999. In her role, she advises and consults with leadership and management on all human resources issues. Her goal is to promote management decision-making that is consistent with Trinity Health values and employment laws, and to foster positive employee relations.

Prior to joining Trinity Health, Allen served in human resources for eight years at the Detroit Medical Center.

Allen holds a bachelor's degree in business administration from Eastern Michigan University. She received certification as a professional in human resources from the HR Certification Institute (HRCI) and the Society of Human Resource Management in 1998. She is considered a generalist with experience in all areas of human resources.

Allen is also a member of the National Association of Health Services Executives, and resides on the board of directors for Leaps and Bounds Family Services, a nonprofit organization founded in Detroit in 1988.

Jocelyn K. Allen was named vice president of communications for OnStar on January 1, 2007. She is responsible for communicating the strategic direction of the brand to all internal and external audiences. She also serves as a member of the OnStar Senior Leadership Board.

Prior to her current assignment with OnStar, Allen was manager of broadcast media relations for General Motors.

She began her career as a freelance production assistant, working on films, commercials and music videos. As a natural progression, she moved on to television to work as a stage manager for the local NBC affiliate, WDIV.

In 2002 Allen founded an organization, Divas4Life. Divas4Life is a not-for-profit program dedicated to fostering determined, inspired, victorious, adventurous (DIVA) young women, ages 8-18, through the instruction of life-sustaining skills.

A native of Detroit, Allen attended Benedictine High School. She received a Bachelor of Arts degree from the University of Notre Dame in 1991, and will receive a master's degree in organizational communications and public relations from Wayne State University in 2008.

DETROIT'S CORPORATE BRASS

Vernon Baker

Senior Vice President
General Counsel
ArvinMeritor, Inc.

Malcolm Blacken

Strength & Conditioning Coach
Detroit Lions

Vernon Baker is senior vice president and general counsel of ArvinMeritor, Inc. In this position, he is responsible for the legal aspects of all ArvinMeritor's global operations and its subsidiaries. In addition, Baker directs all legal activities in the corporation, including corporate governance, acquisitions and divestitures, litigation, business standards compliance, regulatory compliance and intellectual property. He also has functional oversight responsibility for the environmental, health and safety areas.

Before the July of 2000 merger with Arvin Industries Inc., Baker was senior vice president, general counsel and secretary of Meritor Automotive Inc., a global supplier of components and systems for commercial, specialty, and light vehicle OEMs and the aftermarket.

Baker holds a bachelor's degree from Dartmouth College in Hanover, New Hampshire, and a juris doctorate from American University Washington College of Law in Washington, D.C. He was recently honored with the Minority Corporate Counsel Association's Trailblazer Award, which recognizes the outstanding achievements of minority in-house counsels who also act as role models in the legal profession.

Malcolm Blacken enters his seventh year with the Detroit Lions, and is the team's strength and conditioning coach. Throughout the past six seasons in Detroit, he has been instrumental in the transition of a new conditioning program introduced in 2001.

When joining the team in 2001, Blacken added to a resumé that included similar stops at three colleges and his first NFL team, the Washington Redskins. He spent five seasons (1996-2000) as a strength assistant with the Redskins. Before Washington, he was a strength assistant with the University of Virginia's conditioning staff, and worked with all the other sports in the Cavaliers' athletic department.

Additionally, for three years (1992-94), Blacken served as the head strength coach for George Mason University, where his duties included overseeing all conditioning programs for the university's varsity sports. He began his coaching career at the University of South Carolina in 1991.

Blacken graduated from Virginia Tech in 1989 with a bachelor's degree in art. He was a four-time letter winner for the Hokies' football team.

Sandra Boozer

Vice President, Human Resources
Blue Cross Blue Shield of Michigan

Cheryl L. Bowlson

Business Diversity Manager
Barton Malow Company

Sandra Boozer is vice president of human resources for Blue Cross Blue Shield of Michigan (BCBSM). She provides dedicated human resources support to the Operations and Information Technology Division. She also provides oversight to the labor/employee relations and joint programs functions at BCBSM.

Previously, Boozer was vice president of human resources for Blue Care Network of Michigan, the HMO subsidiary of BCBSM. She was responsible for all human resources activities at Blue Care Network, including staffing, employee/labor relations, compensation and benefits, and human resources information systems. Boozer joined Blue Cross Blue Shield in 1972, and has worked in many areas of the company, including operations, marketing, customer service, human resources and union/management relations.

Boozer has a bachelor's degree in business administration from Wayne State University, and is pursuing a master's degree in executive leadership and business administration from the University of Nebraska-Lincoln.

As business diversity manager for Barton Malow Company, one of the nation's largest builders, Cheryl Bowlson directs business and workforce diversity initiatives for the corporation. Her responsibilities include shaping corporate policy, participating in local and national organizations and events, introducing diverse companies to Barton Malow decision-makers, mentoring project teams on proper procedures for diverse inclusion, hosting networking forums and reporting.

Thanks to Cheryl's efforts, Barton Malow is a five-time winner of the Michigan Minority Business Development Council (MMBDC) Corporation of the Year – Construction Sector Award and a six-time choice as one of Greater Detroit's 101 Best Places to Work, including the elite award for diversity and multiculturalism in 2005.

Cheryl holds a Bachelor of Science degree from Michigan State University and a Master of Business Administration degree from Walsh College. She is an active member of MMBDC, the certification committee of the Michigan Women's Business Council and the board of the Booker T. Washington Business Association and New Creation Community Outreach.

Cheryl and her husband, Bertram, are the parents of two adult daughters, Kelly and Shardae.

DETROIT'S CORPORATE BRASS

Denise Brooks-Williams

Vice President, Operations
St. Joseph Mercy Oakland
Trinity Health

Walter R. Brown

Director
Global College Planning

Denise Brooks-Williams is vice president of operations at St. Joseph Mercy Oakland (SJMO), a member of Trinity Health. She is responsible for dietary and environmental services, radiology, laboratory, community programs, advocacy and the employed physician network.

Prior to her most recent role, Brooks-Williams served as vice president of ambulatory services at SJMO, which involved interfacing with key trustees, and community and medical leaders. For several months in 2004, she was the interim chief executive officer for SJMO. Before that, she was vice president at the Health Care Centers of the Detroit Medical Center and served as assistant vice president of ambulatory care operations with the former Sinai Hospital of Detroit.

Brooks-Williams earned bachelor's and master's degrees in health services administration from the University of Michigan. She was a past president of the National Association of Health Services Executives – Detroit, co-chair of the 2005 National Association of Health Services Executives (NAHSE) National Educational Conference, and a member of the Michigan Healthcare Executive Group and Associates. Additionally, NAHSE honored her with the 2004 Young Healthcare Executive of the Year Award.

Walter R. Brown is director of Global College Planning, a nonprofit organization specializing in providing collegiate counseling to students and their families and mentoring them on how to maximize their financial aid and scholarship opportunities. Global College Planning is a member of the Independent Education Counseling Association and the Michigan Association for College Admissions and Counseling.

A former investment Series 7 stockbroker for Investment Diversity Services, Brown has successfully encouraged students to continue their educational commitment by providing recommendations regarding curriculum choices and streamlining the selection process of colleges and universities. He provides a step-by-step college action plan to assist each student in promoting a concise and detailed pathway to meet all aspects of a collegiate school year.

Prior to a successful career at Global College Planning, Brown respectfully served his country as a staff sergeant in the U.S. Army, receiving an honorable discharge for his tour of duty during the Vietnam War. He graduated in 1969 from the University of Lawton in Oklahoma, where he received a Bachelor of Science degree in business.

Kimberly L. Burton

Vice President &
Manager of Community Affairs
Charter One Bank

Joseph Cazeno Jr.

Regional Manager
Corporate & Government Affairs
DTE Energy

Kimberly Burton is vice president and manager of community affairs for Charter One Bank in Michigan. In this capacity, she manages the Charter One Foundation and charitable contributions for the company in Michigan. Prior to joining Charter One, she was the vice president of corporate affairs for Orchards Children's Services, the largest private foster care agency in the state of Michigan.

Burton graduated from the University of Michigan, with a dual Bachelor of Arts degree in psychology and English. Even though she originally hails from Grand Rapids, she has considered the Detroit metro area her hometown since moving to the area to pursue her education.

Burton is deeply committed to the social service needs of the community, and is actively involved with organizations working to improve the social service landscape. As a Leadership Detroit XXIV graduate, she continues to be committed to the economic development of the region. Burton serves as a board member for Grace Centers of Hope, the Gary Burnstein Community Health Clinic and the Neighborhood Service Organization.

An accomplished pianist, Burton enjoys music, reading, theater and dancing.

Joseph Cazeno Jr. is regional manager of corporate and government affairs for DTE Energy, the largest utility supplier in Michigan. In this position, he serves as the company's lobbyist regarding local legislation in counties, cities, townships and villages, and assists the company's state and federal lobbying efforts. He guides the decision-making process on behalf of DTE Energy at government meetings throughout the metropolitan community. Joseph promotes DTE Energy's interests in the areas of electric power generation and transmission, gas production and distribution, nuclear operations, environmental concerns, taxes, media and public relations.

Joseph is a civic leader in the Detroit area, serving on 11 business boards, including the Downtown Detroit Partnership and the Booker T. Washington Business Association. He also works to raise the awareness of organizations that serve and promote diversity and leadership.

He received a Bachelor of Science degree from Lawrence Technological University in Southfield. A native of Detroit, Joseph is the husband of Ardis Cazeno, and the proud father of two sons, Andre and Joseph.

Nancy L. Conyers

Customer Relations Manager &
Vice President
Jaguar of Novi

Burner Crew

Relationship Manager
Public Sector Group
KeyBank

Nancy L. Conyers is the customer relations manager and a vice president of Jaguar of Novi, a Jaguar dealership located in a western suburb of Detroit.

As a result of her efforts and maintaining customer satisfaction scores in the top 10 percent of all Jaguar dealers in the U.S., Jaguar of Novi received the prestigious Pride of Jaguar Dealer Excellence Award three years in a row.

A graduate of the University of Michigan, with a degree in communications, Conyers has honed her skills for more than 26 years in the automotive industry. She has served the industry in various capacities, including as secretary-treasurer, business manager and instructor. As an instructor, Conyers taught employees the customer relationship standards she implemented in numerous dealerships throughout the years.

She has been recognized by the Ford Motor Company, and sought after for speaking engagements nationwide to promote the advancement of minority, female participation within the retail automotive sector.

A native Detroiter, Conyers is the single parent of two school-age children.

Burner Crew is the relationship manager covering Northwest Ohio and Michigan for Public Sector at KeyBank. He joined the Public Sector Group in 2000. His brokerage career began in 1987 with E.F. Hutton, and in 1990 he joined Prescott Ball and Turben. In 1994 he joined McDonald Investments.

Burner serves as treasurer on the board of directors for the Center for Mental Retardation and the John Black Foundation. He is an active member of Beth-El AME Zion Church and the National Association of Securities Professionals. He also serves as a financial analyst for Fox 8 News in Cleveland, Ohio.

Burner holds a bachelor's degree in econometrics from Columbia University, and his securities licenses have included 3, 7 and 63.

Glenn A. Croxton, C.P.M.

Director, Vendor
Compliance & Management
Henry Ford Health System

Olisaeloka I. Dallah

Vice President
Compliance & Security
Greektown Casino

Glenn Croxton was born and raised in Detroit. He attended Detroit Public Schools, and later received a Bachelor of Arts degree from Ferris State University in Big Rapids, Michigan, in 1974.

Glenn began his professional career as deputy purchasing agent for Highland Park General Hospital in 1974. He enrolled as a graduate student at Central Michigan University in 1978, and received a Master of Arts degree in management and supervision with a concentration in public administration in 1980. In 1989 Glenn embarked upon an intensive self-study academic program administered by the National Association of Purchasing Management (NAPM), and received his certified purchasing manager (CPM) designation in 1991.

He joined his current employer, Henry Ford Health System, in December of 2002, and is currently director of vendor compliance and management. In 2004 Henry Ford Health System honored Glenn with its Focus on People achievement award for outstanding contributions to the workplace and community.

Glenn is currently pursuing a doctorate degree in health administration at Central Michigan University.

Olisaeloka I. Dallah's tenure at Greektown Casino began in April of 1999 as the manager of compliance. He was promoted to director and then to vice president of compliance and internal audit. In 2004 he was promoted to vice president of compliance and security. Dallah's responsibilities include developing, administering and interpreting administrative rules from and with the Michigan Gaming Control Board, and other licensing and regulation agencies. He also oversees the completion of all operational compliance reviews and all regulatory divisions.

A Michigan native, Dallah is a graduate of the University of Michigan. He earned dual bachelor's degrees in economics and sociology with an emphasis in finance, business and social welfare.

Dallah's career began at Thyssen Steel Group in the finance and accounting departments. In this capacity, he compiled capital expenditures and corporate investments for the coming fiscal years, reported quarterly to the chief financial officer on capital budget spending for all divisions, and co-managed inspections within the processing center for accreditation.

Dallah enjoys surfing the Internet, building Web pages, and assisting family and friends with financial planning.

Damon A. Davis

Senior Vice President &
Creative Director
GlobalHue

Donald M. Davis Jr.

Vice President
Human Resources & Customer Relations
Health Alliance Plan

Damon A. Davis is senior vice president and creative director of GlobalHue. He oversees the development of print, broadcast, Internet and point-of-sale advertising, as well as marketing collateral for the agency.

In 1990 Damon joined GlobalHue, then known as Don Coleman Advertising. His creative input and vision was instrumental in helping the agency win the DaimlerChrysler account in 1994 as well as various awards over the years, including an American Advertising Federation Mosaic Award, a Mobius Award and an On Wheels Inc. Urban ADvantage Award.

He began his career at D'Arcy, Massius, Benton & Bowles as senior art director, where he gained valuable general market experience by working on projects for the Pontiac Motor Division, Whirlpool, FTD and Detroit Diesel.

In 1986 Damon worked at American Marketing Resources as marketing/art director, and was responsible for collateral and point-of-sales materials for Software City, Monroe Shocks and Automotive, Intertech Electronics and Pepsi-Cola Detroit.

He earned a bachelor's degree at Olivet College and a Master of Business Administration degree at the University of Michigan's marketing school.

Donald "Don" M. Davis Jr. is vice president of human resources and customer relations at Health Alliance Plan (HAP), one of Michigan's largest, most experienced health plans.

Don's expertise extends more than 31 years across all areas of human resources (HR), and includes pioneering efforts to measure the effectiveness of HR. He specializes in organization effectiveness, strategic planning, performance management and leadership development.

Don is active in the HR field locally and nationally. He serves as a national panel member with the Society for Human Resources Management and as a board member for the American Society of Employers.

A trusted community leader, Don is secretary of the board for Detroit Commerce Bank, and co-founder and chair of the Detroit Chapter of the National Association of African Americans in Human Resources. He is also a charter member of 100 Black Men of Greater Detroit, Inc. and an advisory board member at Eastern Michigan University. He served as deputy chief executive officer for HR at Detroit Public Schools from December of 2000 to March of 2001.

Don and his wife, Dolores, have one daughter, Dana.

Marke D. Dickinson

Vice President, Membership
The Auto Club Group

Gail A. Echols

Client HW & SW Engineering Manager
Information Technology
Ford Motor Company

M arke Dickinson is vice president of membership for The Auto Club Group (ACG), a holding company comprised of 4.1 million members, including six AAA clubs: AAA Michigan, AAA Wisconsin, AAA Chicago, AAA Nebraska, AAA North Dakota and AAA Minnesota/ Iowa.

In this position, Dickinson's responsibilities include membership benefits and services, new member acquisition and retention, financial services products and the AAA Driving School.

Prior to this position, he served as ACG's vice president/executive assistant to the president and chief executive officer, following a stint as the organization's chief marketing officer. Before joining ACG in 2002, Dickinson was director of corporate planning and development for TSYS, Inc., and has held various management positions with Accenture, Computer Sciences Corporation and the board of governors of the Federal Reserve System.

He serves on the board of directors of the Detroit Urban League and the Community Alliance Credit Union in Dearborn.

Dickinson holds an MBA from the Harvard Business School, a Master of Public Policy degree from Harvard's John F. Kennedy School of Government and an undergraduate degree, with honors, from Penn State University.

G ail A. Echols is an information technology (IT) senior manager with 16 years of experience in IT infrastructure, networking, manufacturing systems, and security and controls. She is the global client engineering SW and HW manager for Ford Motor Company. Her organization has ultimate responsibility for the PC/Unix hardware standards, operating system images, image/fax and printer strategies, integration lab certification, and software delivery and systems management technology.

Gail has managed multimillion-dollar capital and expense budgets. She has been responsible for all IT applications and infrastructure at the largest manufacturing plant facility in North America. She excels in organization, communication, leadership, team building and project delivery.

Gail holds a bachelor's degree in computer science from Wayne State University. She has been instrumental in IT recruiting and Ford College Graduate mentoring efforts. An active member of the Michigan Council of Women in Technology, she is vice chair of the IT Ford African American Network (FAAN). Additionally, Gail is a member of the Detroit African American Museum Women's Committee, and an active member of her church, Original New Grace Missionary Baptist Church.

Derek L. Edwards

Vice President &
Business Banking Team Leader
Huntington National Bank

Joyce E. Flowers

Director of National Accounts
Grand Rapids
Convention & Visitors Bureau

Derek L. Edwards is vice president and business banking team leader for the north and east districts at Huntington National Bank, where he manages a group of business bankers. With 13 years in banking, Derek has spent the last nine years working with small businesses. With opportunities to originate a large number of SBA lending transactions, working closely with many great resource partners for small businesses, and working directly with the business owners, he developed a passion for small business that continues to grow every day.

Derek became involved with CEED more than 4 years ago. Initially his involvement began with the Micro Loan Program but has grown to include the WBE certification process through the Michigan Women's Business Council, as well as a number of initiatives and events that the organization is involved in.

A born and raised Detroiter, Derek received a bachelor's degree in accounting from Lawrence Technological University and a master's degree in finance from Walsh College. Derek and his wife of 12 years, Charisse, are the proud parents of two lovely daughters, ages 8 and 3 (Drew and Devyn).

Joyce Flowers is director of national accounts in sales and works in the Detroit office for the Grand Rapids Convention & Visitors Bureau. Joyce is responsible for solicitation of new group meetings and conventions from markets in the Detroit metropolitan area including multicultural groups, African-American churches, and corporate, pharmaceutical and women's groups. Her priority in servicing her clients is to work with them to help deliver outstanding meetings and conventions by providing them with access to a portfolio of quality hotels and a state-of-the-art convention center. She is committed to her work and performs it with passion and enthusiasm.

Joyce received her education from Wayne State University. She serves as a board member of the Women of Color Foundation & Health Ministries. She is also a member of Inforum, the Michigan Meeting Professionals International, the Michigan Society of Association Executives, the Michigan Economic Developer's Association, and the National Association of Women Business Owners.

Born and raised in Detroit, Joyce is married to Henry J. Flowers, and is the loving mother of their two children, Kristen Simone and Michael John.

Tamika L. Gaines

Regional Vice President
Primerica Financial Services

Marcia B. Marsh Goffney

Vice President, Secretary &
General Counsel
Yazaki North America, Inc.

Tamika L. Gaines is a recruiting divisional leader for Primerica Financial Services. In this position, she manages, trains and develops leaders who bring financial services to the kitchen table for those who need it most: the working class. Tamika is the leader of Team Divine, which educates people on how to make money and save money.

A graduate of Flint Northwestern Academy in 1991, she received a Bachelor of Arts degree in business management from Wayne State University in 2007.

Tamika is a member of Shiloh Tabernacle Church of God In Christ. She is the proud mother of Tarence Jarise Arrington. Her hobbies are helping people realize there is no task they cannot complete, but that they only need to work longer without quitting. Her favorite quote is from the Bible (KJV) Hebrews 11:1, "Now faith is the substance of things hoped for and the evidence of things not seen."

Marcia B. Marsh Goffney is vice president, secretary and general counsel of Yazaki North America, Inc. (YNA), a multibillion-dollar supplier of wire harnesses, data solutions, and electronic and electrical components to the global automotive industry. YNA is part of the Japan-based Yazaki Group.

Goffney manages all legal services for YNA and Yazaki entities throughout North America, South America, Canada and Mexico. She also oversees governance activities. Previously, she was managing counsel at Dow Corning Corporation.

Goffney co-founded the Charting Your Own Course Foundation for the career advancement of minority lawyers. She is a member of the Executive Leadership Council, and has served on the Michigan Open Justice Commission, and the American Bar Association Ethics and Professional Responsibility Committee. She is an alumna of Leadership America, and serves as a director on the boards of the 20,000-member Association of Corporate Counsel and the Straker Bar Association.

Goffney's awards include the Dow Chemical/Dow Corning Amory Houghton Community Service Award, the Mitten Bay Girl Scout Region's Outstanding Woman of the Year and the Association of Corporate Counsel National Diversity Award.

Paula Green-Smith

Director, Training & Development
Greektown Casino

Jamy P. Hall

Director, Dealer Development
Ford Motor Company

Paula Green-Smith manages the training academy and team member morale programs at Greektown Casino. She joined their executive team in December of 2000, after six years of providing training and mediation services through her consulting firm, The Green-Smith Group. She also spent more than 11 years in community college administration, last serving as associate dean in charge of services for special needs students at Oakland Community College.

Paula has provided training for small businesses and Fortune 500 corporations alike. She also mediated and counseled equal employment opportunity claims for the U.S. Postal Service and the U.S. Army TACOM base in Warren, Michigan. She received a Bachelor of Science degree from Bowling Green State University, and a Master of Arts degree in education leadership from Eastern Michigan University.

A former classical and ethnic dancer, Paula espouses the concept of "edu-training," combining tenets of education and entertainment to the mission of training. She incorporates her innate desire to entertain in developing innovative approaches to train all learning styles.

Paula is a proud Detroiter and the mother of one daughter, Taryn Smith.

Jamy P. Hall is director of dealer development for the Ford Motor Company. She is responsible for assisting qualified dealer candidates in finding and financing dealership investment opportunities, and for enhancing focus on minority dealer operations. She oversees more than 160 dealerships under the Dealer Development Program.

Prior to her current position, Hall was regional manager of the Lincoln Mercury-Detroit Region, responsible for the sale of Lincoln and Mercury cars and trucks in the state of Michigan, northern Ohio and northern Indiana, through a network of 103 dealers.

Before joining Lincoln Mercury, Hall was director of North American business development for the Ford Customer Service Division. She joined the Ford Motor Company in 2001 from Case-New Holland Corporation, where she was senior director of global commercial services and OEM sales.

Born in New York, Hall has a bachelor's degree in industrial engineering from the University of Pittsburgh and a master's degree in marketing from The University of Chicago. She is a member of the Horizons Upward Bound board of directors. In 2002 she received the National Women of Color Technology Award.

Kathryn Bryant Harrison

Vice President &
Chief Public Affairs Officer
The Auto Club Group

Audrey J. Harvey

Vice President, Corporate Services
Blue Cross Blue Shield of Michigan

Kathryn Bryant Harrison is vice president and chief public affairs officer for The Auto Club Group (ACG), the largest AAA club in the Midwest, which serves 4.1 million AAA members. She is responsible for public affairs, public relations, community relations and traffic safety in ACG's eight-state service territory.

Among the many awards Harrison has received are the 2005 Women of Courage – Women of Change Award from the Minerva Education and Development Foundation, a Distinguished Service Award from the Fair Housing Center of Metropolitan Detroit and the Women of Achievement Award from the Anti-Defamation League's Michigan Region.

Some of Harrison's current board and advisory committee participation includes the Motown Historical Museum, the Fair Housing Center of Metropolitan Detroit, Ashland Theological Seminary and the Museum of African American History.

She holds a Bachelor of Arts degree in political science from the University of Michigan, and a Master of Arts degree in radio, television and film from Wayne State University. She is accredited by the Public Relations Society of America, and has earned a certificate in corporate community relations from Boston College.

Audrey Harvey is vice president of corporate services for Blue Cross Blue Shield of Michigan, the state's largest health insurance provider. She provides leadership for facilities management, enterprise security, corporate procurement and communication support services.

Audrey has a track record of improving operations and processes, and developing successful cost-saving strategies in several departments within Blue Cross Blue Shield. She received the Outstanding Achievement Award from the Detroit Chapter of the National Association of Black Accountants, and the designation of certified healthcare insurance executive from the America's Health Insurance Plans Foundation.

Audrey received a Bachelor of Science degree in accounting from Wayne State University, and a Master of Laws degree in taxation and a juris doctorate degree from Wayne State University School of Law. She is licensed as a certified public accountant in Michigan, and is a licensed attorney in Michigan and Illinois.

She is currently serving on several community boards, and is the chair of the Accounting Aid Society in Detroit. A native Detroiter, Audrey is married to Jerome Harvey, and enjoys being a mentor, gardening and traveling.

Edward T. Hightower

Director
AlixPartners LLP

Marc P. Johnson

Director of Real Estate
Strather & Associates

Edward Hightower is a director and senior consultant for AlixPartners LLP. In this role, he helps companies improve profits by reducing costs and growing revenue. He also helps private equity firms evaluate acquisition targets.

Previously, Hightower spent 15 years in the global automotive industry as chief engineer and leader of the $7 billion Expedition and Navigator SUV business for Ford, brand manager of the 5, 6 and 7 Series for BMW in the United States, and as product planning manager of the original Cadillac CTS for General Motors. He has also worked as a consultant and led a start-up business venture in West Africa.

Originally from Chicago, Hightower earned a bachelor's degree in engineering from the University of Illinois at Urbana-Champaign. He also received a Master of Business Administration degree from the University of Michigan (Ross), where he received the 2006 Black Business Alumni Association's Alumnus of the Year Award, and he currently serves on the business school's alumni board of governors. Additionally, he is a lifetime member of the Council on Foreign Relations. Hightower and his family reside in Southfield.

Marc P. Johnson graduated from the University of Detroit Jesuit High School and Florida A&M University. He is one of the leading young entrepreneurs in the city of Detroit. Marc owned and operated a café in Southfield, Michigan, before launching Johnson Enterprise Holdings, a real estate development company, in 2001. As a local real estate investor, he successfully renovates and manages a portfolio of Detroit investment property.

In 2005 Marc joined the staff of local real estate developer, Herbert J. Strather. As director of real estate for Strather & Associates, he helped to secure many high-end developments for the company, such as his role in the extensive renovation of Hotel St. Regis.

As managing partner of the venture, Marc helped to secure Shore Bank as a partner in the $4 million renovation of the hotel. He is currently responsible for Phase II, which will be mixed-use.

Marc invests his time and talents in numerous nonprofits in the city. He is a founder of Legacy, an entrepreneurship training for youth, and has been a big brother for Big Brothers Big Sisters for eight years.

Dichondra Johnson-Geiger

Marketing &
Community Relations Manager
St. John Providence Hospital

Diane Jones

Program Director
Professional Services, Michigan Region
Compuware Corporation

Dichondra Johnson-Geiger is the marketing and community relations manager for St. John Providence Hospital. In this role, she is responsible for marketing hospital initiatives, as well as developing relationships with various external stakeholder groups and the community at large to promote the hospital, St. John Health System and a variety of health awareness programs.

In 2002 the National Association of Performing Arts Presenters named Dichondra Emerging Leader due to her groundbreaking work in the performing arts. Currently, she serves on the Traveler's Aid Society of Metropolitan Detroit board of directors. In addition, Dichondra is co-owner of Verondee Consulting Co., an event management and logistical services company, and a partner with Verondee/Domaine Detroit Productions and Mahogany Tasters, which focuses on wine and spirit education.

Dichondra received a Master of Business Administration degree in marketing and global business from Davenport University. She also holds a Bachelor of Science degree in arts administration and marketing from Eastern Michigan University.

A native of Detroit and East Lansing, Michigan, Dichondra is the wife of Michael Leo Geiger Jr. and proud mother to son Miles Michael.

Diane Jones is program director and senior consultant at Compuware Corporation, after beginning her career with Compuware in 2000. In her current role, she manages a consultant business model, which provides information technology services to Ford Motor Company. Her efforts contributed to Compuware receiving the prestigious ISO 9001:2000 and Ford Q1 awards for its management system standards utilized at Ford Motor Company.

Before joining Compuware, Diane was the associate director of the University Budget Office at Wayne State University, where she received the Presidential Award for high achievement following the successful implementation of the university's financial system.

A trusted community leader, Diane is board treasurer for Detroiters Working for Environmental Justice (DWEJ), a nonprofit organization focused on preventing lead contamination, lead poisoning and pollution, as well as providing training in brownfield redevelopment and hazardous waste awareness.

Diane holds a bachelor's degree from Davenport University and a master's degree from Walsh College.

Tish King

Vice President, Human Resources
Greektown Casino

Dawn K. Lucas

Banking Office Manager
Oakman Office
Huntington National Bank

Tish King joined Greektown Casino's opening team in 1999. As vice president of human resources, she oversees all human resource activities and a multimillion-dollar departmental budget. These activities include recruitment, benefits administration, employee relations, labor negotiations, training and risk management.

A member of the National Political Congress of Black Women, Tish's career began in municipal government. She is a past recipient of the Shirley Chisholm Woman of the Year Award.

Tish earned a Bachelor of Arts degree in public affairs management from Michigan State University and a Master of Arts degree in industrial relations from Wayne State University. Certified by the Society of Human Resources Management, she is a member of several professional organizations and boards working to impact the community and the human resources profession. She is a policy board member of the Detroit Plan to End Homelessness, and a member of the HAP Customer Advisory Board. She is a lifetime NAACP member.

A native Detroiter, Tish lives in the Detroit area with her husband, Edward, and their dog, Tia. She is a member of Oak Grove AME Church.

Dawn Lucas is the banking office manager of the Oakman office of Huntington National Bank in Dearborn, Michigan. In this position, Dawn manages the daily operations of an office with more than $30 million in assets. Her responsibilities include implementing sales and business plans, coaching and developing a staff of 15 and the acquisition of new business.

Dawn has had many accomplishments during her tenure at Huntington, including her recent promotion to assistant vice president. She was one of a select group of bankers named to a recognition program that rewards bankers for outstanding performance for the past two consecutive years.

Throughout her 17-year career in banking, Dawn has remained active in the community. She serves on various volunteer committees and was named one of the 2006 YMCA Minority Achievers.

A native of Detroit, Dawn received a Bachelor of Business Administration degree from the University of Michigan in Ann Arbor. She is the proud mother of one daughter, Jayla.

Navia McCloud

Vice President
Commercial Real Estate
Huntington National Bank

Larry Middlebrooks

Executive Chef
Hyatt Regency Dearborn

Navia McCloud is a vice president and a commercial real estate alternate team leader at Huntington National Bank. In this position, she has a leadership role in the marketing initiatives and development of the relationship bankers within the team, while managing a commercial real estate portfolio in excess of $100 million and acting as an essential partner to local real estate developers.

Navia is the chair of the bank's East Michigan Diversity Council. She has been working to promote diversity awareness at Huntington by participating in and promoting community events, such as the Lawrence Tech Diversity Series and other bank-sponsored awareness activities. Additionally, she sits on the board of visitors for Wayne State University's College of Fine, Performing and Communication Arts.

Navia earned a Bachelor of Science degree in business administration and finance from Saint Louis University in 1998.

She is the wife of Terrence McCloud and the proud mother of two young daughters, Morgan and Mackenzie.

Larry Middlebrooks is the executive chef at the Hyatt Regency Dearborn, a four-diamond hotel with more than 700 rooms. He has worked in many luxurious Hyatt hotels, including Savannah, Atlanta, Virginia, Maryland, New Jersey and Washington, D.C. He is a graduate of the Culinary Institute of America, with honors, in Hyde Park, New York.

Larry has hosted many culinary and charity events throughout the community, such as the American Culinary Federation and Rotisserie Chaine dinners, which are private and exclusive club events. His office walls are filled with various awards and plaques that announce many of his accomplishments throughout the years. These include Chef of the Year, community activist and local culinary school awards for assisting students.

With there being very few minority executive chefs in the large hotel industry, Larry takes pride in mentoring others, inspiring them while enhancing their cooking and managerial skills. His work demonstrates his passion for his craft, which is his secret to success.

DETROIT'S CORPORATE BRASS

Marshalle S. Montgomery

Senior Program Associate
New Detroit, Inc.

Terrina L. Murrey

Director, Human Resources
Compuware Corporation

Marshalle S. Montgomery is senior program associate for New Detroit, Inc. Her position is vital in promoting positive race relations by developing and maintaining relationships that convene the Arab, Chaldean, African-American, Hispanic, Asian and Native American communities throughout southeast Michigan.

As lead facilitator for New Detroit's Multicultural Leadership Series and Emerging Leaders initiatives, Marshalle conducts regional forums with leadership representative from a cross section of businesses, civic groups, educational institutions, health services and community-based organizations. She is committed to cultivating cross-cultural collaboration between diverse communities by developing collective strategies and solutions that affect social equity.

Additionally, Marshalle is a filmmaker. She co-founded Trinity Film Coalition, L.L.C. (TFC) in 2006. This coalition has an ambitious agenda to mobilize and strengthen the film industry in metropolitan Detroit through networking, partnerships and collaborations. TFC provides a platform for independent filmmakers to gain exposure by showcasing their talent. TFC hosted their first annual film festival in Detroit in August of 2007, which featured indie films from around the world.

A graduate of Michigan State University, Marshalle is a native of Inkster, Michigan.

As director of human resources at Compuware Corporation, Terrina L. Murrey's responsibilities include employee relations, training and development, and policy administration for the company's Strategic Services, Technology, Covisint and Product Strategy divisions. She also oversees the employee recognition and internship programs.

A native Detroiter, Terrina is a proud graduate of Cass Technical High School. She earned a bachelor's degree in business administration from Wayne State University, another great Detroit institution.

Terrina is a member of the Society of Human Resources Management (SHRM), and her board and committee affiliations include Metropolitan Detroit's 101 Best and Brightest Companies to Work For, JVS and the Sister to Sister Detroit campaign. She successfully completed the Inform Center for Leadership curriculum and recently participated on the Detroit Road to Renaissance project. She is also a member of Delta Sigma Theta Sorority, Inc.

Terrina continues to reside in Detroit with her husband, Robert, and their two children, Remi and Robert Jr.

Gwendolyn Norman

Vice President
Retail District Manager
Huntington National Bank

Melanie C. Odom

Vice President & Civic Affairs Manager
Comerica Bank

Gwendolyn Norman is vice president and retail district manager of the south retail market in the East Michigan region of Huntington National Bank. In this position, she manages the development of market share for her district and is responsible for staff development of her associates. She has been in the financial services industry for more than 20 years.

Gwendolyn is an active member within the community. She works and currently sits on the local community committee for the United Way of Macomb. Gwendolyn is an alumna of Leadership Macomb. She is also an active member of the Urban Financial Services Coalition and the Detroit Regional Chamber.

A native Detroiter, Gwendolyn is the wife of Jeffrey Norman, whom she has been married to for 21 years. She is the proud mother of three teenage sons, Justin, Marcus and Corey. She and her family are active members of Greater Grace Temple.

Joining the bank in 1996, Melanie C. Odom is vice president and civic affairs manager at Comerica Bank. She is responsible for promoting Comerica as a good corporate citizen. As civic affairs manager, she assists the bank in setting the strategic agenda for relationships with major civic organizations. Odom also manages, tracks and reports on the bank's community involvement and financial education programs. She manages Comerica sections in the *Michigan Chronicle* and *The Michigan FrontPage* publications.

With more than 21 years of experience in financial services, Odom has worked in investment banking, trust, insurance and treasury departments, and served as chief financial officer for a NASD member firm.

A native Detroiter, Odom graduated from Cass Technical High School, and earned a bachelor's degree in accounting from Western Michigan University.

Odom is involved with several civic and professional organizations. She attends St. Stephen AME Church, and is a member of Delta Sigma Theta Sorority, Inc., the Jim Dandy Ski Club and the North Rosedale Park Civic Association. A resident of Detroit, she is the proud mother to 2-year-old Ayana Grace.

DETROIT'S CORPORATE BRASS

Karen Payton

Vice President
OnWheels, Incorporated

Gail Perry-Mason

First Vice President of Investments
Oppenheimer & Co. Inc.

As vice president of OnWheels, Incorporated, Karen Payton interfaces with top industry leaders throughout the world to attract new business opportunities and commitments in such nontraditional areas as recreational vehicles, motorcycles and electronics.

Payton serves as the company's chief business officer, and utilizes the sales, networking and marketing skills honed during her years as a top pharmaceutical sales manager. In April of 2006, she launched Fifty & Fabulous, an event to celebrate top women in and outside the auto industry. The event provides an afternoon of powerful networking while also serving as a fundraiser for the Edward Davis Scholarship Foundation, the philanthropic arm of OnWheels, Incorporated.

Payton more recently made history when she was selected as the first African-American female to join the governing board of the Women's Automotive Association International (WAAI).

Detroiter Gail Perry-Mason is well known in the securities industry, where she has climbed the corporate ladder from receptionist to first vice president of investments at Oppenheimer & Co. Inc. Service, education and economic empowerment are first and foremost for her clients. Gail assists nonprofit and for-profit organizations, and families in their effort to achieve long-term financial goals. She organized and sponsored several trips to annual shareholder's meetings of companies that her clients hold to educate them about the right to vote by owning stock.

Gail founded and directed the first youth investment club through the NAIC, along with the original money camp for teens called Money Matters. This program has instructed more than 5,000 youth locally and nationally.

Her affiliation and membership extends across numerous organizations. She also serves on several boards that assist children, seniors and the homeless. Additionally, she has been honored by many national and local organizations, writes for national magazines, and has co-authored a national bestseller, *Girl, Make Your Money Grow!*

Michael C. Porter

Vice President, Corporate Communications
DTE Energy

Jennel Proctor

Vice President
Community Development
Huntington National Bank

Michael C. Porter is vice president of corporate communications at DTE Energy, a $9 billion diversified energy company involved in the development and management of energy-related businesses and services nationwide. He is responsible for internal and external corporate brand stewardship, including advertising and sponsorships, employee communications, media relations and public information.

Prior to joining DTE Energy, Porter held senior vice president posts in account management and strategic planning at the McCann-Erickson advertising agency. Previously, he was vice president of marketing at Stroh Brewery Company, after beginning his career at American Motors Corporation.

Porter earned a Bachelor of Business Administration degree from the University of Michigan-Dearborn, and a Master of Business Administration degree from the University of Detroit.

He serves on the boards of trustees of the DTE Energy Foundation and the Children's Hospital of Michigan, and on the board of directors of Detroit Public Television and the University of Detroit Jesuit High School. He is a member of the University of Michigan-Dearborn's Citizens Advisory Council, and is chair of the U of M-Dearborn School of Management Dean's Advisory Council.

Jennel Proctor is Huntington Bank's East Michigan community development specialist. With 26 years of dedicated service with Huntington, Jennel has worked in numerous departments and in various capacities. These include customer service, human resources, and as a retail teller trainer and a banking office manager.

As a community development specialist, Jennel coordinates and manages the Community Reinvestment Act program for Macomb, Oakland and Wayne counties. This includes working with various departments within the bank to ensure the delivery of financial products and services. She works in the community to determine their needs and through active business development efforts, markets bank products and services to meet those needs.

Jennel has become a regular face within the community and maintains an open dialogue with government officials, community development corporations, and community and civic leaders. She is also an active board member of numerous community organizations. Her greatest fulfillment is training youth on financial education.

Jennel and her husband of 38 years, Tyrone, are the proud parents of three adult children, six grandchildren and one great-grandchild.

Derrick A. Roman

Partner, Advisory Services
PricewaterhouseCoopers LLP

Gail Ross

Vice President, Customer Service
Blue Care Network of Michigan
Blue Cross Blue Shield of Michigan

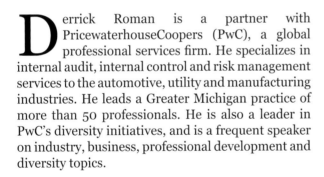

Derrick Roman is a partner with PricewaterhouseCoopers (PwC), a global professional services firm. He specializes in internal audit, internal control and risk management services to the automotive, utility and manufacturing industries. He leads a Greater Michigan practice of more than 50 professionals. He is also a leader in PwC's diversity initiatives, and is a frequent speaker on industry, business, professional development and diversity topics.

Derrick is a board member of the Think-Detroit-PAL, the National Constitution Center (executive committee) and the Philadelphia Police Athletic League. He is a member of the National Association of Black Accountants, for which he co-chaired the 2007 National Convention. He is also a member of the Michigan Association of Certified Public Accountants, the Pennsylvania Institute of Certified Public Accountants and the American Institute of Certified Public Accountants. Additionally, he founded and operated a youth mentoring program that received national recognition in *The Wall Street Journal.*

A graduate of Babson College, Derrick majored in accounting. He resides in Rochester Hills with his wife, Chevelle, and their two children, Alexandra and Derrick Jr.

Gail Ross is vice president of customer service for Blue Care Network of Michigan, the HMO subsidiary of Blue Cross Blue Shield of Michigan.

Ross' career has primarily been spent in leadership roles that have focused on customer service operations, training and development, sales and marketing, project management, process reengineering and business process improvement. She also has extensive experience in labor negotiations, and employee and labor relations.

She holds a bachelor's degree in English from Western Michigan University, and has completed graduate work at Oakland University.

Ross is active in volunteer efforts as a board member for the Detroit Area Council Boy Scouts of America, and previously for the Music Hall Center for the Performing Arts and the YWCA. She also has affiliations with the Women's Economic Club, the Charles H. Wright Museum of African American History and the Western Michigan University Alumni Association. A member of the Business Women's Alliance, she is a lifetime member of the NAACP.

Ross is single and a lifelong resident of the city of Detroit. She currently resides in Royal Oak.

Michele A. Samuels

Vice President & General Auditor
Blue Cross Blue Shield of Michigan

Joseph E. Smiley

Food & Beverage Director
Hyatt Regency Dearborn

Michele A. Samuels is vice president and general auditor for Blue Cross Blue Shield of Michigan (BCBSM). In this position, she oversees the corporate internal audit and quality functions. Samuels started her career at the public accounting firm of KPMG. She has held various positions at BCBSM, including audit, accounting and management information.

She earned an executive Master of Business Administration degree from Michigan State University, and a bachelor's degree in business from the University of Windsor, Canada.

A certified public accountant, Samuels is active in the community for the betterment of youth, and is a board member and past chair of Big Brothers Big Sisters of Metropolitan Detroit. She is co-chair of the BCBSM Physical Activity and Nutrition Committee, which aims to reduce obesity and related chronic medical ailments in Michigan. She also serves on the board of directors of the Greater Detroit Area Health Council, and chairs their Community Health Improvement Committee.

A native of Windsor, Ontario, Samuels is the wife of Paul, and the proud mother of two daughters, Tosh and Cheryl, and one son, Parker.

Born in Wichita, Kansas, Joe Smiley was given the opportunity to travel at an early age. His father was a career U.S. Army officer and his mother was a dean of women at what is now Hampton University. Joe particularly enjoyed living in Germany and Italy, where he was exposed to many cultural and culinary delights.

After graduating from Norfolk State University with a bachelor's degree in hotel restaurant management, Joe became a corporate management trainee for Hyatt Hotels in the Washington, D.C. area. From there, he progressed to several Hyatt properties, including the Grand Hyatt New York and Hyatt Dulles. His crowning achievement was developing Elements on Level One, a contemporary American restaurant and bar at the Hyatt Dulles.

Joe is a 14-year Hyatt veteran and is currently the food and beverage director at the Hyatt Regency Dearborn. He has a wife, Nikki, of seven years and two children, Joie and Styles.

DETROIT'S CORPORATE BRASS

La'Trise Smith

Assistant Vice President
Human Resources
Huntington National Bank

Larry E. Steward

Vice President, Human Resources
DTE Energy

La'Trise Smith is an assistant vice president of human resources for Huntington National Bank in Troy, Michigan. She hires, retains and develops associates to deliver the best customer service when delivering the bank's products and services. La'Trise has also helped develop Huntington's East Michigan region diversity council, where she is committed to providing awareness to all company associates and business partners. Additionally, she volunteers in various community projects and is currently active with the YMCA Minority Achievers program.

La'Trise has a bachelor's degree in human resources from Ferris State University and a master's degree in educational leadership from Western Michigan University. In addition, she currently holds a professional in human resources certificate from the Human Resource Certification Institute.

A native of Detroit, La'Trise is the wife of Edward Smith and mom to her adorable shih tzu, Zyan. She is also very active with her sorority, Zeta Phi Beta Sorority, Inc., where she volunteers countless hours mentoring young women and working within the community. In her spare time, she loves spending time with her family and doing event decorating and wedding planning.

Larry E. Steward is vice president of human resources for DTE Energy, a $9 billion diversified energy company involved in the development and management of energy-related businesses and services nationwide. He is responsible for delivering an integrated human resource strategy that aligns the company's human resource programs and practices with a business strategy focused on aggressive growth.

Prior to joining DTE Energy, Steward was vice president of human resources at Invacare Corporation in Elyria, Ohio. He previously held leadership positions in human resources, labor relations and employee relations at LTV Steel Company in Cleveland, and Mellon Bank Corporation in Pittsburgh. He also served as deputy attorney general for the Pennsylvania Department of Justice.

Steward earned a Bachelor of Arts degree from Antioch College, and a law degree from the University of Toledo College of Law.

He is a board member of the Detroit Youth Foundation and the American Society of Employers. He is vice chair of the American Bar Association's Section of Public Utility, Communications and Transportation Law, and a member of the HR Policy Association board of directors.

Kimberly Turnage

Director, Sales & Marketing
Hyatt Regency Dearborn

Leanora Weaver-Heath

Regional Director
Compuware Corporation

Recipient of the 2006 Director of Sales of the Year award for Hyatt Hotels, Kimberly Turnage is currently the director of sales and marketing at the Hyatt Regency Dearborn, where she manages 772 rooms, 62,000 square feet of meeting space and a sales team of 12.

Kimberly has been in the hospitality industry for 20 years and started her Hyatt career in Chicago as a sales manager. She is currently a member of the National Coalition of Black Meeting Planners, and has the philosophy "You work hard, you play hard."

Kimberly was born in Ann Arbor, but has traveled the United States with Hyatt before finding her way back to Detroit. She currently resides in downtown Detroit with her new husband, Peter.

Leanora Weaver-Heath has more than 25 years of experience in sales, business development and strategic account management. Her career spans numerous Fortune 500 companies, including General Electric and Abbott Laboratories. She currently serves as regional director for Compuware Corporation.

In her current position at Compuware, Leanora actively develops business in public sector accounts, focusing on Michigan and Ohio. As a native Detroiter, she enjoys the opportunity to leverage her sales skills and talents with a Detroit-headquartered corporation.

She is an active member of several professional organizations, including INFORUM, formerly the Women's Leadership Forum; and Detroit Benefits, as a board member. Additionally, Leanora has attained her Green Belt Six Sigma certification. Not surprisingly, she has built her success as a sales professional on a solid foundation of strong discipline, integrity, education and upbringing.

Leanora is married to Michael Heath, and is the proud mother of Jordan and Erica. She enjoys cooking and gardening at her home in Detroit.

Deborah Williams

Human Resource Director
Compuware Corporation

Aiisya Williamson

Executive Director
Mercy Primary Care Center

Deborah Williams has been with Compuware Corporation for nearly ten years, and currently serves as the company's human resource director. In this role, her responsibilities include data management and administration of human resource technology.

Deborah is a graduate of Cass Technical High School and earned a bachelor's degree from Wayne State University. She is currently pursuing a master's degree at Walsh College. She also successfully completed the Inform Center for Leadership curriculum.

Deborah enjoys reading, gardening, and spending time with family and friends. She loves mentoring and volunteers her time to Big Brothers Big Sisters of Metropolitan Detroit. A native Detroiter, Deborah resides in Lathrup Village, and has two adult sons, Eric and LaRon.

Aiisya Williamson is executive director of Mercy Primary Care Center in Detroit, a ministry of Trinity Health providing free medical services to uninsured adults who do not have private health insurance and do not qualify for Medicare or Medicaid. In this role, she provides strategic leadership for program advocacy, operations management, community relations and budgetary oversight.

Prior to leading Mercy Primary Care Center, Williamson served as a senior planning analyst at Trinity Health, the fourth-largest Catholic health system in the nation, where she redesigned volume forecasting and budgeting processes to assist facilities with developing effective budgets. Her career has also included planning positions at the University of Michigan Health System and the Detroit Medical Center.

Williamson holds a bachelor's degree in sociology from the University of Michigan and a master's degree in health services administration from the University of Michigan School of Public Health. Her involvement with civic and professional organizations includes the Infant Mortality Program, the Michigan Society for Healthcare Planning and Marketing, and the National Association of Health Services Executives.

Ron Wood
Vice President, Underwriting
Blue Cross Blue Shield of Michigan

Kenyea J. Zimmermann
Senior Associate & Operations Manager
Aegis Group Search Consultants, LLC

Ron Wood is vice president of underwriting for Blue Cross Blue Shield of Michigan (BCBSM). In this position, he provides executive leadership in the areas of small and middle groups, key accounts and multistate underwriting. He joined BCBSM in 1979.

Ron is co-founder and past president of the Wayne State University Black Alumni Association. He has served on a variety of boards and committees, including the Wayne State University College of Lifelong Learning advisory board, Historic Trinity, Inc. and the NFWB softball association. He is a graduate of Leadership Macomb, Leadership Detroit and Leadership Michigan, and is a lifetime member of the Michigan chapter of the NAACP.

Ron earned both a bachelor's degree in mathematics and a master's degree in applied mathematics from Wayne State University. He also has a master's degree in advanced management from Michigan State University.

Kenyea J. Zimmermann is a senior associate and operations manager for Aegis Group Search Consultants, LLC, a retained executive search firm specializing in the recruitment of executives and physician executives for a wide array of sectors in health care. In this role, she oversees the daily operation and search projects for the company. She has successfully recruited department chairs and senior level executives for numerous academic medical centers and health care systems.

For more than ten years, Kenyea has been a leader in the human resources field. She is a member of the Society for Human Resource Management and the National Association of African Americans in Human Resources. She is also an active member of Hope United Methodist Church and serves on various ministries.

Kenyea received a bachelor's degree in human resources and society from Michigan State University. She also holds a master's degree in organizational management and an MBA with a concentration in human resources management from the University of Phoenix.

A native of Saginaw, Kenyea enjoys reading, dancing, and spending time with family and friends.

meticulous

compassionate

DETROIT'S
DOCTORS

empathetic

precise

intuitive

benevolent

attentive

decisive

magnanimous

**Deloris Ann
Berrien-Jones, M.D.**

Associate Medical Director,
Southern Region
Henry Ford Medical Group

Dr. Deloris Ann Berrien-Jones is associate medical director, southern region of the Henry Ford Medical Group (HFMG). She is also physician-in-charge for the Henry Ford Medical Center – Fairlane, a large multispecialty outpatient facility.

Deloris received a bachelor's degree from the University of Michigan and a Doctor of Medicine degree from Michigan State University, College of Human Medicine. She completed her internship and residency in internal medicine at Henry Ford Hospital. Since 1999, she has been a member of the Henry Ford Wyandotte Hospital board of trustees.

Deloris assumed the role of physician champion for the Diabetes Initiatives for HFMG, one of the systemwide chronic care initiatives culminating in the re-establishment of patient Diabetes Self-Management Education programs. For the last two years she has participated in faith-based initiatives and local health fairs, and has spoken at metropolitan Detroit churches.

Deloris received the Governor's Award of Excellence for improving preventive care in an ambulatory setting, and was voted Best Downriver Doctor by *The News-Herald*.

A Detroit native, she is the proud mother of two daughters, Jessica and Aubrey.

Stanley M. Berry, M.D.

Chairman, Department of
Obstetrics & Gynecology
William Beaumont Hospitals

Dr. Stanley M. Berry is chairman of the Department of Obstetrics and Gynecology at William Beaumont Hospitals in Royal Oak and Troy, Michigan. He is responsible for overseeing all of the medical care provided to obstetrical and gynecological patients. His educational responsibilities include teaching medical students, residents, nurses and attending physicians. He is also a professor at Wayne State University.

Berry practices the subspecialty of maternal-fetal medicine, which encompasses the care of high-risk obstetrical patients. These patients include women who have medical illnesses such as diabetes, hypertension or disorders unique to pregnancy. Within this subspecialty, his expertise includes fetal diagnosis and fetal therapy.

Berry attended Macalester College in St. Paul, Minnesota. In 1984 he earned a medical doctor degree from Mayo Medical School in Rochester, Minnesota. He completed his residency at Saint Louis University in 1988, and finished a fellowship in maternal-fetal medicine at Wayne State University in 1990.

A native of Minneapolis, Berry is the proud father of one son, Akin, and two daughters, Niambi and Ayanna.

D r. Margaret Betts is the medical director of Betts Medical Group, and has specialized in internal and holistic medicine for more than 20 years. She makes house calls and visits nursing homes, as well as attends to patients in her private practice. Parent, friend, speaker, teacher, mentor, black doll collector, political advocate and school board member are a few of the hats she has worn on her quest to strengthen her community.

Betts is dedicated not only to increasing awareness on health issues, but also to improving the quality of education in Detroit. She shares diagnoses and medical advice with listeners in plain English as host of *The Best Medicine for You* and as medical correspondent for *Inside Detroit* on News Talk 1200 WCHB AM. As founder and chief executive officer of the Willie Betts Foundation, she provides scholarships to inner-city middle and high school students.

Betts is a member of Delta Sigma Theta Sorority, Inc. and the Detroit Branch NAACP, and is a trustee of Hartford Memorial Baptist Church. She is the mother of three and the grandmother of four.

Margaret Louise Betts, M.D.

Medical Director
Betts Medical Group

D r. Paul Edwards believes in giving his patients the highest possible quality care, and providing them with information about their disorders so they can make better-informed decisions. In partnership, together, they take better care of the problem.

Edwards is the distinguished Cornelius E. McCole chair of ophthalmology and eye care services at Henry Ford Hospital. He is responsible for one of the largest eye care departments in the United States. In partnership with Henry Ford OptimEyes, Henry Ford has 375,000 patient visits per year for eye care.

A graduate of the University of the West Indies, Edwards completed his residency in ophthalmology at Henry Ford Hospital and a research fellowship at the National Eye Institute. He is named as one of America's Top Ophthalmologists by the Consumer Research Council of America and by *Hour Detroit* magazine as a Detroit Top Doc.

In addition to his medical career, Edwards co-founded two charitable nonprofit organizations, and currently serves as president of Student Mentor Partners.

He resides with his wife, Jennifer; daughters, Nikeisha and Tiffany; and son, Paul II, in West Bloomfield.

Paul A. Edwards, M.D.

Chairman, Department of
Ophthalmology &
Eye Care Services
Henry Ford Hospital

DETROIT'S DOCTORS

Thomas M. Flake Jr., M.D., F.A.C.S.

General Surgeon
Harper University Hospital
Sinai-Grace Hospital

A dedicated surgeon, a compassionate listener and a skilled clinician, Dr. Thomas M. Flake Jr. is the son of Dr. Thomas M. Flake Sr. and Margaret P. Eaton-Flake. He completed medical school at Wayne State University (WSU) School of Medicine in 1979 and began his residency there. When Flake completed the WSU Residency Program in 1984, it made him and his father the first father-son duo to complete both the School of Medicine and Residency Program at WSU in the 20th century. In 1984 he became a member of Harper University Hospital and Sinai-Grace Hospital.

Flake is a promoter of women's health, and his practice concentrates on the treatment of breast disease. He continues to offer the latest technological advancements in breast care and treatment of breast cancer.

Involved in the community, Flake has been the football team physician for the Inkster High School Vikings for three seasons. He also volunteered in the same capacity for 17 years at St. Martin De Porres High School.

He is the proud father of three and has always been devoted to his children.

Cheryl Gibson Fountain, M.D.

Chief of Staff
Obstetrician & Gynecologist
St. John Detroit Riverview Hospital

Dr. Cheryl Gibson Fountain is chief of staff and attending physician in obstetrics and gynecology at St. John Detroit Riverview Hospital. She is also a clinical preceptor at Wayne State University College of Pharmacy and Health Sciences.

Gibson Fountain's primary interests are adolescent medicine, teenage pregnancy and menopause. Extending her genuine regard for the community, she partnered with her late husband, Pastor Renzo L. Fountain Sr., to provide free annual health screenings, immunizations and clothing drives for local residents, and obstetric and gynecologic care to women in Nigeria during a medical mission.

Gibson Fountain is board-certified in obstetrics and gynecology. She completed undergraduate studies at the University of Michigan, received a medical degree from Wayne State University, and completed ob-gyn residency at Hutzel Hospital in Detroit.

A native Detroiter, she is a member of the American College of Physician Executives, the National Medical Association, the American Medical Association, the Michigan State Medical Society, the Wayne County Medical Society, the Detroit Medical Society, and a lifetime member of the NAACP.

Gibson Fountain resides with her daughter, Anne Marie.

Dr. Raechele Cochran Gathers is board-certified by the American Board of Dermatology, and is a senior physician with the Henry Ford Medical Group. She completed her undergraduate training at Cornell University, and received a medical degree from the University of Michigan School of Medicine. She completed her postgraduate dermatology residency training at Henry Ford Hospital, where she served as chief resident.

As a member of Henry Ford's Multicultural Dermatology Center, Gathers specializes in treating diseases of the skin, hair and nails in people of color. Her research focuses on the treatment of hair loss in African-American women, and she has been featured in print, television and radio. Additionally, her research has been presented at both regional and national scientific meetings.

Gathers is a member of the American Academy of Dermatology, The Skin of Color Society, the Michigan Dermatological Society, the Michigan State Medical Society and the American Medical Association. She has also received numerous awards for her commitment to superior dermatologic care.

A native of Detroit, Gathers is an avid writer and runner.

Raechele Cochran Gathers, M.D.

Dermatologist & Senior Physician
Henry Ford Medical Group

Dr. Herman Gray Jr. is president of Children's Hospital of Michigan, the only freestanding children's hospital in Michigan. He is the first African American in the history of the hospital to serve as president. At Children's, Gray established innovative programs, such as the hospital's first sleep apnea program to monitor babies for sudden infant death syndrome; family-centered care to engage families in the decision-making process of their child's medical care; and a school-based health clinic in Detroit.

Previously, Gray held leadership roles with Michigan SIDS Center, Project Uptown and the Pediatric AIDS Prevention and Control Program. He also served as the first medical director of children's special health care services at the Michigan Department of Public Health. Gray also served on numerous national and international committees to improve health care services and access for children. He has been repeatedly recognized for his humanitarian efforts on pediatric health care.

Gray earned a medical degree from the University of Michigan and a physician executive Master of Business Administration degree from the University of Tennessee.

He and his wife, Shirley Mann Gray, have two daughters.

Herman B. Gray Jr., M.D.

President
Children's Hospital of Michigan

Ebonie Harris, M.D.

Obstetrician & Gynecologist

Dr. Ebonie Harris is an obstetrician and gynecologist in practice in Southfield. She is committed to providing gentle, compassionate and high quality obstetric and gynecologic care for women of all ages, with a special interest in adolescents. With her strong medical training and unwavering faith in God, she promotes preventative medicine and treats diseases that may affect women's reproductive health.

Harris received a Bachelor of Science degree in biology from the University of Michigan and a Doctor of Medicine degree from Wayne State University School of Medicine. She completed her medical training in obstetrics and gynecology at St. John Providence Hospital, Southfield, in which she proudly served as administrative chief resident.

Harris resides in the metro Detroit area with her husband, Terrance Harris, and son, Colin. She is a member of Word of Faith International Christian Center in Southfield.

Herbert L. Isaac II, M.D.

Chief Executive Officer
Herbert L. Isaac II,
Family Medicine PLLC

Dr. Herbert L. Isaac is a family physician practicing in Pontiac, Michigan. Herbert is continuing a tradition of delivering quality health care to the underserved populations of Pontiac. The practice was established by his father, Herbert L. Isaac Sr., who served the community for 37 years until his passing in December of 2005. Herbert's practice is an office and hospital-based. He also does house calls and nursing home visits.

Herbert is on staff at the Detroit Medical Center, Oakwood Hospital, St Joseph's Mercy Hospital, North Oakland Medical Center and Southeast Surgical Hospital. He is a member of the American Academy of Family Physicians, the Michigan State Medical Society and the Oakland County Medical Society.

Herbert received a Bachelor of Science degree from Howard University and a medical degree from Wayne State University College of Medicine. He completed his internship and residency at Martin Luther King/Charles R. Drew Medical Center and Oakwood Hospital.

On February 14, 2007, Herbert exchanged wedding vows with Danielle McPhail.

Dr. Mary Jackson-Hammond is president of Jackson Health Services and former chief of staff at Mercy Hospital. She established a clinic to provide quality health care for displaced patients when Mercy Hospital closed its doors in 2000. She is a board-certified physician in both occupational and family medicine.

As a lieutenant colonel in the United States Army, Jackson-Hammond has earned many military medals, and most recently, completed a tour of duty in Afghanistan. She is a past recipient of the Spirit of Detroit Award, the Michigan State Legislature Special Tribute and the Millikin University Alumni Merit Award.

Jackson-Hammond is a loyal member of the Detroit Medical Society, the National Medical Association, the NAACP, Top Ladies of Distinction, Delta Sigma Theta, Inc. and Gamma Phi Delta, Inc.

She received both a Doctor of Medicine degree and a Master of Public Health degree from the University of Illinois. She currently resides in Detroit with her family.

Mary Jackson-Hammond, M.D.

President
Jackson Health Services

Dr. Melanie Jessup received her medical training at Temple University School of Podiatric Medicine in Philadelphia, Pennsylvania. She completed a three-year residency program in podiatric medicine and surgery at Botsford Hospital in Farmington Hills, Michigan.

Jessup has a special interest in all areas of podiatric medicine, including foot and ankle surgery, diabetic foot care, limb salvage and sports medicine. She is a member of the American Podiatric Medical Association, the Michigan Podiatric Medical Association, and the American College of Foot and Ankle Surgeons.

Melanie R. Jessup, D.P.M., AACFAS

Podiatrist
Foot and Heel Pain
Institute of Michigan

DETROIT'S DOCTORS

Ray H. Littleton, M.D.

Urologist & Director,
Lithotripsy & Endourology
Henry Ford Health System

Dr. Ray Littleton is American board-certified in urology with clinical and special medical interest in renal calculus, prostate diseases and sexual dysfunction.

Littleton is a graduate of the University of Michigan Medical School. He completed a residency in urology at Henry Ford Hospital and has been on staff there since 1980. He has been practicing medically for 31 years, and is currently director of endourology and lithotripsy with Henry Ford Health System's Vattikuti Urology Institute.

Littleton's clinical and special medical interests are renal calculus disease, endourology, laparoscopic urology, percutaneous renal surgery, prostate diseases and sexual dysfunction. His patient care philosophy is to preserve renal function, prevent renal stone disease with minimally invasive surgery and help eliminate urological malignancy.

Littleton and his wife, Marcia, have been married 36 years. They have three sons, Dr. Jason Littleton, a physician at St. Joseph Mercy Hospital in Ypsilanti; Attorney Ray Littleton II of Dickinson Wright PLLC; and Kevin Littleton, a recent graduate of Yale University.

Shari L. Maxwell, M.D.

Senior Staff Obstetrician &
Gynecologist
Henry Ford Health System

Dr. Shari L. Maxwell is a board-certified obstetrician and gynecologist in Detroit. She has been on staff with the Henry Ford Health System (HFHS) for more than 15 years. During this time, Shari has held positions in leadership, and was HFHS' first African-American female who held a leadership position in a surgical subspecialty.

Additionally, Shari is a part of the teaching staff at Henry Ford and is active in her community. Over the years, she has done many public speaking engagements, and has been interviewed by local newspapers and magazines. Shari was featured in the "Minds of Medicine" television segment on menopause, and was recently interviewed by *Essence* magazine regarding women's health care needs. She has also published articles in medical journals.

Shari received a Bachelor of Arts degree from the University of Michigan and a medical degree from Wayne State University. She completed her training in obstetrics and gynecology at Henry Ford Hospital, where she was chief resident.

A native of Flint, Michigan, Shari is single, and her interests include exercising, fashion, music, theater and design.

D r. Thomas David Mays Jr. is a board-certified family physician and has been practicing medicine in the Detroit metropolitan area for more than 25 years. He received undergraduate and medical degrees from Michigan State University. He is a member of the American Medical Association, the Wolverine Medical Association and the Detroit Medical Association. Mays is affiliated with the Sinai-Grace Hospital.

In addition to providing quality medical care for patients at his Southfield, Michigan, office, Mays makes house calls to senior citizens and the disabled. He is a member of New Bethel Baptist Church, where the Reverend Robert Smith Jr. is the senior pastor. He volunteers his time by giving informative lectures on health care issues at his home church as well as other churches in the community. Mays is also a significant contributor to the scholarship program at New Bethel.

Mays has been recognized as an outstanding father and community supporter. He and his wife, Vanessa Miree Mays, are the proud parents of a son, David Joseph.

Dr. Thomas David Mays Jr.

Family Physician
Sinai-Grace Hospital

D r. Sharon Minott serves as the medical director of the Michigan Interventional Pain Associates. There, she is committed to improving patients' quality of life and helping patients to maintain an active lifestyle. She and her partners have a noted reputation of excellent care. The Michigan Interventional Pain Associates treat pain conditions with interventional and conservative management. Their state-of-the-art practice focuses on various neuropathic pain syndromes, pain conditions of the axial skeleton and many musculoskeletal disorders. The goal is to bring back quality to the patients' lives through technology, professional excellence and compassion.

Minott is a graduate of the University of Michigan School of Medicine. She is a board-certified anesthesiologist, with an additional certification in pain medicine. She enjoys her work as an anesthesiologist at Huron Valley-Sinai Hospital, where she has worked since 1999.

Minott is a native of Detroit, Michigan, and enjoys yoga, traveling and cooking.

Sharon D. Minott, M.D.

Medical Director
Michigan Interventional
Pain Associates

Earlexia M. Norwood, M.D.

Physician-In-Charge
Henry Ford Medical Center – Troy

Dr. Earlexia M. Norwood is physician-in-charge of the Henry Ford Medical Center – Troy and division head of family medicine for the northeast region. She is a family physician who balances caring for patients and providing administrative leadership. Her professional memberships include the board of governors for the Henry Ford Medical Group, AMA, NMA, DOCSS and the American College of Physician Executives.

Norwood's honors include the Top Doc Award from *Hour Detroit* magazine, the People Award, Who's Who, the Distinguished Alumni Award and the Robert E. Birk Award for Excellence in Research.

A Jackson State University (JSU) graduate of the W.E.B. Du Bois Honors College, Norwood earned a medical degree from the University of Iowa. She is chair of the JSU Kids Kollege national board of directors, captain for UNCF, chair of Your Journey to Wellness and vice president of the Medical Advisory Board of Straight Gate International Church.

Robert is her husband, and Gabriel and Mikhaella are their two gifts from God. The family is her most precious asset and her number one priority, outside of her relationship with Jesus Christ.

Michael H. Rainer, M.D.

Senior Associate Physician
Rehabilitation Medical
Specialists, LLC

Dr. Michael H. Rainer is the senior associate at Rehabilitation Medical Specialists, LLC. He recently left the academic department of physical medicine and rehabilitation at the Detroit Medical Center (DMC) for private practices, but continues his affiliation with the DMC. He evaluates and treats patients with musculoskeletal, neurologic and trauma-related conditions, and provides pain management.

Rainer graduated from Wayne State School of Medicine in 1988. He completed two-and-a-half years of core general surgery residency at the DMC. He subsequently worked at Detroit Mercy's emergency room for five years. Additionally, Rainer finished a residency in physical medicine and rehabilitation at the University of Pittsburgh, and is board-certified. He was an associate professor at UT Southwestern, where he was medical director of a 14-bed inpatient unit, a multi-disciplinary spine/injection clinic and an amputee clinic.

His clinical interests and expertise include the evaluation and treatment of musculoskeletal conditions, neck and back pain, arthritis, headache management, sports medicine, EMGs evaluations and interpretation, and treatment of spasticity.

D r. Vanessa L. Robinson is senior staff physician and section head of New Center One, Department of Internal Medicine of Henry Ford Hospital. She was appointed to membership on the board of governors of the hospital in November of 2005.

Robinson completed her internship and residency in the Department of Internal Medicine at Henry Ford Hospital in 1984 and became chief medical resident. In 1985 she advanced to senior staff physician and became board-certified in geriatrics. Shortly following that, she earned the distinction of fellow in the American College of Physicians.

She is a member of the executive committee of the Henry Ford Hospital Medical Association, the American Medical Association and the Wayne County Medical Society.

Robinson is an evangelist with the Greater Grace Temple Ministerial Alliance and deputy director of Christian education.

She is a graduate of the University of Michigan with a Bachelor of Science degree in zoology in 1977 and a Doctor of Medicine degree in 1981.

Vanessa L. Robinson, M.D., F.A.C.P.

Senior Staff Physician & Section Head
New Center One
Department of Internal Medicine
Henry Ford Health System

D r. Tara Long Scott, owner and chief executive officer of the Foot and Heel Pain Institute of Michigan in Southfield, is a graduate of the Ohio College of Podiatric Medicine. She completed her first podiatric residency at the Baltimore V.A. Hospital in Maryland. She completed a two-year surgical residency at Kern Hospital in Warren, Michigan.

Although she specializes in conservative and surgical treatment of the foot and ankle, Scott has a special interest in diabetic patient education and wound care. She is a frequent lecturer on the prevention and management of diabetic complications. She is chief of podiatry at Providence Hospital in Southfield.

Scott is a fellow in the American College of Foot and Ankle Surgeons, board-certified by the American Board of Podiatric Surgery, a member of the American Podiatric Medical Association, and a member of the Michigan Podiatric Medical Association, Southeast Division.

She was appointed to the Michigan Board of Podiatric Medicine and Surgery, and the Controlled Substances Advisory Commission to represent the Michigan Board of Podiatric Medicine and Surgery.

Tara Long Scott, D.P.M., FACFAS

Owner & Chief Executive Officer
Foot and Heel Pain
Institute of Michigan

DETROIT'S DOCTORS

John W. Sealey, D.O.

Medical Director
Vascular Surgery Education
Detroit Medical Center
Sinai-Grace Hospital

Dr. John W. Sealey, F.A.C.O.S., has more than 30 years of experience as a board-certified vascular and thoracic surgeon. He is the medical director of vascular surgery education for the Detroit Medical Center Sinai-Grace Hospital, and maintains a thriving private practice in the city of Detroit.

Sealey received a bachelor's degree in organic chemistry from North Carolina Central University, and in 1973 he enrolled in Michigan State University College of Osteopathic Medicine, completing a degree in 1976. He specializes in general thoracic surgery and peripheral vascular surgery.

Sealey's contribution to vascular surgery has earned him a reputation among his colleagues that is very well respected. His interest in raising the standard of care for vascular patients is equal only to his long-standing commitment to minority health issues and research.

A recipient of numerous honors and awards, Sealey enjoys golfing and reading, and is a member of the American Osteopathic Association, the American College of Osteopathic Surgeons and the Michigan Osteopathic Association.

Richard E. Smith, M.D.

Chairman, Board of Governors
Henry Ford Medical Group

A native Detroiter, Dr. Richard E. Smith completed an undergraduate education at the University of Michigan in Ann Arbor; a medical degree, with honors, from Howard University College of Medicine in Washington, D.C.; and residency in obstetrics and gynecology at Wayne State University. He is a senior staff physician at Henry Ford Hospital. During his 27-year tenure, Smith has delivered more than 7,000 babies and has served as medical director of obstetrics.

Smith played a leading role in advocating for state and federal legislation that improved prenatal care for women and teens across the country. He has also been honored by *Hour Detroit* magazine as one of Metro Detroit's Top Docs, and by the Detroit Board of Education for his work as chairman of the Health Education Advisory Committee. As chair, he helped to establish the middle school health curriculum.

Smith is a member of many professional societies. He is a past president of the Wayne County Medical Society of Southeast Michigan, and serves on the board of directors of the Michigan State Medical Society.

D r. Natalia M. Tanner is a pediatrician with a subspecialty in adolescent medicine. She is an attending physician at Children's Hospital in Michigan and clinical professor of pediatrics at Wayne State University School of Medicine.

In 50 years of practice, Tanner has been the recipient of many national awards and honors for contributions, mentoring and the recruitment of minorities. She has served on national boards and committees, and has been a contributing author to textbooks of adolescent medicine.

Tanner was recognized in 1951 as Michigan's first board-certified African-American pediatrician, and the first female African-American fellow of the American Academy of Pediatrics (AAP). She was later elected president of the Michigan Chapter of the AAP.

Tanner received her premedical training from The University of Chicago, and a Doctor of Medicine degree, with honors, from Meharry Medical College.

She and her husband, surgeon Waldo Cain, M.D., have two daughters, Anita Cain Long, M.D., and Sheila T. Cain, Esq.

Natalia M. Tanner, M.D.

President
Pedi-Center Associates, P.C.

D r. Michele Thomas is a private practitioner in obstetrics and gynecology. She began her private practice in 2004 after being employed for six years.

Thomas is a board-certified obstetrician and gynecologist serving the metropolitan Detroit area. The specialty of ob-gyn focuses on health care for women of all ages. She has received many awards and honors for her commitment to teaching residents.

Thomas obtained an undergraduate degree from the University of Michigan with a Bachelor of Science degree in biology and psychology. She attended the Medical College of Ohio for medical school, and completed her residency training at Wayne State University/Hutzel Hospital. Her hospital privileges include Providence Hospital and Hutzel/Harper.

Thomas is a member of the American College of Obstetricians and Gynecologists, the National Medical Association and the Michigan State Medical Society. She is also a member of Delta Sigma Theta, Inc.

Thomas is married with two children. Her outside interests include working with the health care ministries at her church, New Hope Missionary Baptist Church. She also enjoys traveling, gardening and spending precious time with friends and family.

Michele Thomas, M.D.

Owner &
Obstetrician and Gynecologist
Michele Thomas, M.D., P.L.C.

DETROIT'S DOCTORS

Thomas J. Trueheart, M.D., FACAAI

TrueCare Asthma and
Allergy Center

D r. Thomas J. Trueheart is board-certified in pediatrics and in adult allergy and immunology. His goal is to provide personal, quality and effective care for all persons, of all ages, in the treatment of asthma and allergies. His office motto is, "Not only do we treat, but we teach."

To his credit, Trueheart has a published writing, "The Improvement of Intractable Asthma with Treatment of Gastroesophageal Reflux." Presently, he serves as a Pfizer-physician consultant, a fellow in the American College of Asthma Allergy and Immunology, and a member in the American Academy of Asthma Allergy and Immunology. His active civic duties include Hope United Methodist Church and the NAACP. He is also a 33rd degree Prince Mason.

Trueheart holds a bachelor's degree from Canisius College, a master's degree from Roswell Park Memorial Cancer Institute, and a medical degree from The State University of New York Upstate Medical University. His medical training was conducted entirely at the Detroit Medical Center.

Trueheart and his wife, Kimberly, are the proud parents of Janelle, Marcus and Nia.

Eleanor M. Walker, M.D.

Director, Breast Radiation Oncology
Henry Ford Health System

D irector of breast radiation oncology for the Henry Ford Health System (HFHS), Dr. Eleanor M. Walker is board-certified in radiation oncology and active in integrative medical research. She received a grant from the Susan B. Komen Breast Cancer Foundation examining acupuncture in the treatment of hot flashes in women with breast cancer.

Walker is active in many medical organizations, including the National Medical Association, the Radiation Therapy Oncology Group, the Southwest Oncology Group, the American Society for Therapeutic Radiology and Oncology, the American Medical Association, and the Wayne County and Michigan State medical societies.

A graduate of the University of Notre Dame, Walker is active in the alumni association, and serves on the College of Science advisory board. She received a medical degree from Washington University, and completed an internship at Vanderbilt University and residency at the University of Maryland.

Walker is active in the community through her church and through HFHS, educating African Americans about cancer. Her hobbies include traveling, scrapbooking, reading and jazz. She is a native of Brooklyn, New York.

Stephen Wilson, M.D.

Chief Executive Officer
Advanced Physical Medicine, P.C.

Dr. Stephen Wilson is chief executive officer of Advanced Physical Medicine, P.C. He is board-certified in physical medicine, and rehabilitation and pain management. He is also certified in medical acupuncture. He incorporates the use of traditional and complimentary medicine to improve the quality of life for his patients.

Wilson was honored in the 2004-2005 edition of *Guide to America's Top Physicians*, and also among the October 2005 and 2006 *Hour Detroit* magazine's Top Docs, as voted by doctors and nurses. He then received a Proclamation Award from the City of St. Clair Shores, Michigan, to publicly recognize his dedication and concern for others.

Wilson received a Bachelor of Science degree from the University of Detroit in 1989 and a Doctor of Medicine degree from Wayne State University in 1993. He completed his medical internship at Grace Hospital and his residency at Schwab Rehabilitation Hospital in Chicago.

A native of Detroit, Wilson is the husband of Maria and the proud father of two children, Stephen and Isabella.

Amanda F. Yancy, M.D.

Co-Founding Member
Physicians For Women, PLLC

Dr. Amanda F. Yancy is one of the co-founding members of Physicians For Women, PLLC, a private obstetrics and gynecology practice serving the Greater Detroit metropolitan area.

Yancy is a junior fellow of the American College of Obstetricians and Gynecologists, and holds staffing privileges at several hospitals. She is committed to educating her community, and has spoken for numerous outreach programs, schools, health fairs, expos and radio programs.

Yancy is a native of California and grew up in Los Angeles. She earned a Bachelor of Arts degree in biochemistry and cell biology from the University of California, San Diego, with a minor in African-American studies. She migrated to Michigan to attend Wayne State University School of Medicine. Thereafter, Yancy completed her ob-gyn residency training at Hutzel Woman's Hospital in the Detroit Medical Center.

During medical school, she met her husband, Lee A. Yancy III. In her free time, she enjoys traveling, rollerblading, running and Caribbean music.

benevolent

principled

DETROIT'S

COUNSELORS AT LAW

vested

democratic

accomplished

mediator

advocate

litigator

arbiter

Linda D. Bernard

Principal
Linda D. Bernard J.D., LL.M.
and Associates

Paul Bryant

Partner, Attorney at Law
Plante & Moran, PLLC

Linda Bernard, principal in the law firm Linda D. Bernard J.D., LL.M. and Associates, specializes in business, labor, contract and entertainment law. An excellent business strategist, she excels in problem solving, dispute resolution and litigation and business planning, which achieves and often exceeds client objectives.

Linda personally argued and won three precedent-setting cases in the Michigan Supreme Court, and has broad public and private sector experience as a business leader, general counsel and corporate president. She is a licensed attorney in Michigan, Massachusetts, Pennsylvania, and Washington, D.C., as well as the U.S. Supreme Court, the U.S. Court of Claims, the U.S. Court of International Trade and various federal, district and circuit courts. She has received numerous professional awards, and serves on various local and national boards.

Linda received bachelor's and juris doctorate degrees from Wayne State University and a Master of Laws degree from the University of Pennsylvania Law School. She hosted her own radio and television shows, and is an editorial columnist, arbitrator, mediator and Michigan Civil Rights Commission hearings referee. She is the first City of Detroit administrative hearings officer.

Paul Bryant is the first African-American partner at Plante & Moran, PLLC, the nation's 11th-largest public accounting and professional services firm. As partner, he provides assurance services to clients in the K-12 education, manufacturing and not-for-profit industries. He also assists these clients with general business consulting.

Paul is a member of the firm's Single-Audit Compliance Team, which provides training to staff and functions as a resource for newer staff. He is also a member of Plante & Moran's Diversity Council, which strives to guide the firm toward long-term success and growth by identifying opportunities to engender a thriving and diverse environment. He is very active in the firm's recruiting efforts.

Paul is a member of the American Institute of Certified Public Accountants, the Michigan Association of Certified Public Accountants and the National Association of Black Accountants. He also serves as chair of the Academy of Finance at the Golightly Career and Technical Center.

Paul received a Bachelor of Business Administration degree from Eastern Michigan University. He resides in Farmington Hills with his wife, Pam, and children, Lauryn and Justin.

Alan L. Canady

Member, Attorney at Law
Clark Hill PLC

George A. Chatman

Principal Attorney
George A. Chatman and Associates

Alan L. Canady is a member of Clark Hill's government policy and practice group, and specializes in government relations and legislative affairs. Prior to Clark Hill, he served as chief of staff to several Michigan leaders, including Michigan House Democratic leader Dianne Byrum, former Michigan House Democratic leader Kwame Kilpatrick and former Democratic leader Buzz Thomas.

Canady joined government in 1987 as an attorney and policy analyst for the Michigan State Senate in the areas of local government and taxation. He was appointed Senate Democratic counsel in 1989, where he served as chief legal counsel and parliamentarian for the Senate Democratic Caucus. Canady advised the caucus on all legal matters as well as Senate rules, parliamentary procedure, campaign finance and election law. In 1998 he was given the title of deputy chief of staff by then Senate Democratic leader John Cherry.

Prior to working in the government, Canady was in private practice in Lansing, specializing in litigation within state and federal courts.

Canady earned a bachelor's degree from the University of Michigan, and a juris doctorate degree from George Washington University.

George A. Chatman is principal attorney at George A. Chatman and Associates. His law practice includes criminal, personal injury, family law and appeals. He has more than 25 years of trial experience. In 2004 he was a candidate for judge of the 36th District Court, and was rated Outstanding by the Detroit Metropolitan Bar Association.

George has received many awards during his legal career, including Lawyer of the Year, 1989-1990, by the Wolverine Bar Association; WCNLS Private Attorney Involvement Program Award for 1986-1987; Certificate of Appreciation from the Southern Poverty Law Center in 2004; and Certificate-Volunteer from the Legal Aid and Defender Association, Inc. in 2005.

George graduated from Cass Technical High School, and received a Bachelor of Science degree from Wayne State University. He received master's and juris doctorate degrees from the University of Detroit. He has also consulted on two high school textbooks, *Law in American History* and *American Government – Principles and Practices*.

George is married to Marian Williams-Chatman, and has one daughter, Sharyl, a graduate of Spelman College.

DETROIT'S COUNSELORS AT LAW

Reginald G. Dozier

Shareholder & Corporate Secretary
Lewis & Munday, P.C.

Arthur Dudley II

Shareholder, Attorney at Law
Butzel Long

Reginald G. Dozier is a shareholder and the corporate secretary of the firm Lewis & Munday, P.C. Reginald is a 1985 graduate of the Detroit College of Law. He was the former president of Dozier, Turner & Braceful, P.C., and the commanding officer of the Detroit Police Department's Legal Advisor Section.

Reginald represents Fortune 500 corporations, municipal corporations and small businesses in premises and personal injury matters, as well as commercial, contract and condemnation matters.

Reginald is licensed to practice in Michigan, federal courts and the U.S. Supreme Court. He is the past chair of the State Bar of Michigan's Law Practice Management Section Council, and is a former member of the board of directors of the Wolverine Bar Association. He was highlighted in *Crain's Detroit Business'* 40 Under 40 in 1997.

Reginald attended Howard University, and received a Bachelor of Arts degree from the University of Michigan-Dearborn in 1980. He is involved in numerous professional and community activities. A native Detroiter, he is the husband of Dr. Karen Gunn and the father of MaToya, Reginald II and Karla.

Arthur "Art" Dudley II is a shareholder in Butzel Long's Detroit office. He has practiced law for more than 26 years, specializing in securities law, mergers and acquisitions, executive compensation, emerging growth companies and general corporate representation.

Art received a juris doctor degree from Yale Law School and a master's degree in economics from Yale University. He attended Harvard College as a National Merit Scholar, graduating cum laude with a bachelor's degree in economics.

Art is involved in numerous civic and charitable organizations. He is a graduate of Leadership Detroit, a member of the Michigan Minority Business Development Council (MMBDC), the current chair of the CIC Professional Services Sector and the recipient of the MMBDC's 7 GEMS Award. He is a director of the Legal Aid and Defender Association, a past vice chair of the Detroit Urban League, a past chair of the Black United Fund of Michigan and a recipient of its Hampton Award. Art's passion is to increase minority wealth through economic development.

Art and his wife, Doreen, are the proud parents of two sons, Alexander and Frederick.

Stephen C. Glymph, Esq.

Chief Financial Officer &
General Counsel
The Basketball Warehouse, LLC

Enrique R. Griffin, Esq.

Attorney at Law
Enrique R. Griffin, P.C.

Stephen Glymph is a member, chief financial officer and general counsel of The Basketball Warehouse, LLC. The Basketball Warehouse is an indoor sports and entertainment company, with the mission of providing clean, safe, affordable, and accessible recreation and entertainment facilities in urban communities. It employs a business model that focuses on building partnerships with local government, community-based nonprofit organizations, schools and churches.

The Basketball Warehouse opened its first location, a 33,000-square-foot facility on Detroit's East Side in February of 2006. Children of all ages can enjoy activities such as pick-up basketball, leagues, tournaments, instructional camps, boxing, volleyball, weight training and batting practice. The facility includes a family entertainment center, snack shop, barbershop and retail sports apparel shop, making The Basketball Warehouse the first of its kind in Detroit.

A native of Detroit, Stephen received a Bachelor of Science degree in mechanical engineering from Michigan State University, and a juris doctorate degree from William and Mary School of Law in Virginia.

Stephen manages The Basketball Warehouse with fellow members and native Detroiters Jermaine Woods, chief executive officer, and Terrence Willis, chief operating officer.

Enrique R. Griffin focuses his practice in the areas of business law, intellectual property, technology, real property, and trust and estate planning. He is admitted to practice in the state of Michigan and the U.S. District Court for the Eastern District of Michigan. He is a member of the Michigan Bar Association, Business, Real Property and Computer Law sections; and the American Bar Association, Business Law, and Science and Technology sections.

Griffin provides pro bono services to the Christian Legal Society and Wayne County Legal Services, and is counsel to the Detroit Full Gospel Business Men/Women organization. He is also an active member of his church, serving as a leader in the outreach ministry and chairing the Faith Christian Academy Dad's Club. He has lectured and counseled large municipalities throughout the country regarding Internet privacy and the formation and enforcement of information security policy and procedures.

Griffin received a bachelor's degree from Lawrence Technological University and a juris doctorate degree from the University of Detroit Mercy School of Law. A native of Colón, Panama, he is married with two children.

DETROIT'S COUNSELORS AT LAW

Frank Westley Jackson III

Assistant General Counsel
Blue Cross Blue Shield of Michigan

John E. Johnson Jr.

Corporation Counsel
City of Detroit

Frank Westley Jackson III leads the Employment Law Relations section for Blue Cross Blue Shield of Michigan (BCBSM). He is the principal attorney to the senior vice president of human resources, and coordinates legal services to the Human Resources Division. Jackson started working at BCBSM in September of 1990 after working 17 years at the City of Detroit Law Department.

Jackson received a law degree from the University of Michigan in 1973 and a bachelor's degree in political science from Wayne State University in 1970. He served in the U.S. Army Reserves from 1974 to 1991, obtaining the rank of major. While in the military, he graduated from the U.S. Army Command and General Staff College and the Defense Equal Opportunity Institute.

Married to Frances Jackson, Ph.D., an associate professor of nursing at Oakland University, Jackson has two married children, Frank IV and Alaina, and four grandchildren.

Placing great emphasis on the need to assemble the best legal minds to address challenges in creating the NEXT Detroit, Mayor Kilpatrick appointed John E. Johnson Jr. as corporation counsel for the City of Detroit. Johnson brings more than 25 years of legal expertise to the Kilpatrick administration along with a career that exemplifies legal advocacy on behalf of the public.

Having spent most of his legal career representing the indigent and middle class, Johnson is perfectly qualified to protect and represent the best interests of the citizens of Detroit. Serving as corporation counsel and director of the law department, Johnson is responsible for helping manage the city's legal matters, while reducing its caseload.

Johnson's background in the legal arena and civic and community affairs has uniquely qualified him for his role in Mayor Kilpatrick's cabinet team. From running one of the nation's largest legal aid programs to serving as past president of both the Michigan Coalition for Human Rights and the Wolverine Bar Association, Johnson is a respected legal mind and civic activist in Detroit.

Nicole Y. Lamb-Hale

Office Managing Partner
Foley & Lardner LLP

Claire Mason Lee

Attorney at Law
Plunkett Cooney

Nicole Y. Lamb-Hale is the office managing partner of Foley & Lardner LLP's Detroit office. She counsels corporate clients on significant business transactions and legal issues, including business restructuring.

Nicole received a law degree from Harvard Law School and an undergraduate degree from the University of Michigan. She is active in several bar associations, including the Detroit Metropolitan Bar Association, where she co-chairs its Debtor/Creditor Section; and the American Bankruptcy Institute, where she serves as an advisory board member of its Central State Conference.

Active in the community, Nicole serves on the boards of the Michigan Land Bank Fast Track Authority and Leadership Detroit. She is also a life member Delta Sigma Theta Sorority, Inc. and a member of The Links, Inc.

Nicole was recognized by *Crain's Detroit Business* as one of its 40 Under 40, and most recently, as one of its Most Influential Women in 2007. A graduate of Leadership Detroit, she is a fellow of the Michigan State Bar Foundation. She was recognized in 2006 and 2007 as one of Michigan's Super Lawyers in the practice of bankruptcy law.

An attorney in the firm's Detroit office, Claire Mason Lee focuses her practice in the area of medical liability defense. She has prepared and argued case evaluation summaries and summary disposition motions on behalf of numerous clients in the public and private sectors.

Claire is a member of several local, state and national professional organizations. Most notably, she serves as a board member of the Wolverine Bar Association's Summer Clerkship Committee, and is a member of the board of directors for Ben Ross Public School Academy. Additionally, she received the YMCA Minority Achiever award for 2003-2004, served as a member of the Race Relations & Diversity Task Force in the Birmingham-Bloomfield area, and is a life member of the NAACP.

In 2004 Claire graduated from the University of Detroit Mercy School of Law, where she received several academic awards. She received a Master of Public Administration degree with a concentration in health care administration from Southern University and A&M College in 1997, and an undergraduate degree from Louisiana State University and A&M College in 1993.

David Baker Lewis

Chairman & Chief Executive Officer
Lewis & Munday

Denise J. Lewis

Partner, Real Estate
Honigman Miller Schwartz and Cohn LLP

David Baker Lewis is chairman and chief executive officer of Lewis & Munday (L&M), a professional corporation. He received a bachelor's degree from Oakland University, and an MBA from The University of Chicago Graduate School of Business. He was also awarded a juris doctorate degree from The University of Michigan Law School.

David chairs L&M's Corporate Services Practice Group, and has specialized in municipal finance law since 1974, serving as L&M's lead attorney on numerous and diverse municipal bond offerings. A past director of the National Association of Bond Lawyers, he is a former chairman of the National Association of Securities Professionals.

David has served on the boards of numerous professional, educational and civic organizations. Particularly noteworthy is his service as a former assistant professor at the Detroit College of Law, and as former member and chairman of the board of trustees for Oakland University. Currently, David serves on the board of directors of The Kroger Company and H&R Block. He is a former director of Comerica, Inc., TRW, Inc., LG&E Energy Corp., M.A. Hanna Company and Consolidated Rail Corporation (Conrail).

Denise J. Lewis is a partner in the Real Estate Department of Honigman Miller Schwartz and Cohn LLP's Detroit office, and a member of the firm's board of directors. She represents and counsels real estate developers, owners and investors with projects ranging from retail, office, multifamily, industrial, single-family and mixed-use hotel/office development. Lewis focuses on projects in urban centers involving public/private partnerships and issues of redevelopment and restoration, environmental planning, land use planning, brownfield financing, tax abatement and tax increment financing.

Lewis is the first woman and the first African American from Michigan elected to membership in the American College of Real Estate Lawyers. She has been recognized in the 2007 Super Lawyers for Michigan listing, the *Chambers USA: America's Leading Lawyers for Business*, the 2007 Lawdragon's top Dealmakers in America and in *Crain's Detroit Business* as Most Influential Women Leaders and Outstanding Black Business Leaders.

Lewis earned a juris doctorate degree, cum laude, from the University of Michigan Law School, a Master of Arts degree from Wayne State University, and a Bachelor of Arts degree, cum laude, from Columbia University.

Angelique Strong Marks

Vice President, General Counsel
Handleman Company

A'Jené M. Maxwell

Attorney at Law
Real Estate Department
Honigman Miller Schwartz and Cohn LLP

Angelique Strong Marks serves as Handleman's vice president, general counsel. Handleman is a $1.2 billion (revenue) music distribution company with operations in the United States, Canada and the United Kingdom. She is Michigan's only African-American female general counsel of a publicly traded company.

Marks is an ABA Business Law Section Ambassador, a *Michigan Lawyers Weekly* board of editors director, an Oakland County Women's Bar Association advisor and a Save Kids of Incarcerated Parents (S.K.I.P.) director. She has also served as a State Bar of Michigan commissioner, the State Bar of Michigan Young Lawyers Section chairperson, an American Bar Association House of Delegates' Michigan delegate and the D. Augustus Straker Bar Association president.

Marks has been honored as one of *Michigan Lawyers Weekly*'s Up and Coming Lawyers (2004), *Crain's Detroit Business'* 40 Under 40 (2005) and the State Bar of Michigan's Citizen Lawyer (2006). She received a Bachelor of Science degree in finance from the University of Akron, a Master of Business Administration degree in finance and management from Miami University, and a juris doctorate degree from The Ohio State University.

A'Jené M. Maxwell is an attorney in the Real Estate Department of Honigman Miller Schwartz and Cohn LLP's Detroit office. He concentrates his practice in commercial, office, and residential real estate transactions and financing of such transactions.

Maxwell has experience in various conveyance, leasing and lending matters for clients, including leasing of Detroit's Renaissance Center and Millender Center for Riverfront Holdings, Inc.; various leasing, real estate acquisitions and land use matters for Steelcase Inc. (and related entities); shopping mall leasing throughout the United States for Taubman entities; leasing for automotive supplier DBM Technologies; and HUD and MSHDA-related lending for St. James Capital. He has also had numerous appearances before Detroit's City Council and substantial experience with other City of Detroit agencies.

Maxwell is a member of the Wolverine Bar Association, where he serves on the Summer Clerkship Committee. He is also an active volunteer of the Ministry of Helps for Word of Faith International Christian Center.

He earned a juris doctorate degree, cum laude, from Wayne State University, and a Bachelor of Business Administration degree from Grand Valley State University.

Laurel F. McGiffert

Partner, Attorney at Law
Plunkett Cooney

Sharon McPhail

General Counsel
City of Detroit

A partner since 1991, Laurel F. McGiffert concentrates her practice in the areas of medical liability, labor and employment law, municipal law and general litigation. She has extensive litigation experience, and is one of the firm's senior trial attorneys. She also serves as an arbitrator and mediator in alternative dispute resolution cases.

Laurel is a member of the Detroit Metropolitan, Wolverine, Michigan and American bar associations, as well as the Association of Defense Trial Counsel. She currently volunteers for the American Heart Association, and she previously served on the board of directors for Wayne County Easter Seal Society, Gracious Savior Lutheran Church, and the Caring Athletes Team for Children's and Henry Ford Hospitals.

For more than 15 years, Laurel has been an instructor on numerous topics for the Michigan Institute of Continuing Legal Education (ICLE), including motion and discovery practice, deposition skills, anatomy of a lawsuit, practical evidence, demonstrative evidence, ultimate trial notebook, and common settlement and trial problems.

Laurel received a law degree in 1980 from Wayne State University Law School and an undergraduate degree from Vassar College in 1970.

L egal expertise will play a critical role in creating the NEXT Detroit. Understanding the fundamental need to assemble some of the best and brightest legal minds, Mayor Kilpatrick appointed former city council member Sharon McPhail as general counsel in the Office of the Mayor. McPhail's 30-plus years practicing law and her extensive knowledge of city government makes her uniquely qualified for this important cabinet post.

McPhail's portfolio includes law, human rights, and the workforce planning and development departments. These departments will be critical to helping improve antiquated systems and outdated work processes that have challenged city government for decades. Her expertise in practicing law includes work as a trial lawyer, an assistant U.S. attorney, a division chief in the Wayne County Prosecutor's Office, corporate counsel with Ford Motor Company and partner in a local law firm.

McPhail has also served in several quasi-judicial capacities including that of hearing officer for the Michigan Civil Rights Commission, and arbitrator and mediator in both Wayne and Oakland counties.

Alex L. Parrish

Partner, Corporate & Securities
Honigman Miller Schwartz and Cohn LLP

Marlo Johnson Roebuck

Founder & Attorney at Law
Roebuck Legal Counseling PLC

Alex L. Parrish is a partner and serves on the board of directors for Honigman Miller Schwartz and Cohn LLP. He is a key legal adviser to more large minority- and women-owned companies than perhaps any other corporate attorney in the country. He also represents a number of Fortune 500 manufacturing and services companies and major financial institutions. Parrish concentrates his practice in transactional matters including capital formation, mergers and acquisitions, joint ventures, securities regulations and general corporate matters. Additionally, he has significant experience with business reorganizations, workouts and bankruptcies.

Parrish is active in a number of Michigan civic and charitable institutions, and is currently chairman of the board of Detroit's Music Hall Center for the Performing Arts. He has been named in the *Best Lawyers in America* 2006, and as one of Michigan's outstanding business leaders in *Crain's Detroit Business* and *Corp!* magazines.

Parrish earned a juris doctorate degree from Harvard University Law School in 1980, and a Bachelor of Arts, summa cum laude, from Howard University in 1977.

Marlo Johnson Roebuck, a native Detroiter, is the founder of Roebuck Legal Counseling PLC, a law firm that specializes in assisting small- and medium-sized companies during company formation and growth periods, and on a project-by-project basis. Her practice centers on commercial, corporate and employment matters. Roebuck also has extensive experience representing corporate clients in the automotive, retail, real estate, education and manufacturing industries. She has successfully taken cases from inception to jury verdict.

Prior to founding Roebuck Legal Counseling, Roebuck was an associate at Kienbaum Opperwall Hardy & Pelton in Birmingham, Michigan, which was named by *Chambers USA* as the No. 1 labor and employment firm in Michigan. She was also an associate for Sonnenschein Nath & Rosenthal in Chicago, an international firm of more than 500 attorneys.

Roebuck received a juris doctorate degree, with honors, from DePaul University College of Law. While there, she was the business manager, and the articles and notes editor of the *DePaul Law Review*, and was awarded the Order of the Coif distinction. She received an undergraduate degree from the University of Michigan.

DETROIT'S COUNSELORS AT LAW

Herbert A. Sanders, Esq.

Founder & Attorney at Law
The Sanders Law Firm, P.C.

Jacqueline H. Sellers

Member, Attorney at Law
Clark Hill, PLC

Herbert "Herb" A. Sanders founded The Sanders Law Firm, P.C. in 1995. He is admitted to practice law in Michigan and the District of Columbia. In his current legal practice, he places special emphasis on civil litigation, and labor and employment relations.

Herb is a former Robert Millender fellow, and after completing the Millender Fellowship, he served as an assistant to Mayor Coleman A. Young.

In 2002 The Sanders Law Firm, P.C. became the first predominantly African-American law firm to be retained to provide continued representation to a major labor union within Michigan. Recently, Herb won a $1.8 million verdict on behalf of a member of a teacher's union. The verdict was recognized as the highest in Michigan's history in regard to a union member's effort to exercise his First Amendment right to freedom of speech and association.

In 2005 Herb was selected as one of the Best Dressed Real Men in America by *Esquire* magazine. Involved in various social and professional organizations, he enjoys playing tennis, riding bikes, reading, and spending quality time with his wife, Danielle, and his son, Anthony.

Jacqueline H. Sellers is a member at Clark Hill, PLC, where she serves as the practice group leader for the firm's Litigation Management Group. She primarily focuses her practice in the areas of warranty, product liability, commercial litigation and premises liability.

Sellers has substantial experience in serving as national alternative dispute resolution and national coordinating counsel in managing and defending warranty, fire and accident claims on behalf of automobile manufacturers, dealerships and finance companies.

Following law school, Sellers clerked for then Michigan Supreme Court Justice Dennis W. Archer. She is a mediator for the Wayne County Circuit Court Mediation Tribunal, and is a certified general civil case mediator.

Sellers is an executive director and secretary on the board of Forgotten Harvest, the nation's third-largest food rescue organization. She is also an active member of the Renaissance Chapter of The Links, Inc.

Lionel Sims Jr.

Assistant General Counsel
Detroit Board of Education

Richard T. White

Senior Vice President, Secretary
& General Counsel
The Auto Club Group

Lionel Sims, assistant general counsel to the Detroit Board of Education, concentrates his practice in the areas of commercial litigation, labor and employment, and contractual litigation. He is lead counsel on many litigation matters, including a million-dollar lawsuit filed on behalf of the Detroit Board of Education. He has also co-authored a chapter on public employers' drug testing policy.

A recipient of the Wolverine Bar Foundation Scholarship, Sims earned a law degree from the University of Detroit Law School in 2000. He holds a Bachelor of Science degree in corporate finance from Wayne State University. Sims is a member of the State Bar of Michigan and the National Bar Association. He also serves as president of the Wolverine Bar Association and general counsel for the International Detroit Black Expo.

Recently, Sims formed GGE Management, a sports management company tailored to provide legal service, real estate purchasing and financial guidance to professional athletes. He is certified by the National Football League as an agent and contract advisor, and has successfully negotiated contracts for basketball players in South America and Europe.

Richard T. White is senior vice president, secretary and general counsel of The Auto Club Group (ACG), the largest AAA club in the Midwest, with more than 4.1 million members in eight states. He is responsible for legal, governance and government relations.

Prior to joining ACG, White was in private practice as a founding and managing partner with the firm of Lewis, White & Clay (Lewis & Munday) where he specialized in corporate, mergers/acquisitions, health care and insurance law.

In 2007 White was elected chair of the Association of Corporate Counsel, the in-house bar association comprised of chief legal officers and attorneys who practice in legal departments and other private sector organizations worldwide.

He served as a commissioner of the Foreign Claims Settlement Commission from 1996 to 2002 and also as a commissioner and vice chair of the Michigan Transportation Commission from 1991 to 1997.

White received a Bachelor of Arts degree from Morehouse College, with honors, and is a graduate of Harvard Law School. He is a member of the Michigan and District of Columbia bar associations.

THE DETROIT TIGERS SALUTE "HOMETOWN HERO" WILLIE HORTON

tigers.com

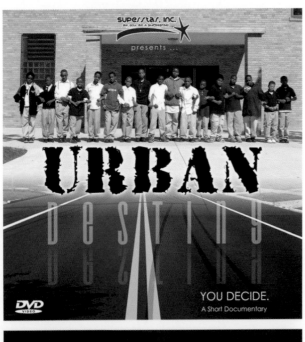

perform

elevate

DETROIT'S

Academia

ACADEMIA

phenom

scholar

prodigy

mentor

merit

value

attain

Alfred E. Baylor III, M.D.

Assistant Professor
Department of Surgery
Wayne State University

D r. Alfred Eugene Baylor III is an assistant professor in the department of surgery at Wayne State University (WSU). He is also a general surgeon and attending staff physician for the Detroit Medical Center, with special interest in trauma and critical care. Alfred has been actively involved as a captain in the U.S. Army National Guard/ Reserve since 1988, and holds the position of assistant chief medical officer of the MEPS in Troy.

Alfred received a baccalaureate degree from Hampton University in 1991. He subsequently received a Doctor of Medicine degree from Georgetown University in 1998. Of note, he was the first African-American male class president in its more than 150-year history. He successfully completed his internship and residency at WSU, where he is currently a doctoral candidate with emphasis in immunology and microbiology. He is a member of several local and national medical associations and societies, and has authored and co-authored several peer-reviewed publications in medical journals.

A native of Oxon Hill, Maryland, Alfred is the husband of Michelle and the proud father of three daughters, Amber, Ashley and Alexis.

Rosalind Brathwaite

Principal
HEART Academy

R osalind Brathwaite is the principal of HEART Academy located in Harper Woods. Rosalind serves as the educational leader, implementing the policies, programs and curriculum in a manner that promotes the educational development of each student. This high school has a specialized curriculum that integrates health concepts with traditional education classes.

Rosalind received a bachelor's degree from Chicago State University, where she was awarded scholarships to participate in track and field and volleyball. In 2004 she received a master's degree in administration and supervision from the University of Phoenix. She has been an educational leader for more than ten years.

Rosalind enjoys volunteering her time coaching track and field with Think Detroit PAL, where she coaches more than 140 athletes. Born in Milledgeville, Georgia, she is the wife of Kevin Brathwaite of Detroit SWAT and the proud mother of one daughter, Jasmine Brathwaite, the 2007 AAU Junior Olympic gold medalist in the 100-meter dash.

Jan Lewis Cardwell is campus director of University of Phoenix – Metro Detroit. She oversees six learning centers across metro Detroit with 200 administrative employees and approximately 300 adjunct instructors. She is also responsible for delivering higher education to more than 3,500 active students who attend classes at local learning centers or online.

Jan holds a bachelor's degree in business management and a Master of Business Administration degree in global management. She is currently a doctoral learner for a Doctor of Philosophy degree in instructional design for online learning.

Jan has 25 years' experience in education and corporate training. Her previous employers include the Detroit Public Schools and the former Michigan Bell Telephone Company, now AT&T.

Jan and her husband have a merged family of two daughters, two sons-in-law, two teenage granddaughters and four grandsons. She is a current member of the Tee Shots – Women's Golf Club, the Second Sunday Brunch Investment Club and the Central C.M.E. Church.

Her personal mission statement is a quote from Napoleon Hill: "Don't search for opportunity in the distance—recognize it and embrace it—right where you are."

Jan Lewis Cardwell

Campus Director
University of Phoenix –
Metro Detroit

Gloria Causey-Johnson is a special education teacher with the Detroit Public Schools. Born and raised in the Detroit area, she received Bachelor of Science and Master of Education degrees in special education from Wayne State University. She worked for the Wayne County Association for Retarded Citizens prior to her teaching career.

On June 25, 2002, Causey-Johnson was given a Teacher of the Year Award from The Arc Detroit in recognition of her outstanding and dedicated service to disabled students in the community. In June of 2007, she received an award from the Detroit Public Schools Wayne County RESA Superintendent's District Initiative for service and commitment to the children at her school.

Causey-Johnson is the very proud daughter of the late Andy James Causey and the late Alma Ruth Jackson, and the mother of Scot and Taji.

Gloria Causey-Johnson

Special Education Teacher
Detroit Public Schools

Janice E. Hale, Ph.D.

Professor &
Founding Director, Institute for the
Study of the African American Child
Wayne State University

Dr. Janice E. Hale is professor of early childhood education and founding director of the Institute for the Study of the African American Child (ISAAC), a national research institute at Wayne State University. She has written numerous articles and three books in her field. *Unbank the Fire: Visions for the Education of African American Children* and *Learning While Black: Creating Educational Excellence for African American Children* were both nominated for the Pulitzer Prize. Her book *Black Children: Their Roots, Culture and Learning Styles* is required for courses at more than 125 universities.

Hale received a bachelor's degree from Spelman College, a master's degree in religious education from the Interdenominational Theological Center and a doctoral degree in education from Georgia State University. She completed post-doctoral work at Yale University. In 1981 she was named Distinguished Alumna of the College of Education at Georgia State University, and in 2007 she received a Spelman College Alumnae Achievement Award.

Hale is the daughter of the Reverend and Mrs. Phale D. Hale. Her son, Keith Benson, is a scholarship basketball player at Oakland University and majoring in pre-medicine.

Randy Hayward

Superintendent
Marvin L. Winans Academy of
Performing Arts

Randy Hayward is superintendent of the Marvin L. Winans Academy of Performing Arts school district, which serves more than 1,100 students. He works with students, staff and families to build a community of academic and performing arts excellence. Since 1998, he has worked at the Academy in various capacities, including dean of students, assistant principal and principal. Among his proudest accomplishments at the Academy is traveling with students to Italy, where they performed at the Vatican.

A native of Detroit, Randy is a veteran of the United States Air Force. He received Bachelor of Liberal Arts and Master of Education degrees from Harvard University. In 2006 he received a certificate of completion from the National Institute for Urban School Leaders through Harvard's Principal Center.

Randy is a member of Perfecting Church. He is also a member of Phi Delta Kappa, a professional fraternity in education. He and his wife, Shuna, have four children, Randy Jr., Jasmine, Rayna and Jordan.

D r. Deborah Hunter-Harvill is currently the principal of Owen Academy at Pelham K-8. In this position, she serves as the educational leader, responsible for student achievement, parental involvement, staff development and providing a safe learning environment that meets the approved curricula and mission of the school.

Hunter-Harvill is a member of Delta Sigma Theta Sorority, Inc. She will serve as president of the National Alliance of Black School Educators from November of 2007 through November of 2009.

Hunter-Harvill received an educational doctorate degree from Wayne State University in Detroit, Michigan, in 1994. She received a master's degree in special education and a bachelor's degree in elementary and middle school education at Marygrove College in Detroit. She has also studied at Harvard, Brown University, the Michigan Institute for Educational Management, SUPES Academy and the Michigan Quality Council.

Hunter-Harvill is the wife of Walter and the proud mother of two children, a son, Jevin, and a daughter, Krystle.

Deborah Hunter-Harvill, Ed.D.

Principal
Owen Academy at Pelham K-8

V ivian R. Jackson is the principal of Chandler Park Academy's elementary, middle and high schools. She has nearly 40 years of service in public education. During her years with Chandler Park, she led the school to receive the Skillman Foundation's grant for Good Schools Making the Grade, and helped the staff and students meet the state requirement of proficiency on the MEAP test.

Jackson has been nominated for the 2007 Administrator of the Year for MAPSA, and was named Teacher of the Year in 1998 by the Area C Office of the Detroit Public Schools.

Receiving a Bachelor of Arts degree from Wayne State University and a master's degree in early childhood development from the University of Detroit Mercy, she has done post-graduate work at the University of Michigan, Eastern Michigan University and Oakland University. Additionally, Jackson is a member of Delta Sigma Theta Sorority, Inc.

Born in South Carolina but reared in Detroit, Jackson is the wife of the Reverend Jeff Jackson, the proud mother of Brennan and Jason, and stepmother of Faith, Tracy and Cynthia.

Vivian R. Jackson

Principal
Chandler Park Academy

Deshawn Johnson

Director, Human Resources
Lawrence Technological University

Deshawn Johnson is the director of human resources at Lawrence Technological University, where she incorporates progressive human resources practices with an emphasis on policy development and administration.

With the growth of Lawrence Tech's student body, advanced employee processes and leadership programs play a major role in the success of the university. Johnson designed and implemented the foundational infrastructure of the human resources department to align with the university's mission of developing leaders through innovative and agile programs. She implemented a multimillion-dollar HRIS system and directed the development of Lawrence Tech's internal leadership training program to augment employee expertise and enhance their skill sets.

Johnson is a member of the Society of Human Resources Association, the Greater Detroit Chapter of the Human Resources Association, the American Association for Affirmative Action, and Delta Sigma Theta Sorority, Inc. She received a bachelor's degree from Spring Arbor College in Michigan, and earned a master's degree from Central Michigan University. In 2000 she was nationally certified as a professional of human resources by the Society of Human Resources Management.

Malesa Owens McGhee

District Communications Director
Detroit Academy of Arts and Sciences

Malesa Owens McGhee came to the Detroit Academy of Arts and Sciences (DAAS) after nearly 15 years in the public relations and film industry. She has worked with 20th Century Fox's *Minority Report*, Disney's *Tuck Everlasting*, HBO's *Taxicab Confessions*, BET and ESPN, to name a few.

At DAAS, Malesa strategically plans and leads the communications and education efforts to support the mission of the school district. She raises monies for scholarship and sponsorship programs that send students to college and on educational tours throughout the world, and give hands-on experience with performing arts companies.

Malesa received a bachelor's degree in broadcast journalism and a master's degree in operations in film from Howard University. Her memberships include the National Association of Executive Women, the UNCF, the NAACP, the NABJ, the NEA and Concerned Citizens for Higher Education.

Her professional career also includes event planning, freelance writing and various national radio, television and film projects. A patron of the arts, Malesa loves to mentor and encourage young people, travel, cook, and have quality time with family and friends.

Dr. Delila Owens is assistant professor of counselor education at Wayne State University. In her position, she is responsible for training school counselors, and providing service to the college and the community. She has also co-authored articles and book chapters with nationally and internationally acclaimed scholars. Their works appear or are scheduled to appear in the *Midwestern Educational Researcher*, *Gifted Child Quarterly* and the *Journal of Counseling and Development*.

Owens was recently reappointed to the Michigan Board of Counseling by Governor Jennifer Granholm, and is a member of the Rosa Parks Scholarship Foundation Board. She is also president-elect elect of NCACES, a regional association of counselor educators and supervisors whose members represent 13 states.

In her commitment to continued excellence in education, Owens developed the Paul Winfred Owens Memorial Book Scholarship Fund at Ferris State University in memory of her grandfather.

She received a bachelor's degree from Ferris State University, a master's degree from Central Michigan University and a doctorate degree from Michigan State University at the age of 27.

Dr. Delila Owens

Assistant Professor
Counselor Education
Wayne State University

Jonathan Powell currently heads the Workforce Development and Continuing Education Division of Special Projects at Wayne County Community College District's Western Campus in Belleville, Michigan. In that capacity, he is responsible for customized contract training, career and professional development and training, personal and leisure programs, summer camps programs for youth, mature learners, as well as special guest lectures, seminars and workshops.

A native of St. Louis, Missouri, Jonathan obtained an undergraduate degree from Webster University in media communications, with a focus in public relations and a minor in English. He is also pursuing a graduate degree in educational administration.

Jonathan has served as a member of the following organizations or chambers: the NAACP, the Belleville Michigan Chamber of Commerce, the Canton Michigan Educational Committee, and an ambassador for the Belleville Michigan Chamber of Commerce.

In the past, Jonathan's career choices have allotted him the opportunity to work for such companies as the Edison Brothers Stores, Inc., Big Brothers Big Sisters, Goodwill Industries, the United Negro College Fund, the Catholic Youth Council and SER Metro Detroit.

Jonathan T. Powell

Development Specialist
Workforce Development &
Continuing Education Division
Wayne County Community College District

JuJuan C. Taylor, Ph.D.

Professor & Department Chair
Communication Arts
Schoolcraft College

D r. JuJuan C. Taylor is professor and department chair of communication arts at Schoolcraft College in Livonia, Michigan.

Taylor is frequently invited to speak and serve on academic panels throughout the metro Detroit community. She has been the keynote speaker for the National Association of Negro Business and Professional Women's Clubs, the Greater Mt. Olive Baptist Church and the Sacred Heart Catholic Church in Detroit.

As a professor, Taylor has taught Introduction to African Studies, Black Women in America and the Harlem Renaissance within the department of African-American studies at Wayne State University (WSU). She has also taught for several years within WSU's Graduate School of Teacher Education.

Taylor has been selected during consecutive years for inclusion within the national edition of *Who's Who Among America's Teachers*, making her among "only 2 percent of U.S. teachers to be honored in more than one edition."

She is the author of *Effective and Professional Speech Communications for Future Leaders in the 21st Century.*

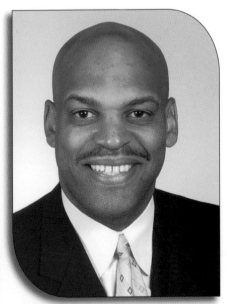

Tyrone E. Winfrey

Associate Director
Undergraduate Admissions,
Detroit Office
University of Michigan

B orn and raised in Detroit, Michigan, Tyrone E. Winfrey is married to Janice Winfrey, the Detroit city clerk. They have three children, Chad, Lauren and Tyrone Jr. He is a member of Greater Grace Temple of the Apostolic Faith.

After graduating with a Bachelor of Science degree from the University of Wyoming, Tyrone returned to Detroit. He attended Wayne State University and then graduated with a Master of Arts degree in counselor education. Later, Tyrone began studies toward a doctoral degree.

In 1990 Tyrone's higher education career began through a position at Michigan State University Extension. Eventually, he helped initiate the Michigan State University – Detroit Outreach Admissions Office.

Currently, Tyrone is associate director in the office of undergraduate admissions and director of the University of Michigan's Detroit admissions office, which addresses academic preparation, admissions and advancement of higher education in urban communities. Furthermore, Tyrone was elected to the Detroit Board of Education in November of 2005. He is chair of Academic Achievement, Curriculum Development and Information Technology as it relates to Curriculum Committee for the board.

earnest

merciful

DETROIT'S
SPIRITUAL LEADERS

faithful

consecrated

virtuous

dedicated

wise

benevolent

honorable

Dr. Charles G. Adams

Senior Pastor
Hartford Memorial Baptist Church

Dr. Charles G. Adams has been senior pastor of Hartford Memorial Baptist Church since 1969. He has led the church in outstanding Christian witness, community outreach and social justice advocacy. He organized the Hartford Agape House, a social service agency serving northwest Detroit and encompassing Head Start to a senior center. Hartford's Economic Development Program has developed neglected urban property to commercial use, creating hundreds of jobs and providing needed retail services.

As professor of the practice of ethics and ministry at Harvard University Divinity School, Adams heads the Harvard Summer Leadership Program, a collaborative program taught by Harvard Business and Divinity schools. Clergy and laypersons from around the country attend intense two-week sessions on church economic development.

Highly acclaimed as a preacher, speaker and writer, Adams has preached on every continent and has published widely. He is the recipient of more than ten honorary doctorate degrees, and a graduate of the University of Michigan, Ann Arbor and Harvard Divinity School.

Adams is married to Agnes Hadley Adams and is the father of Dr. Tara Adams Washington and the Reverend Charles Christian Adams.

Rev. Ortheia Barnes

Founder & Chief Executive Officer
I Believe Ministries

The Reverend Ortheia Barnes is chief executive officer and founder of I Believe Ministries (A Ministry Without Walls) and I Believe Coalition. She is doing ministry and mission work in Japan, Europe, Egypt, Sweden, the U.S., Canada and Africa. She recently partnered with Hosanna Outreach Ministries of Emmanuel to "dig wells in Kenya," making two trips a year and servicing thousands spiritually and physically. Ortheia was featured in the *Michigan Chronicle* as Pastor of the Week.

I Believe Coalition is a coalition of eight community organizations which host programs to bring solutions to community issues and needs in the areas of education, homelessness, substance abuse and violence.

Ortheia is also known as an international recording artist, with numerous recordings and commercials such as: "I Really Love the Lord," "Stranger in Town," K-Mart, McDonald's, and "It's a Great Time in Detroit." She has been a solo vocalist for Nelson Mandela, Bishop Desmond Tutu and Pope John Paul II. A recipient of numerous awards for being a business owner and community and social activist, Ortheia says that the greatest award is to serve God's people.

Bishop P.A. Brooks is one of the 12 members of the presidium of the Church of God in Christ, Inc., headquartered in Memphis, Tennessee. In this position, he helps to direct six million members worldwide, with churches in the United States and in more than 57 foreign countries. He is co-author of *Understanding Bible Doctrine as Taught in the Church of God in Christ*, a widely used training manual for ministry leaders and new converts.

Brooks is the recipient of an honorary doctorate degree from the Lewis College of Business. He also serves as president of the New St. Paul Tabernacle Non-Profit Housing Corporation, and as chief executive officer of Faith Community Mortgage, which is licensed to operate in 50 states.

A native of Chicago, Brooks and his wife, Doris, are celebrating more than 56 years of marriage. They are the parents of Evangelist Faithe Brooks, hostess of the *Faithe to Faith* television broadcast; and Minister Phillip Brooks III, a musician and recording artist.

Bishop P.A. Brooks

Member, National General Board
Church of God in Christ, Inc.

David Bullock is the senior pastor of Greater St. Matthew Baptist Church. In this position, he manages the holistic and life changing ministry of this growing urban congregation. He also serves as an adjunct professor in philosophy at Wayne State University and Wayne County Community College District. He is also the chairman of a community development corporation that is building a 15,000 square-foot community center in Highland Park.

A published author, he is a noted speaker and founder of the Superstar Mentoring Group.

David received a Bachelor of Arts degree from Morehouse College, and Wayne State University awarded him a master's degree in philosophy. He is currently in the final stages of dissertation preparation at Wayne State University and pursuing a Doctor of Philosophy degree in philosophy.

David Bullock

Pastor
Greater St. Matthew
Baptist Church

Dr. Samuel H. Bullock Jr.

Pastor
Bethany Baptist Church

D r. Samuel H. Bullock became pastor of Bethany Baptist Church of Detroit, Michigan, in 1982. He was called and ordained to the gospel ministry while he was a member of the New Mount Vernon Baptist Church of Ferndale, Michigan.

Bullock received an Associate of Arts degree from Highland Park Community College and a Bachelor of Science degree from Wayne State University. He continued his education at Andover Newton Theological School in Massachusetts and at Drew University in New Jersey, where he received Master and Doctor of Ministry degrees.

Bullock is highly involved in the church and community, serving as president of the Joan Ann Bullock Academy, the Spear Community Development Corporation, and the Council of Baptist Pastors of Detroit and Vicinity, Inc. He also sits on the board of directors for the Red Cross of Southeastern Michigan, New Detroit, Inc. and the Detroit Medical Center. He is a past president of the Michigan Progressive Baptist Convention, the Southeast Area American Baptist Churches Ministers Council and the West Detroit Interfaith Community Organization.

Bullock is married with four sons and two grandchildren.

Rev. Dr. Nathaniel Caldwell

Pastor
Greater Burnette Baptist Church

T he Reverend Dr. Nathaniel Caldwell is pastor of the Greater Burnette Baptist Church, succeeding his father, the Reverend Dr. J. Allen Caldwell, who founded the church 54 years ago. Growing up in a Christian family, Nathaniel Caldwell was called to preach at 19 years of age.

He received a bachelor's degree from Bishop College, a Master of Divinity degree from Virginia Union University, and a doctorate degree in theology from Philadelphia Bible College and Seminary.

Caldwell served as pastor and co-pastor in Dallas, Texas, and Richmond, Virginia, prior to returning to his hometown of Detroit in 2000 to co-pastor with his father. In 2005 he was elected and installed as pastor of the Greater Burnette Baptist Church. During his short tenure, he has implemented ministries that address the holistic needs of the church and community. They include a food and clothing program as well as the development of a transitional housing program.

The foundation of Caldwell's being is Christ-centered, Bible-regulated, prayer-minded, Spirit-filled and willfully giving.

He is the father of three daughters and two sons, three of whom are ordained ministers.

Joyce C. Driver is pastor of For Such A Time As This Deliverance Center in Detroit. This ministry was founded on Esther 4:14. Driver is currently celebrating eight years of serving as a pastor. She is a full-time pastor, wife of Elder Jimmie Driver, mother of four children and grandmother of 11.

During her years as pastor, Driver has been involved in 30 years of international radio outreach ministry. She has a special mandate to minister to those who are hurting, suffering, lonely, bitter and unsaved.

Driver also serves as chair for Detroit's Annual Operation Rescue, which feeds and clothes hundreds of less-fortunate senior citizens and children of Detroit and its surrounding areas. Additionally, she has served on the governor of Michigan's re-election committee, as well as participated in other political functions in Detroit.

Joyce C. Driver

Pastor
For Such A Time As This
Deliverance Center

Bishop Dr. Keith Farmer is founder and senior pastor of Cathedral Center Church in Detroit, Michigan. He is also the founder of The C3 Agency, an advertising agency connecting the church to the community. His latest project is producing the show *Celebrate Live* with the TCT Network, that reaches 75 million homes showcasing different pastors and Christian authors around the world. Every year, he works with Bob Bauer's Marathon for Meals, feeding more than 200 families in the state of Michigan.

Farmer worked with such organizations as Gospel Music Workshop of America and the Quaker Oats Voices of Tomorrow. He has worked with such great gospel recording artists as Vickie Winans, Dottie Peeples, Beverly Crawford and Bishop "Mr. Clean" White.

Farmer has a doctorate degree from New Life Theological Seminary. A native of Detroit, he is the husband of Tiffany Walters-Farmer and father of Keith II, Jaquata, Jaylin and Chase.

**Bishop Dr.
Keith A. Farmer**

Pastor
Cathedral Center Church

Rev. Dr. Cecelia E. GreeneBarr

Pastor
Trinity AME Church

The Reverend Dr. Cecelia GreeneBarr is pastor of Trinity AME Church in Detroit. As pastor, she is the communicator of the congregational vision, developing goals, operating plans, policies and objectives. She provides spiritual nurture through prayer, preaching, teaching and pastoral care. GreeneBarr also represents the congregation to denominational, ecumenical and financial communities, government agencies and the general public. She is also president of GreeneHouse, providing publishing services, ministerial development training and leadership coaching.

An author, GreeneBarr's book, *Guide My Feet: Ministry Transformed through Mentoring*, discusses her specialty in clergy mentoring. Her additional publications include *The African American Pulpit* and *This is My Story: Testimonies and Sermons of Black Women in Ministry*.

GreeneBarr has earned a Bachelor of Science degree from North Carolina A&T State University, a Master of Divinity degree from Princeton Theological Seminary, and a Doctor of Ministry degree from Ashland Theological Seminary. She is a Roothbert fellow and a life member of Delta Sigma Theta Sorority, Inc.

A native of Chapel Hill, North Carolina, GreeneBarr is married to Theron Barr Jr., and they are the parents of Cecelia II and Theron-Howard.

Apostle Nina D. Hall

Founder & Pastor
Ark of the Covenant Ministries of
the Apostolic Faith

Apostle Nina Hall was one of the first black women to sell cars in Michigan, and has been a trailblazer for women in the ministry in both the Baptist and Apostolic church since 1975. She is founder and pastor of the Ark of the Covenant Ministries of the Apostolic Faith, located in Sinai-Grace Hospital, one of the largest medical centers in Detroit. This non-traditional, mega-media ministry reaches a captive audience of more than 28,000 people a month, and Hall's sermons bring hope and encouragement to the sick. She pastors many of the doctors, nurses, chaplains and staff who are unable to attend traditional church services.

Hall is also the founder and prelacy of five Christian organizations, and the Midwest regional apostle of the Homi Fellowship in Chicago. Her street ministry has provided food and community resources to more than 190,000 people in Detroit. She has been honored by mayors, city councils, governors, senators and the House of Representatives.

Educated in Detroit, Hall attended Wayne State Community College, and has three children.

James A. Jennings Jr. is pastor of Shield of Faith Ministries in Detroit. There he preaches and teaches the word of God, counsels, mentors and nurtures the congregation. Shield of Faith is an empowerment ministry teaching principles of faith and successful living.

Jennings received an honorary Doctor of Divinity degree. He was the recipient of the highest civilian award by the late Mayor Coleman A. Young and the Detroit City Council. He also received the 1994 Reverend C.L. Franklin Preaching Award for his inspirational style of preaching.

Jennings completed his undergraduate studies at Macomb County Community College and Wayne State University. He received a Bachelor of Arts degree from the American Baptist Theological Seminary, in Nashville, Tennessee. Additionally, Jennings pursued a Master of Divinity degree at Southern Baptist Theological Seminary in Louisville, Kentucky. He also earned Master of Arts degrees at Wayne State University and the University of Louisville.

A native of Forkland, Alabama, Jennings grew up in Detroit. He is a husband, father and grandfather. He is married to Helen Watkins-Jennings.

James A. Jennings Jr.

Pastor
Shield of Faith Ministries

The Reverend James C. Jones is a remarkable man of God. He is currently pastor of Williams Chapel Missionary Baptist Church, and began pastoring there on January 1, 2006, at the "ripe old age" of 27.

Jones has based his ministry entirely on the Lord's will and not his own. He is not only concerned with the physical needs of people but their spiritual needs as well. Saving the lost at any cost and baptizing and equipping the saints for service are the significant focuses of his ministry. The vision of the chapel is to be a place where God's people will be spiritually fed and become completely focused on evangelizing, equipping, developing and maintaining a personal spiritual relationship with God, based upon the principles and sureness of God's holy word through the Lord Jesus Christ.

Under his leadership, the membership at Williams Chapel has doubled in size. A native of Detroit, Jones is a graduate of Detroit's Central High School, and is currently attending Ecumenical Theological Seminary.

Rev. James C. Jones

Pastor
Williams Chapel Missionary
Baptist Church

Rev. Dr. Joseph Ralph Jordan

Pastor
Corinthian Baptist Church

The Reverend Dr. Joseph Ralph Jordan was born in Jasper, Georgia, on April 29, 1936, the son of Mr. and Mrs. Jimmie Jordan. His higher learning experience began at Wayne State University in Detroit, Michigan. Educational pursuits were continued at Payne Theological Seminary in Wilberforce, Ohio. He earned a master's degree from the University of Detroit Mercy in Detroit, Michigan, and a doctorate degree from Drew University in Madison, New York.

On February 28, 1968, Jordan accepted the call to God's ministry. The membership of Corinthian Baptist Church, in Hamtramck, Michigan, called him to be their new pastor in October of 1973.

Jordan is a leader and member of numerous civic and professional organizations, including president of the Todd-Phillips Children's Home; a member of the executive committee of the Greater Detroit Area Health Council, Inc.; president of the Grand Haven-Dyar-Dequindre Corporation; and chair of the Coalition for Healthcare Equity. He has many other past and current affiliations and memberships.

Jordan is married to Bobbie Drake Jordan, and they are the parents of three children, Anthony, Kimberly and Sandra, and a granddaughter, Ashante.

Larry T. Jordan

Founder & Senior Pastor
Family Victory Fellowship Church

Larry T. Jordan is founder and senior pastor of Family Victory Fellowship Church in Southfield. The church is a family-oriented ministry with the vision of building, strengthening and restoring families.

Jordan is chief executive officer and founder of Generation 2 Generation, Inc., a youth development organization focusing on maximization of individual potential. He is also founder of Children's Technological Academy, a Christian school committed to training children to be leaders in society. He currently serves as a chaplain with the City of Southfield Police Department.

Jordan is a graduate of Lawrence Technological University, earning a degree in architecture. Prior to the pastorate, he was a senior staff architect with Albert Kahn Associates.

Jordan is a member of the board of trustees for several organizations, including the St. Johns/Providence Hospital Community Affairs. He is also founder of the Covenant Pastor's Association, a network of senior pastors and their spouses in the metropolitan Detroit area.

Entrepreneur, author and life coach, Jordan is married to Southfield Councilwoman Sylvia Jordan, and is the father of two children.

The Reverend Robert Kennerly, known as "Pastor Bob," is founder of SpiritLove Ministries International. He is also executive officer of I Believe Coalition, comprised of eight community organizations that host programs providing solutions to community issues and needs in the areas of education, homelessness, substance abuse, violence and much more.

Pastor Bob hosted a radio and television program called *Come Out Men's Ministry* to help bring men back to the place God has called them to be. He is a minister of ministers for pastors, bishops and apostles across the U.S. and Canada, providing counsel, setting up men's ministries and homeownership.

Pastor Bob is owner and chief executive officer of TJ Mortgage Solutions, Inc., and branch manager for Reliance Financial. It is his goal to help people realize the dream of homeownership, and make it possible for them to have payments within their budgets.

A native of Detroit, Pastor Bob is a husband, father and grandfather. He is married to the Reverend Ortheia Barnes.

Rev. Robert Kennerly

Executive Officer
I Believe Coalition

Innovative, anointed and Bible-based, Kevin Lancaster founded and pastors Love Life Family Christian Center in Eastpointe, Michigan. With continuous growth of the ministry, Love Life offers a diverse environment accommodating all walks of life.

Obtaining two associate degrees in design and engineering, Kevin worked at Ford Motor Company for more than 15 years. In 1999 he became partner of the first 100 percent African-American-owned engineering firm called MENC (Minority Engineering Networking Consortium). Compelled to go into ministry, he left MENC to have more time to commit to building the ministry of Love Life.

A member of the Eastpointe Networking Forum, and Police and Community for Equality, Kevin is sincere and dedicated to bringing about godly changes. He is a devoted husband to Kathy, and they are proud parents of three children, Patrick, Krystal and Kiara.

Holding a bachelor's degree in divinity, Kevin makes teaching, preaching and living God's word a personal commitment that he will not compromise.

Kevin Lancaster

Pastor & Founder
Love Life Family Christian Center

DETROIT'S SPIRITUAL LEADERS

Rev. Orville K. Littlejohn

Pastor
Messiah Baptist Church

As a native of Dayton, Ohio, the Reverend Orville K. Littlejohn was born on the evening of July 8, 1959 as the second of five sons to Abraham and Julia V. Littlejohn. In April of 1967, he accepted Christ as his personal Savior. In October of 1989, he accepted the call to the prophetic ministry, and on the night of November 5th, he preached his first sermon.

Littlejohn attended Sinclair Community College, where he completed an associate degree in quality engineering in 1989 and an associate degree in business administration in 1995, graduating with honors. He attended Wright State University, where he achieved a bachelor's degree in business management in 1999. That same year, Littlejohn was inducted in the National Honorary Fraternity Sigma Iota Epsilon. He is presently continuing his studies in the Master of Divinity program at Ecumenical Theological Seminary.

Littlejohn has enjoyed a music ministry for more than 20 years with his brothers known as the Littlejohn Brothers. His life was enriched when he united in the holy bond of matrimony with his wife, Cheryl, who is also from Dayton, Ohio.

Andrew Merritt

Bishop & Founder
Straight Gate International Church

Andrew Merritt is a bishop, author, city statesman, business owner and visionary leader. In 1978 he and his wife, Viveca Merritt, founded the Straight Gate International Church in Detroit, Michigan, with only three members. The church has experienced phenomenal growth with eight church moves and now serves the needs of the emerging congregation of more than 6,000 today.

A respected minister and community leader, Merritt has prayed with Presidents Clinton and Bush, as well as Michigan's Governor Jennifer Granholm and Detroit's Mayor Kwame Kilpatrick. In 2004 he and his wife launched the international annual conference, One In Worship, which gathers thousands from the body of Christ in one accord for the sole purpose of praise and worship.

Merritt's family-managed record company, Bajada Records, has produced numerous gospel and inspirational recordings as well as Stellar-nominated hits. He is a family-based minister and is the proud father of six children and five grandchildren. Merritt is a pastor of pastors and is acknowledged nationwide as a spiritual father and covering in the church because of the anointing on his life.

The third son to Dr. Luvenia Miles and the late Apostle Charles O. Miles, Prince A. Miles was born in Detroit on July 8, 1956. He is married to Lady Monica Miles, and is father to three sons, Matthew, Joseph and the late Prince A. Miles II.

A graduate of Southfield High School, Miles attended Detroit Business Institute. In 1975 he was called into the ministry, and in 1977 he was ordained to preach. He attended William Tyndale College, and received a Doctor of Divinity degree in 1990 from the United Bible College and Theological Seminary. In 1999 he received the Spirit of Detroit Award and a certificate of recognition from the mayor.

The pastor of International Gospel Deliverance Center in Southfield, Miles was consecrated as an apostle on July 8, 2006. He serves on the executive council of the National Clergy Council and as chaplain for MADD of Wayne and Oakland counties. A leader and shining light in the community, he is a witness for Jesus Christ, with a desire to see lives changed by his saving grace.

Prince A. Miles

Pastor
International Gospel
Deliverance Center

The Reverend Dr. James C. Perkins has served as pastor of Greater Christ Baptist Church in Detroit, Michigan, for 25 years. An internationally recognized minister, he fulfills speaking engagements at churches, seminaries and conferences across the United States and abroad.

Perkins is the author of *Building Up Zion's Walls: Ministry for Empowering the African American Family*, published by Judson Press. His other writings, as well as profiles of his ministry appear in both secular and Christian publications, including *Black Enterprise, USA Today, Ebony*, and the best-selling *Success Runs in Our Race* by George Fraser.

Perkins has established numerous enterprises that support his vision for community redemption. In 1992 he founded the Fellowship Nonprofit Housing Corporation as a vehicle for community economic development. Perkins also instituted the Benjamin E. Mays Male Academy in 1993. This Christian school for boys offers kindergarten through sixth grade.

Currently, Perkins is serving as second vice president of the Progressive National Baptist Convention.

Rev. Dr. James C. Perkins

Pastor
Greater Christ Baptist Church

Anthony D. Shannon Sr.

Senior Pastor
Beyond the Veil
International Christian Church

The gifts that extend from this powerful man of God are pastor, teacher, evangelist, prophet, motivator, author and Christian business owner. Anthony Shannon is an ordained pastor of the gospel of the kingdom of Jesus Christ and deeply committed to sharing the word of God with revelation. He serves as senior pastor and founder of Beyond the Veil International Christian Church. Anthony is a dynamic man with a positive message for this generation. He is a respected preacher and teacher to churches, colleges, schools and businesses.

Anthony is a member of the Association of Independent Ministers (AIM) under Bishop I.V. Hilliard. He is president and founder of God's Gear Gospel Wear and first assistant to Bishop Michael Jones, the international bishop of the Ministerial Alliance for the Full Gospel Baptist Church Fellowship. He is also a host of *TCT Alive* and *Ask the Pastor* on TCT Television in Detroit.

Anthony is a devoted husband to his lovely wife, Glynis, and a father of three children, Anthony Jr., Kendra and Balint.

J. Drew Sheard

Senior Pastor
Greater Emmanuel Institutional
Church of God in Christ

Intelligent, confident and diligent are three of the many words used to describe J. Drew Sheard, senior pastor of Greater Emmanuel Institutional Church of God in Christ in Detroit. His awesome leadership abilities have established his position as one of the most influential leaders in the Church of God in Christ (COGIC).

As the current president of COGIC's International Youth Department, Sheard is an advocate for youth and wayward souls, and has implemented several programs during his tenure. He also serves as chairman of the Auxiliaries in Ministries (AIM) Convention, superintendent of the Emmanuel District and administrative assistant of the North Central Ecclesiastical Jurisdiction of Michigan.

Sheard has held several other positions on national, jurisdiction and local levels within COGIC, including national adjutant overseer, executive secretary of the International Youth Department and vice president of the AIM Convention.

Graduating from Wayne State University, Sheard received a bachelor's degree in education and a Master of Education degree in mathematics. He is the dedicated husband of Evangelist Karen Clark-Sheard, and is father to Kierra Sheard and J. Drew Sheard II.

Deborah L. Shumake, Ja`Phia, a visionary, preacher, teacher, playwright, author and businesswoman, pastors Greater One Ministries and co-pastors Christian Temple Baptist Church.

Deborah owns GW Publishing, Inc. Co., a printing and design company that has developed creative products for MBC cable network, Cecil Fielder, Evander Holyfield, other major corporations and many churches. She received the Woman in the Light Award for her business astuteness.

She is the publisher and executive editor of *God's Woman*, the magazine for women who love and serve Jesus Christ, and the host of *God's Woman On The Air*, a radio talk show aired on WPON. Deborah is a featured contributor in the *Woman of Color Study Bible, World Bible, Sister To Sister Volume 2: Devotions For And From African American Women* (Judson Press), and the *Sister to Sister Journal* (Judson Press).

Deborah is on the Leadership Circle – Council of Clergywomen of Metropolitan Detroit, in partnership with the Office of the Mayor, Faith Based Affairs. She is also an executive board member of the Shumake Family Foundation and the Robert S. Shumake Scholarship Relays.

Deborah L. Shumake, Ja`Phia

Pastor, Author & Owner
GW Publishing, Inc. Co.

The Reverend Dr. Dana L. Teamor is pastor of Mt. Calvary House of Prayer and program manager of information technology within the Detroit Public Schools. In addition to her present positions, she has served as region operations coordinator at IBM, and as product manager and director of marketing at Achip Technologies, Inc. She has authored three books, *A Harlem Love Song, Womanchild: A Rebirth* and *Because Our Story Will Never End*, and was a featured vocalist on the CD *He's Worthy* by Victory in Praise.

Teamor has received awards and recognitions from numerous organizations, including IBM, Business Professionals of America, Wayne County RESA, the Detroit Association of Black Social Workers, Detroit Compact, and the Detroit, Southfield and Birmingham public schools. Additionally, she is a member of the Metro Detroit Council of Pastors, Amnesty International, and is a lifetime member of Optimists International.

Teamor holds bachelor's and master's degrees in business administration, and a doctorate degree in business marketing. Having completed her first doctorate degree at 25, she is currently completing a second doctorate degree in systematic theology.

Rev. Dana L. Teamor, Ph.D.

Pastor
Mt. Calvary House of Prayer

Curtis C. Williams

Pastor
Aijalon Baptist Church

Curtis C. Williams has served as pastor of Aijalon Baptist Church for 17 years and administrator of Trinity Chapel Funeral Home for 18 years. He is active in the religious community, serving as one of the directors of the Concession Committee for the National Baptist Convention, USA, and as president of the Congress of Christian Education in the Michigan Baptist District, encompassing an association of 27 churches. He also serves on the Citizens Review Panel, and is a police chaplain with the Detroit Police Department, spring chair of the Metropolitan Boy Scouts of America, and a member of the board of directors for CareFirst, promoting Comerica Bank in commercials.

Williams graduated from Highland Park High School, received a bachelor's degree from the Detroit College of Business, a master's degree in pastoral ministry from Marygrove College and a Doctor of Divinity degree from the Tennessee School of Religion.

A native of Detroit, Williams is the husband of Joyce and the father of Jaclyn, Curtis and Janel.

Marvin L. Winans

Pastor
Perfecting Church

Pastor Marvin L. Winans has focused his life on bringing joy and good works to his community, people and country. Growing up in a musical and religious family, he is the youngest twin, and the fourth of ten children. The Winans are well known as the First Family of contemporary gospel, and have gained international acclaim. Three generations have earned numerous Dove and Stellar awards, and more than 20 Grammys.

Winans acknowledged his ministry call in the 1970s, delivering his first sermon on December 18, 1976. On May 27, 1989, he founded Perfecting Church in Detroit. The Lord has blessed Perfecting to grow into a ministry campus of more than 165,000 square feet with 3,500 members.

In 1992 Winans created Perfecting Community Development Corporation to ignite economic growth, offer transitional housing and provide recreational activities for youth. In 1997 he established the Marvin L. Winans Academy of Performing Arts for students in grades K-12.

Although amassing numerous awards and accolades, Winans' greatest joy is to see people come into the full knowledge of Jesus Christ and live victoriously forever.

D ouglas and Cathy Wray have often been dubbed as the "leaders of leaders," ministers and motivational speakers. They have a remarkable ability to preach and teach a powerful message based solely on the word of God. They are cutting edge motivators, with more than 30 years of ministry experience, and experts at challenging others to pursue their God-given purpose.

Douglas and Cathy maintain a very busy schedule, speaking at conferences, church services and training seminars all across the country. They are regular hosts for Total Christian Television's (TCT) international broadcast *TCT Alive*, which reaches more than 4.5 billion viewers worldwide. They are also regular guests on *The Joys of Oneness*, which is also a TCT broadcast. While doing all this, they still serve faithfully in various departments at their home church, Word of Faith International Christian Center in Southfield, Michigan, under the leadership of Bishop Keith A. Butler.

The Wrays reside in East Lansing, Michigan, and are the parents of five adult children, Leon (wife Tiffanie), Durrell, Daryl, Gerald and Jasmine. They are also the very proud grandparents to Halee and Alia.

Douglas & Cathy Wray

Founders
Living In The Overflow Ministries

noble

caring

Community DETROIT'S
COMMUNITY LEADERS

self-sacrificing

generous

empowering

heroic

philanthropic

humanitarian

altruistic

Tonya Allen

Vice President, Program
The Skillman Foundation

Tonya Allen is vice president, program, at The Skillman Foundation, a private independent foundation whose mission is to improve the lives of children in southeast Michigan. She is the architect of the Foundation's ten-year, $100 million Good Neighborhoods program, and helps oversee all three of the Foundation's main program areas and investments.

Named to this year's *Crain's Detroit Business'* 40 Under 40 list, which recognizes Detroit's emerging leaders, Allen attended the University of Michigan in Ann Arbor, where she completed a Bachelor of Arts degree in sociology and African-American studies. She also holds master's degrees in public health and social work from the University of Michigan.

Allen, who joined Skillman's staff in 2004 as a program director, has also worked for the C.S. Mott Foundation and the Plymouth-based Thompson-McCully Foundation. She was also the executive director of the Detroit Parent Network.

Allen lives in Southfield with her husband, Louis, and their daughters, Phylicia, Brianna and Alanna.

Paul Bridgewater

President & Chief Executive Officer
Detroit Area Agency on Aging

Paul Bridgewater is president and chief executive officer of the Detroit Area Agency on Aging. He has established one of the country's largest Holiday Meals on Wheels programs, trained hundreds of seniors in computer technology and created a regionwide Medicare/Medicaid counseling program. The agency runs one of Michigan's top care management and home-care support services, and also transitions nursing home residents back into the community.

Bridgewater spearheaded research through Wayne State University on health disparities among Detroit's elderly. The final report, *Dying Before Their Time*, led to government initiatives for long-term care reform. The agency received a $13.1 million demonstration grant to establish a "Single Point of Entry" for long-term care, one of four sites in Michigan.

Bridgewater has a master's degree in public administration from Oakland University and a bachelor's degree in political science from Saginaw Valley State College. He teaches gerontology courses at Wayne County Community College District.

Bridgewater was appointed to the 1980, 1990 and 2005 White House Conference on Aging by Congresswoman Carolyn Cheeks Kilpatrick, and to the 1998 White House Conference on Social Security by President Clinton.

Elizabeth "Betty" W. Brooks is a patron of the arts and a tireless community services leader. She writes inspirational poetry and is a columnist for a local newspaper.

Elizabeth is a member of the board of directors of the Michigan Opera Theatre, the Music Hall for Performing Arts, the Charles H. Wright African American History Museum, the Michigan Humanity Council and the Greening of Detroit. She is also chair of the board of directors for the Sphinx Organization and the After School All-Stars. Additionally, she chairs the UNCF Black and White Scholarship Ball, and the Council for African American Dance at the Detroit Opera House. An advisory board member for the Metro Parent Publishing Group, she serves on the Belle Isle Women's Committee. She has also chaired fundraising for the Motown Museum.

Elizabeth was appointed by Governor John Engler to three terms as a member of the Michigan Council for the Arts and Cultural Affairs. She is the recipient of many awards, including the Shirley Chisholm Award of recognition as the 1997 Woman of the Year.

Elizabeth W. Brooks

Philanthropist &
Community Leader

Dorothy Burrell is chairperson of the Social Action Committee of the Detroit Alumnae Chapter of Delta Sigma Theta Sorority, Inc. This committee ensures the awareness and involvement of the sorority in critical and pertinent political and social issues affecting its community. It has partnered with the Detroit-Wayne County Community Mental Health Agency to present several community forums on depression awareness and suicide prevention.

Additionally, Dorothy serves as chair of the City of Detroit Board of Canvassers. This board is responsible for the certification of the City's election results.

Dorothy is the fifth vice chairperson of the Michigan Democratic Party 14th Congressional District, and serves on screening committees for endorsements of political candidates. She is retired as a department manager from Wayne County government.

Dorothy received a Bachelor of Science degree in business administration and a Master of Arts degree in industrial relations from Wayne State University.

A native of Murfreesboro, Tennessee, Dorothy is the wife of John Burrell, the mother of Sharon Burrell and Donna Burrell-Jones, and the grandmother of Raven Careathers.

Dorothy Burrell

Chairperson,
Social Action Committee
Detroit Alumnae Chapter
Delta Sigma Theta Sorority, Inc.

Annie Carter

Board Member, District 3
Detroit Board of Education

Annie Carter is a certified board member of the Detroit Board of Education for Detroit Public Schools (DPS). As an elected official, she represents District 3 for the DPS and is the chairperson of the Committee on Parent and Community Involvement, Title I. Additionally, she is an activist for children.

Annie has served, past and present, for many organizations, including the National School Board Association (NSBA); the NSBA Council of Urban Boards of Education; the Michigan Association of School Boards (MASB); the District Parent Advisory Council; the Citywide Parent Organization; a Chapter 1 parent delegate for the State of Michigan; the Juvenile Accountability Advisory; the NAACP; the National Coalition of Title I; a delegate for the State of Michigan; the 14th Congressional Democratic Party; a former union member of DFT; the United Dairy Workers; Barton McFarlane Neighbor Association; Hope United Methodist Church; and many other committees within the Detroit Board of Education.

Annie has received several certificates, such as a leadership MASB in business industry. A native of Georgia, she is the proud wife of 39 years and mother of four children.

Harriet Carter

Director, Bureau Services
Detroit Metro Convention &
Visitors Bureau

Harriet Carter is director of bureau services for the Detroit Metro Convention & Visitors Bureau (DMCVB). She began her career with the DMCVB in 1989 as a sales account executive.

In her current role, Carter is responsible for developing customer service and membership programs and initiatives. Her position is critical in developing and maintaining relationships with customers such as the Society of Automotive Engineers, Alpha Kappa Alpha Sorority, Inc., the National Urban League and the National Baptist Convention, USA, whose choice of Detroit as a meeting destination brought considerable economic impact to the Detroit economy.

Carter has received several awards for her efforts in bringing major conventions to Detroit. She has been featured in several national publications, such as *Meetings & Conventions* magazine and "Who's Who in the Travel Industry" in *Dollars & Sense* magazine.

A graduate of Michigan State University, Carter has a Bachelor of Arts degree in international relations. She also earned two professional designations, certified meeting planner (CMP) and certified hospitality sales professional (CHSP).

Andrea Cole is the new executive director and chief executive officer of the Detroit-based Ethel & James Flinn Foundation. She is the first African American to hold this position. The Foundation is committed to improving the quality of life of those with mental illness by improving the quality, scope and delivery of mental health services. Andrea will provide the necessary leadership and vision to foster the growth and recognition of the Foundation as Michigan's philanthropic leader in the mental health field.

She was previously the first African-American chief financial officer of The Skillman Foundation, where she was responsible for all financial operations.

Andrea received both a master's degree and a Bachelor of Science degree in finance from Wayne State University. She is actively involved in her community and serves on several boards. She is also a member of the National Black MBA Association, the Institute of Management Accountants, the Foundation Financial Officers Group, the Association of Black Foundation Executives and Women in Philanthropy.

Married to Kelvin Cole, Andrea is the proud mother of two sons, Brandon and Christopher.

Andrea M. Cole

Executive Director &
Chief Executive Officer
Ethel & James Flinn Foundation

Bamidele Agbasegbe Demerson is director of exhibitions and research at the Charles H. Wright Museum of African American History. Prior to this, he served as the museum's curator of education.

A graduate of the University of Michigan, Demerson has conducted anthropological fieldwork in Nigeria, Brazil and the United States. His research interests include African-American culture and history, comparative social organization in Africa and the African diaspora, and political consciousness in visual art created by African Americans. Presented at domestic and international conferences, his research also appears in anthologies and periodicals.

Demerson has curated numerous exhibitions, including "New Eyes for Ancient Gods: Yoruba Orisa in Contemporary Art," and "Unmasked: Stereotypes in American Material Culture." He also collaborated in the development of the 22,000-square-foot, long-term exhibition, "And Still We Rise: Our Journey Through African American History and Culture" at the Wright Museum.

Demerson participates in the Paradise Valley Commemorative Park Working Group, serves on the board of directors of the National Conference of Artists, Inc., and provides consultative services to the Edo Arts and Cultural Heritage Institute, USA.

Bamidele Agbasegbe Demerson

Director, Exhibitions & Research
Charles H. Wright Museum of
African American History

DETROIT'S COMMUNITY LEADERS

Dr. Brazeal W. Dennard

Artistic Director Emeritus
The Brazeal Dennard
Choral Ensembles

Dr. Brazeal W. Dennard attended Detroit Public Schools, and completed his formal education at Wayne State University, earning a Master of Music Education degree. A retired supervisor of music from Detroit Public Schools, he also served as president of the National Association of Negro Musicians Inc. and the Detroit Musicians' Association.

Some of the honors Dennard has received include the Maynard Kline Choral Award from the Michigan chapter of the American Choral Directors Association, the Distinguished Alumni Arts Award from Wayne State University and the Dr. Alain Locke Award from Detroit Institute of Arts. He also received the Lifetime Musical Achievement award from the Detroit Symphony Orchestra, the Metropolitan Arts Complex Award and the African Diaspora Living Legend Award from California State University. He is also the founder of the *Classical Roots Series*.

Dennard received a Doctor of Humane Letters degree from Marygrove College. He also received an honorary Doctor of Music degree from Olivet College.

His choral arrangements are published by Shawnee Press, GIA Publishing Co. and Alliance Music Publications Inc. Alliance has established a choral series named for Dennard.

Dr. Alison J. Harmon

Program Director
The Skillman Foundation

Dr. Alison J. Harmon is a 30-year veteran educator. She has a Doctor of Education degree in educational administration, a Master of Education degree and a Bachelor of Science degree in education. Currently, she is a program director and education specialist for The Skillman Foundation, a private grant-making foundation that applies its resources to improve the lives of children in metropolitan Detroit.

Harmon is committed to participating in community activities. She is president of the Delta Research and Educational Foundation and a national executive board member of Delta Sigma Theta Sorority, Inc. She is also a member of the board of directors of the Detroit Area Pre-College Engineering Program and the Coleman Young Foundation, and an active member of Trinity Missionary Baptist Church in Pontiac.

Harmon is married to Robert F. Harmon Sr. They have two sons, Aaron, 21, an honors student at Bowling Green State University, and B.J., 25, a law student at the University of Michigan.

D r. Cassandra Joubert is vice president for community investment at the Community Foundation for Southeast Michigan. In this role, she oversees the foundation's $30 million annual grantmaking program. The foundation awards grants in the areas of arts and culture, economic development, education, health and human services in seven counties in southeast Michigan.

Prior to joining the Community Foundation, Joubert was senior program officer with the Ruth Mott Foundation in Flint, Michigan, where she managed the foundation's health promotion portfolio. She also served as director of strategic planning for Mott Children's Health Center, and as acting chief for the Michigan Office of Minority Health. Earlier this year, Joubert was appointed senior community fellow at Michigan State University. She is the author of an upcoming book, "Losing Control: Loving and Parenting a Black Child with Bipolar Disorder."

Joubert received a Doctor of Science degree in maternal and child health from the Johns Hopkins University School of Hygiene and Public Health, and a Bachelor of Science degree in psychology and child development from Howard University.

Cassandra Joubert, Sc.D.

Vice President, Community Investment
Community Foundation for
Southeast Michigan

V ersandra Jewel Kennebrew is executive director of Health and Fitness ICU, an association of holistic health professionals. In this position, she manages the Wellness Resource Center, which provides personal development and financial literacy coaching, and holistic health services in a relaxing environment. Under Versandra's leadership, ICU has introduced the concept of a holistic approach to optimal health to thousands through health fairs, life camps and expos across metro Detroit. She received the Spirit of Detroit Award in 2005 for her leadership and commitment to enhance the lives of Detroit residents.

Her media appearances include *The Detroit News*, the *Michigan Chronicle*, WXYZ Channel 7, *WGN Morning News*, *Access Health and Fitness Show*, *Mind Body & Soul*, *Cream of the Crop* and *MASSAGE Magazine*.

Versandra's most fulfilling role is teaching. Her instruction at the National Institute of Technology and Irene's Myomassology Institute has produced many massage professionals. She loves traveling, exploring the world, and teaching professionals and novices alike the art of touch.

Versandra Jewel Kennebrew

Executive Director
Health and Fitness ICU

Sgt. Richard C. Knox

Administrative Sergeant
Child Abuse
Detroit Police Department

Sergeant Richard C. Knox is a 24-year veteran of the Detroit Police Department. A native Detroiter, he is proud to be married to the beautiful and loving Alice Faye, and is the father of two lovely daughters, Amelia and Lydia Shine.

Promoted to the rank of sergeant in 2004, Richard is currently the administrative sergeant at Child Abuse. Child Abuse is responsible for the investigations of cruelty or neglect issues concerning the children of Detroit. Child Abuse also has a close working relationship with Protective Services in helping families when the need arises.

Richard received a bachelor's degree in criminal justice administration from the University of Phoenix, and is a candidate for an MBA in the summer of 2008. He is a member of Kappa Alpha Psi Fraternity, Inc. He attends The Church of Jesus Christ of Latter-Day Saints in northwest Detroit, where he serves as the elder quorum president.

Richard's philosophy is very simple, and is expressed by what George Benson said in song, "I believe the children are our future. Teach them well and let them lead the way."

Lt. Ilaseo Lewis

Central Events
Detroit Police Department

Lieutenant Ilaseo Lewis was born in 1953 to Paul and Arcola Lewis. His parents, lured by the automobile industry, came to Detroit from Alabama in 1949. The Lewis family grew and thrived around the influence of Ilaseo's father's involvement with Local 600 of the United Auto Workers. His parents were active in the labor movement and the civil rights movement. In later years, Ilaseo also became active in political and social causes.

Ilaseo graduated from Cass Technical High School. In 1972 he attended Wayne State University, where he served on the Student Faculty Council, was president of the Association of Black Students and was a founding member of the Association of Black Communicators. In the mid-70s, he worked for several years as a volunteer with WDET-FM radio station and with Project BAIT (Black Awareness in Television).

Ilaseo is currently a 25-year veteran lieutenant with the Detroit Police Department. He considers himself an ambassador for the city of Detroit. He can often be seen in downtown Detroit at major events wearing a white hat and a welcoming smile.

K. Kendall Mathews is a major in The Salvation Army. He was commissioned as a Salvation Army officer in 1991 from the Central Territory College for officer training in Chicago. He is also a certified social worker manager within the National Network for Social Work Managers, and has been a certified social worker in Michigan since 1983. Additionally, he has a diplomate status with the American Psychotherapy Association and is a certified relationship specialist.

Mathews has served in The Salvation Army as a corps officer (pastor) in the inner city of Detroit for five years and at the Pontiac Corps of North Oakland County for five years. He has served as the divisional secretary for the Eastern Michigan divisional headquarters in the central territory of The Salvation Army since 2001. He was assigned to be the Detroit city commander and the metro Detroit area coordinator.

Mathews has written several articles for *Officer Magazine* and *The War Cry* of The Salvation Army, and is known for his passionate spirit for the lost. He and his wife, Major Katrina Mathews, have five children.

K. Kendall Mathews

Major
The Salvation Army

Tracey Theodoria Miree-Marks assumes many responsibilities in her commitment to achieve full accessibility by connecting the global hearing majority to the deaf, hard of hearing and deaf/blind minority cultures.

Tracey is actively implementing services in the Detroit Public Schools to provide visual language education interpreting, while setting precedents in the Wayne County Judicial System for legal interpreting services. She plays a vital role in the Homeland Security CEPIN Project, protecting the safety of the communities. Successfully petitioning to the Detroit City Council, she has made a tremendous impact with her "campaigning for full accessibility."

Tracey has received numerous awards and honors for her professional community affiliations and involvement, and is now making her mark on Capitol Hill by lobbying and advocating for the rights of the people she serves. She is a member of the Disability Task Force, and a member of DDOT's Paratransit Appeals Board and the Citizens Review Committee.

Tracey is inspirited by the enormous support from both the hearing and nonhearing communities to be the best at creating value in our society.

Tracey T. Miree-Marks

Founder & President
Connections for Deaf Citizens, Inc.

Sgt. Elton Moore

Commanding Officer,
Tactical Operations Unit
Detroit Police Department

Sergeant Elton Moore is the commanding officer of the Detroit Police Tactical Operations Unit. Detroit Police Tactical Operations is responsible for the assistance in planning all large-scale events that occur in the city of Detroit. Such events include the Detroit Free Press Marathon, the International Fireworks, the Thanksgiving Day Parade and the Belle Isle Grand Prix, to name a few.

A 30-year veteran of the Detroit Police Department, Moore has had the pleasure of working at the 4th Precinct, the Tactical Services Section, Court Liaison and Tactical Operations.

Moore believes in the city of Detroit. While in the planning stage of events hosted by the city, he and Tactical Operations try to place Detroit in the brightest light possible, so the world can recognize a true gem.

Rev. V. Lonnie Peek Jr.

District Director of Comparative
Religious and Cultural Studies
Wayne County Community
College District

The Reverend V. Lonnie Peek Jr. is an instructor, professor and ordained minister. A previous department chair of the Black Studies Department, he is currently district director of religious studies at Wayne County Community College District. Peek founded and served as the first president of Wayne State University's Association of Black Students in 1967, serving as a springboard into Detroit's political and civic arena. He later founded the Concerned Citizens Council, a citywide advocate organization.

Peek serves on the board of New Detroit, the Detroit Economic Growth Corporation and the Detroit Riverfront Conservancy. He has worked with mayors Coleman Young, Dennis Archer and Kwame Kilpatrick; served as executive assistant to Governor James Blanchard; and is chief executive officer of eBusiness Strategies and Diversified Temporaries. He serves on the executive committee of the Council of Baptist Pastors, and is the assistant pastor at Greater Christ Baptist Church.

Peek is a radio talk show host and columnist with the *Michigan Chronicle*, appearing on local and national television. Married to Eunice, he has four children, Monique, Lonnie III, Ricky and Ki.

Sergeant Conway Petty has been a member of the Detroit Police Department for 30 years. He has had a variety of assignments, including, but not limited to, precinct patrol, special crimes (gang squad), homicide and organized crime, and is currently assigned to the Tactical Operations Unit. The Tactical Operations Unit has the task of planning and assessing major events hosted by Detroit. Some of those events include the N.A.I.A.S. (North American International Auto Show), as well as visits of foreign dignitaries and heads of state. This division also assists in local emergency evacuation and international emergency evacuation training for the Canadian border.

At the end of the day when his job is complete, Petty believes that any patron attending an event within the great city of Detroit, no matter what their geographic background, will leave feeling they came to the greatest city in the country and had the greatest time.

Sgt. Conway Petty

Tactical Operations Unit
Detroit Police Department

Arlene M. Robinson, the first black Girl Scout executive in Michigan, has served as chief executive officer of the Girl Scouts of Metro Detroit (GSMD) Council since 2001. Of 312 councils nationwide, GSMD is the seventh-largest, providing opportunities to more than 30,000 girls in the metro area. Girls, ages 5 to 17, take advantage of programs, including computer safety, diversity awareness, human sexuality, substance abuse prevention, conflict resolution and a myriad of age-appropriate services.

Previously, Robinson served as a City of Detroit mayoral appointee, building the Youth Department from the ground up. Her past positions include administration vice president of the Detroit Economic Growth Corporation, president of Efficacy Detroit and president of the Community Training & Development Corporation.

A licensed counselor, Robinson holds a Master of Arts degree from the University of Detroit, and a Wharton School executive leadership development certificate. She has advanced education in business administration from Wayne State University.

Robinson served as the first black working president of the Junior League of Birmingham. She works on numerous boards, commissions and committees, and has received recognition for her community service.

Arlene M. Robinson

Chief Executive Officer
Girl Scouts of Metro Detroit Council

Janice L. Rowley

Founder & Executive Director
Amachi, Incorporated

Janice L. Rowley is founder and executive director of Amachi, Incorporated, a nonprofit 501(c)(3) educational corporation whose mission is to provide young people with the self-knowledge and life skills they require to bring forth the blessing of their fully realized potential. Through a series of workshops, adult facilitators enlighten, encourage and empower young people to make good decisions about their lives and the lives of those around them.

Janice received a Bachelor of Arts degree in humanities from Michigan State University, and a Master of Arts degree in American history and black studies from The Ohio State University. She is currently completing the coursework for a Doctor of Philosophy degree in history. She has been teaching and mentoring for more than 20 years on the collegiate and high school levels.

A native of Detroit, Janice is also a high school English and history teacher with Detroit Public Schools. She has been recognized by students and administrators as a dedicated and influential teacher, and has been featured multiple times in *Who's Who Among America's Teachers*.

Claudette Y. Smith, Ph.D.

Executive Director
Coleman A. Young Foundation

Dr. Claudette Y. Smith is executive director of the Coleman A. Young Foundation. In this role, she oversees an organization that provides college scholarships and other programs for personal and academic growth to Detroit's youth.

Before joining the Coleman A. Young Foundation, Smith was program officer at The Skillman Foundation. She came to Skillman after ten years in various positions with New Jersey's Department of Higher Education. She previously worked as a statistician/demographer for the United Nations in New York City.

Smith earned a doctorate degree in sociology and demography from Princeton University, a master's degree in demography from the London School of Economics and Political Science, and a bachelor's degree from the University of the West Indies. She is an adjunct professor of Wayne State University's sociology department. She sits on several boards, and is a graduate of Leadership Detroit Class XXV.

Smith is married to Locksley A. Smith, and is the proud mother of a daughter, Najwa Smith Schmookler, who is married to Benjamin; and a son, Dia Smith.

D r. Gerald K. Smith has spent his entire professional life as an advocate for families, youth and communities, making a substantial difference in the lives of many young people. As president and chief executive officer of the Detroit Youth Foundation, and in his day-to-day development of comprehensive, collaborative, community-based initiatives, he has capitalized on his passion for providing resources and services for young people.

Smith is the recipient of numerous awards and honors, and serves on the following boards that are committed to addressing the needs of young people, families and communities: Health Alliance Plan, New Detroit, Inc., Black Family Development, Inc., the United Way for Southeastern Michigan and the National Association of Black Social Workers.

Smith holds a bachelor's degree in history and government education from Ohio University, a master's degree in education administration and guidance counseling from Xavier University, a master's degree in sociology and urban affairs from the University of Detroit Mercy, and a Doctor of Education degree in administration and supervision from Wayne State University.

He is the husband of Dr. Ann C. Smith.

Gerald K. Smith, Ed.D.

President & Chief Executive Officer
Detroit Youth Foundation

M arie L. Thornton is a certified board member at-large of the Detroit Board of Education for Detroit Public Schools (DPS). As an elected official, she is committed to improve her board leadership skills, and she received three outstanding achievement awards from the Michigan Association of School Boards: an Award of Distinction, an Award of Merit and a Certified Board Member Award.

Marie has two sons that attended DPS. As a parent, she was actively involved in her children's education, attending PTA, LSCO and school board meetings on a regular basis. She learned about school policies, procedures and Title I programs, and educated many parents on school policies and procedures. Marie is an advocate for both regular and special education students.

In 1996 she spoke out against the state takeover of DPS, and in 2005 she helped organize citizens in and around the city of Detroit to prevent the continuation of the state takeover after six years, by defeating Proposal E. Currently, she hosts a weekly talk show on WHPR 88.1/TV33 to share educational update information with citizens of Detroit.

Marie L. Thornton

Board Member At-Large
Detroit Board of Education

Ophelia Twine-Henry

Program Associate
Community Capacity Building
New Detroit, Inc.

Ophelia Twine-Henry is an accomplished sales and marketing professional and consultant who has switched to the nonprofit sector. Starting with New Detroit, Inc. in 2006 as conference coordinator for the Leadership Summit on Race, she currently serves as program associate for the Community Capacity Building Focus Area. She works with community and faith-based organizations to help build, strengthen and enhance their organizational capacity to meet the needs in their community.

Ophelia's success and longevity in the hospitality industry can be attributed to building rapport with clients, having clients feel appreciated and taking care of clients with respect and integrity. She volunteers her spare time as a board member for the Wayne County Chapter of Mothers Against Drunk Driving, and will serve as the liaison with the Michigan Baptist Fellowship as Detroit hosts the National Baptist Congress on Christian Education in 2009.

A native of Milledgeville, Georgia, Ophelia is married to Edward, and is a mother of three adult children and a grandmother of five.

Alison Vaughn

Founder & Chief Executive Officer
Jackets for Jobs, Inc.

Alison Vaughn is the founder and chief executive officer of Jackets for Jobs, Inc., which is a nonprofit organization that provides employment etiquette, career skills training and professional clothes to low-income individuals. Since opening the doors in 2000, the organization has assisted more than 6,000 individuals with employment. This organization has been supported and applauded by Donald Trump, ABC's *The View*, NBC's *Today* show and Oprah's *O* magazine. A highlight of her career was the distinct honor of ringing the closing bell on NASDAQ.

Alison received a Bachelor of Science degree from Michigan State University, and graduated from The Women's Campaign School at Yale University. She is active with the NAACP and was a candidate for the 2006 Michigan Senate.

A former model, Alison was a Miss America Petite Pageant contestant, *Jet* magazine beauty, auto show model and high school homecoming queen.

In her spare time, she enjoys traveling, reading and attending sporting events. She is a loyal Detroit Lions season ticket holder, and is a member of the Top Ladies of Distinction and Distinguished Women in International Service.

Kimberly Minter Walker is Eastern Regional director of Operation HOPE – Banking on Our Future program. She oversees the nationally recognized premiere financial literacy program for low- to moderate-income youth in Detroit, Baltimore, Atlanta, New York, Philadelphia, Pittsburgh, Boston and Washington, D.C. She supervises staff in the areas of partnership recruitment and retention, volunteerism and fundraising efforts.

Kimberly is a member of the Black MBA Association, a graduate of Leadership Macomb, and has served as a board member for several nonprofit organizations.

A native Detroiter, Kimberly (whose maiden name is Stodghill) still remains loyal to the many friendships and memories from Gesu and Immaculata High School. She received a Bachelor of Arts degree in economics and English from Albion College in Albion, Michigan. She also received Master of Business Administration and Master of Public Administration degrees in finance and urban planning from Seattle University in Seattle, Washington.

Married to William Walker, Kimberly is the proud mother of Jerome Hayward Minter II, Kristopher Ian Minter, Kaelin Iman Minter and William Benjamin Walker.

Kimberly Minter Walker

Eastern Regional Director
Banking on Our Future
Operation HOPE

Geneva J. Williams, president of City Connect Detroit, continues to be a catalyst for positive change in Detroit. Under her leadership, City Connect Detroit has evolved into an organization recognized for its cross-sector collaborative work, convening nonprofit, private and public sectors to address pressing community issues.

With more than 25 years of leadership experience, Geneva has led three major nonprofits in Detroit. She was co-founder, and vice president and chief operating officer of United Way Community Services. She was also the first African-American, and first female president and chief executive officer of United Community Services of Metropolitan Detroit.

Appointed to Governor Granholm's Mentor Michigan Leadership Council, Geneva serves as the education chair of Mayor Kilpatrick's NEXT Detroit Transformation Team. She is also on the board of directors for New Detroit, the Detroit Economic Growth Corporation and the Music Hall.

Recently identified by the Black Women Contracting Association as Detroit's Best Community Leader, Geneva received a master's degree from Bryn Mawr College and an undergraduate degree from Morgan State University.

She resides in Detroit with her husband, Otha, and they have three children.

Geneva J. Williams

President
City Connect Detroit

Quarter to Midnite

Quarter to Midnite is one of the top Jazz/R&B bands in the City. What makes this band so unique is their down-to-earth appeal. It's not only the smooth sound of the music, but their ability to transfer their energy and enjoyment to their audience in every performance.

For your next event, spend an evening with us.

WWW.QUARTERTOMIDNITE.COM • MIDNITEONE4U@YAHOO.COM

(313) 445-1831

enliven

recreate

Media

DETROIT'S
MEDIA PROFESSIONALS

inspire

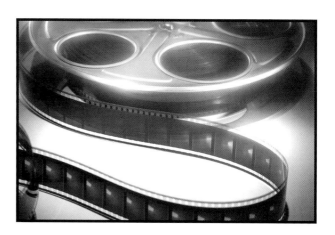

captivate

delight

imagine

amuse

illuminate

innovative

Karen Addison

Director of Music & Promotions
WGPR "The Rhythm" 107.5 FM

D. Michelle AliDinar

President &
Chief Executive Officer
Educational Television Programs
Public Access Channel 68

Karen Addison is director of promotions and music for WGPR "The Rhythm" 107.5 FM in Detroit. In this position, she oversees the schedule in which all the music played over the WGPR airwaves is ordered. Also, as the promotions director, she oversees all promotions carried out for WGPR. Every promotion that is carried out with "The Rhythm" must receive her approval.

As a stand-up comedian, Addison has graced comedy stages on HBO's *Def Comedy Jam*, BET's *Comic View*, MTV and A&E, and reigned as a three-time *Star Search* champion.

Currently, Addison performs at the comedy cafe every Friday inside of Greektown Casino in downtown Detroit.

A native of Seattle, Washington, Addison is the proud mother of one, Michael Addison Jr. She loves being all natural, simply organic.

Michelle AliDinar is president and chief executive officer of educational television programs. She is also the executive producer and news anchor of *Empowerment News* on Comcast Cable's Public Access Channel 68, and brings more than 15 years of television experience to Comcast viewers with national and international reporting.

Michelle has recently returned to her native Detroit after spending three years working as an executive television producer and host in Dubai, United Arab Emirates. Upon returning, she witnessed the plight of many people in the Detroit area and created *Empowerment News*. The program is designed to connect people with resources by disseminating news and information to empower viewers educationally, financially and socially. She is pleased that *Empowerment News* makes a positive impact on people's lives.

Michelle also sits on the board of directors of a nonprofit organization that offers shelter and legal assistance to women and children of domestic violence, and is active in many volunteer projects in the community.

Sharif AliDinar

Vice President
Educational Television Programs
Public Access Channel 68

David Bangura

General Sales Manager
WMYD-TV20 Detroit

Sharif AliDinar is the vice president of educational television programs for Public Access Channel 68. He is also co-producer and news anchor on *Empowerment News*, a community service news program that has been in production since 2005 and airs on Comcast Cable's Public Access Channel 68. His mission is to provide news and information to adults and youths regarding scholarships, financial assistance and events that help viewers become self-sufficient and active in the community.

A native of Los Angeles, California, Sharif has traveled extensively internationally. He studied in Spain for two years, and lived in Dubai, United Arab Emirates prior to coming to Michigan in 2004. He encourages all students to consider a study abroad program in their academic curriculum.

Sharif is currently a Phi Theta Kappa honor student at Wayne State University and the recipient of the Presidential Scholarship. He has served as vice president and treasurer of the Student Government Association at Wayne County Community College District, and has received several awards for volunteering in the community.

Since March of 2005, when David Bangura was elevated to the position of general sales manager for WMYD-TV20 Detroit, he has been leading the station's sales team. With his forward-thinking strategies, he is strengthening TV20's position in the advertising and business community, and taking the station to the next level.

Bangura previously served as local sales manager, and later as national sales manager, for TV20. He then joined WKBD-TV as general station manager before returning home to TV20. Prior to joining the staff at TV20, Bangura worked for five years as a senior account executive at WJBK-TV Fox 2. His extensive background includes experience in investment finance.

Bangura holds a degree in business administration from Wayne State University. He is a member of the Adcrafter Club, and is involved in various youth education projects in the Detroit community.

Bangura was born and raised in Dublin, Ireland, until age ten, when his family moved back to Sierra Leone, West Africa. Later, he spent two years in Berlin, Germany, before coming to Michigan. He is fluent in German and Creole.

Chuck Bennett

Society Columnist
The Detroit News

Jay Black

On-Air Personality
WDMK 105.9 Kiss FM
Radio One Detroit

Chuck Bennett's journalism career is a series of firsts. He was the first to contribute regular R&B record reviews to *The Detroit News*. He went on to gain notoriety at *The Detroit News* for innovative fashion presentations that always used multicultural models, another rarity for that publication.

Today, still trailblazing, Bennett is the only African-American male in the country working as a society columnist for a major metropolitan daily. His column appears every Tuesday in *The Detroit News*. He is also editor-in-chief of *The Real Scoop*, Detroit's sassy online magazine.

Bennett was a fundraising consultant for Detroit Holiday Meals on Wheels, and more than $1 million was raised during his five-year tenure. He teamed with Christian Dior to raise money for Beaumont Women's Heart Center and Lighthouse PATH, and planned successful fundraising events for Detroit Community Health Connection, and the City of Detroit's HIV/AIDS Awareness and Prevention Program.

In addition to his community involvement, Bennett was honored in Martell's Rise Above campaign, and is a highly sought-after emcee for many of the most prestigious fundraising events in southeast Michigan.

Jay Black is a connoisseur of music. His broad music knowledge has enabled him with the opportunity to make his presence known and felt during some of the highest profile industry events in the metropolitan area.

A native Detroiter, Jay got his start in the industry by working as a disc jockey (DJ) everywhere he could. His DJ skills afforded him the nickname the "Junglist." He says he got the name by being the first DJ at the time to make jungle music, a form of music found and played widely in Europe, and acceptable for clubs and radio in the U.S.

Jay has been with Radio One Detroit for nine years. He can currently be heard during *Kisses After Dark* on WDMK 105.9 Kiss FM, weeknights from 7 p.m. to 12 a.m.

Sheri Clark Brooks

Filmmaker & Host
DWIFTV/WHPR 88.1 TV 33

Travon P. Brooks

General Manager
WLPC-TV26 Detroit

Sheri Brooks is host and executive producer of the award-winning literary and entertainment television show *Wordz in Motion*, and is chief executive officer of Dynasty Publications, an independent press. The principal of Hot Property Entertainment, LLC and managing partner of Kinfolk Castle Films, she recently completed the documentary *Film Diva Dossier: A Modern Perspective on Female Filmmakers in Michigan*. As a television producer and filmmaker, Sheri is responsible for developing and producing quality entertainment projects that have a positive impact on the community.

Sheri is actively involved with several organizations, including NABW, Writer's Legacy and the National Association of Black Female Executives in Music and Entertainment. As executive chair of Michigan's Women in Film and Television, she uses her position to help educate and create positive images of women in the media. Further promoting Detroit, in June of 2008 DWIFTV will host the first annual Detroit Oscar's honoring achievements of women in film and television.

The native Detroiter is an advocate for literacy and host for the Writer's Legacy Annual Conference and Awards Gala. She resides in Michigan with her family.

Travon P. Brooks is general manager for WLPC-TV26 Detroit, an affiliate of the Christian Television Network (CTN). In this capacity, she oversees the daily operations of the station, managing more than ten personnel. Travon's career began as an intern with CTN, and she later became the production coordinator. In 2000 she became station manager for WLPN-TV61 New Orleans, and in 2005 she assumed general manager duties at WLPC. In June of 2006, she was featured in the *Michigan Chronicle* for her accomplishments at the station.

Travon often volunteers as a career exploration speaker through the Learning for Life program, sharing her experience of earning a Bachelor of Science degree in chemical engineering from Michigan Technological University and working in communications. She is also pursuing a certificate in worship arts at Destiny School of Ministry in Roseville, scheduled for completion in May of 2008.

Travon is the proud daughter of Victoria Forte, with whom she enjoys teaching Sunday school at Second Canaan Baptist Church, and Ronald Brooks, a Ford Motors employee of more than 25 years.

Katrina Brown

President & Chief Executive Officer
City Talk Magazine

Gary Chandler

Disc Jockey
WHTD-FM HOT 102.7
Radio One Detroit

Katrina Brown is president and chief executive officer of *City Talk Magazine*. She has a talented board, and with community influence, this nonprofit organization has assisted in the growth of Detroit. Katrina is also chair of City Talk Future Leaders Program, an apprenticeship program for youth in the community to assist in their career path and address the overall image of today's youth.

In 2005 Katrina developed Expertise Services Consulting Group, which is a business-consulting firm. After working in the community, she realized that the majority of minority-owned businesses were failing due to a lack of structure in their organizations. Using thought and consideration, she developed a plan to assist the community by creating tips and techniques to influence productivity through a free monthly publication called *City Talk Magazine*.

Katrina began her education at Alabama State University and majored in biology education. She later returned to Detroit, and earned a Bachelor of Science degree in business management and a Master of Business Administration degree from the University of Phoenix.

Born and raised in Detroit, Katrina has a daughter, Kayla.

"Detroit's Bad Boy" DJ Gary Chandler has been in and around the music business for 23 years. Best known for his versatility, Gary can rock a party whether the attendees are 8 or 80.

The way he got started is a little unconventional. His best friend, who was a local DJ at the time, left town and happened to leave his turntables with Gary. Once he returned, he was astonished to see that Gary was even better than he was.

Capitalizing on his newfound skill, Gary soon hit the streets, clubs, and any party that would have him. After becoming the house DJ for the well-known Club UBQ, his reputation began to precede him. In 1991 a local urban radio station contacted Gary and asked him to come onboard.

Gary has been with Radio One Detroit for four years. In his spare time, he enjoys collecting eclectic music, DVDs (he is a movie buff), hanging out with family and friends, and shopping. Look for him in his next life move as a music producer.

COCO

On-Air Personality
FM 98 WJLB

Frankie Darcell

On-Air Personality
WMXD Mix 92.3 FM

COCO is an on-air personality on the very popular morning show of FM 98 WJLB. Being on the air with Detroit's No. 1 station for hip-hop and R&B has afforded COCO the opportunity to spread her message of strength, love and empowerment to her female listeners, as well as reach out to her male fans. She has productively utilized her status and influence to not only entertain, but to also educate and inspire. The response received from on-air segments like "COCO's Community Cypher" led her to start an initiative called COCO's House: Where Love is More Than a Word.

COCO has received numerous awards for her craft, as well as for her community involvement, investment and activism. She has received recognition from listeners, peers, city council, the mayor of Detroit and the governor of Michigan.

A native of Highland Park, Michigan, COCO is mother to Tyffanie, and grandmother to the wonderfully active Jakob.

Before moving to Detroit in 1993, Frankie Darcell started her career at Morgan State University's WEAA FM in Baltimore as an engineer. Since then, she has worked in Raleigh-Durham and Charlotte, North Carolina, as a music director and assistant program director.

Frankie is the host of the award-winning shows *The Mid-day Mix* and *Sunday Morning Talk of the Town*. An author, lecturer and businesswoman, she has appeared on four magazine covers, and has been featured in more than 65 newspaper articles and publications. Frankie also appears frequently on local and national television and radio programs, discussing topics that matter to the community, specifically, issues relating to the quality of life for women and children. She has a unique way of inspiring and empowering her listeners and readers, often with great humor.

A graduate of Morgan State University, Frankie has a Bachelor of Arts degree in telecommunications. She is a member of Alpha Kappa Alpha Sorority, Inc., and the recipient of several major industry awards and recognitions. Her greatest achievement is being a mom. Her daughter, Phallon, gives her the greatest joy.

Claudette de la Haye

Owner & Editor-in-Chief
MetroCosmo, Detroit-Windsor Edition

Karen Dumas

President
Images & Ideas, Inc.

Claudette de la Haye is owner, freelance reporter, photographer and editor-in-chief of the first and only transcontinental, intermodal magazine in metro Detroit. The magazine, entitled *MetroCosmo, Detroit-Windsor Edition*, is attributed to her beloved late father, Lewis de la Haye, of Port Morant, Jamaica. The ambassadorial civic sense of pride Louis shared with Claudette was a constant source of adventure, tourism, cricket, soccer and other sports shared throughout the family, church and community.

Claudette's love for speaking French, European culture, haute cuisine, couture and design in fashion print is a testament to her patriotic commitment to Ontario and Michigan. Her gumption, commitment and integrity are keys to the success of the online *MetroCosmo* magazine.

Born and raised in the United Kingdom, this Afro-Caribbean European native resides in Oak Park, Michigan. Claudette has matriculated her studies in accounting, computers, economics, French, sociology, and English literature and language between two continents.

Claudette is the proud grand aunt of Mya, Alyssia, Kymani and Kyle Smith. She is striving to share family values and traditions throughout the history of the de la Haye family.

Karen Dumas is a columnist for the *Michigan Chronicle* and *The Michigan FrontPage*, host of the television show *Next Detroit*, co-host of *The Art Blackwell* radio show, host of radio programs *Artifacts* and *Jazz at the Center*, and president of her own public relations firm.

She served as director of culture, art and tourism for the City of Detroit, and as director of community relations for Mayor Kwame M. Kilpatrick.

Dumas joined the Kilpatrick administration after serving as president of her public relations firm for more than 14 years, where she served an impressive list of corporate, entertainment and community clients. She returned to private practice after finishing her tenure with the Kilpatrick administration and having her own talk radio show, *Up Front with Karen Dumas*.

Dumas serves on the Michigan Film Commission and the Communication Committee for the Detroit Riverfront Conservancy. The City of Detroit, State of Michigan and several Who's Who entities have recognized her achievements.

Dumas graduated with a bachelor's degree in merchandising from Michigan State University. She and her husband, Timothy Cook, reside in Detroit with their two children.

Greg Dunmore

Co-Partner
Pulsebeat.tv
Jazzjewels.tv

Mildred Gaddis

Host, *Inside Detroit*
News Talk 1200 WCHB AM
Radio One Detroit

Greg Dunmore is co-partner with Joel Boykin of Pulsebeat.tv and Jazzjewels.tv, an online broadcast quality entertainment media outlet and special markets promotional agency. This Web-based media outlet has worked in partnership with such companies as Toyota Motor's Scion Division and Comcast Cable. Dunmore is also co-chair of the Arts and Entertainment Task Force for the National Association of Black Journalists.

Ivy-League-educated and multitalented, Dunmore graduated from Cornell University and the National University of Mexico. He is the former "On Detroit Hot Happenings" columnist for *The Detroit News*, and producer and writer of the Emmy-nominated *Detroit Jazz Jewels* television special, starring pianist and singer Jo Thompson and vocalist Harvey Thompson.

Dunmore is the former vice chair of the Detroit Cable Commission, and a former correspondent for BET. He co-published with Kim Moore the *Hue* and *Venhue* magazines. Additionally, he is remembered by many Detroiters as being the "About Town" columnist for the *Michigan Chronicle*.

Dunmore's most recent accomplishment is being selected by Aretha Franklin to help cast her upcoming musical life story.

A 29-year radio veteran, Mildred Gaddis has been described by the *Detroit Free Press* as one of ten African Americans to watch in Detroit.

Listeners consistently tune in to her sometimes no-nonsense, but warm and inspiring style, as the host of *Inside Detroit* on News Talk 1200 WCHB AM weekday mornings from 6 to 10 a.m. According to Arbitron Ratings Services, Gaddis continues to rank as the top morning show host with listeners who spend the longest time listening.

A native of Hattiesburg, Mississippi, Gaddis arrived in Detroit 18 years ago, building an immensely successful career in Detroit radio. Her skills earned her the opportunity to travel to China with former Detroit Mayor Dennis Archer and former Michigan State Governor John Engler.

Gaddis was named Professional Woman of the Year by the National Association of Negro Business Women's Organization. She is also a member of the Detroit Urban League board.

A graduate of Texas Southern University, Gaddis is the proud parent of Khia, a freshman newly enrolled at a historically black college/university.

Gary Gunter

General Sales Manager
WDMK 105.9 Kiss FM
Radio One Detroit

Angelo B. Henderson

Host, *Your Voice with Angelo Henderson*
News Talk 1200 WCHB AM
Radio One Detroit

Gary Gunter is a 12-year veteran of radio sales/marketing, and has received numerous awards and accolades for his accomplishments and sales successes in the media industry. Prior to coming to Radio One Detroit, Gary started his own marketing solutions firm, GEE Media Group, in Chicago, Illinois. The company specialized in providing multi-platform marketing solutions for Fortune 1000 companies utilizing event, print, direct mail and grass roots marketing.

Gary began his career as a sales account executive for Clear Channel Radio Chicago in 1995. He caught on fast to the newly created term in the radio industry "NTR," non-traditional revenue, and began to develop record-breaking NTR numbers for the company.

In 1999 Clear Channel promoted Gary into sales management as local sales manager for its top radio property in Detroit, FM 98 WJLB. In 2003 Cox Broadcasting recruited Gary to general sales manager for the top adult urban radio property, WCFB Star 94.5FM in Orlando, Florida.

Gary has a Bachelor of Science degree in radio and television communications, with a minor in journalism, from Southern Illinois University in Carbondale, Illinois.

Your Voice with Angelo Henderson airs weeknights on News Talk 1200 WCHB AM from 7 to 9 p.m.

The Pulitzer Prize-winning host has a wealth of experience in journalism, ranging from *The Wall Street Journal* to *The Detroit News*, the *St. Petersburg Times* in Florida, and *The Courier-Journal* in Louisville, Kentucky. Named one of 39 African-American Achievers To Watch In The Next Millennium by *Success Guide* magazine, Angelo has also been honored by Columbia University as one of the nation's best reporters on race and ethnicity in America.

He was an ordained deacon at Hartford Memorial Baptist Church in 1999, and was ordained and licensed as a member of the clergy under Pastor Charles G. Adams in December of 2003. Now, Angelo is the associate pastor of worship, vision and emerging ministries at Hope United Methodist Church in Southfield.

Angelo earned a Bachelor of Arts degree in journalism in 1985 from the University of Kentucky, and is a member of Phi Beta Sigma Fraternity, Inc.

He is married to Felecia Dixon Henderson. The couple and their son reside in Pontiac, Michigan.

DJ Jinx

On-Air Personality
WHTD-FM HOT 102.7

Carolyn Johnson-James

Program Director &
Executive Director Assistant
WPGR "The Rhythm" 107.5 FM

D J Jinx has been in the music business since 2001. He is one of the youngest disc jockeys (DJ) in Detroit to be on the radio.

Jinx was inspired by the DJ battle scene in the movie *Juice*. He would mimic the scratches and tricks for weeks at a time. After months of practicing, he met one of the members of the Mixx Mobb, Gary Chandler. Chandler and his friends repeatedly pushed Jinx to enter DJ competitions around Detroit.

Capitalizing on his newfound skill, Jinx started throwing parties, entering battles and making a name for himself. He became a house DJ for different Detroit clubs, and his reputation began to precede him. In 2005 he won a DJ competition for 105.9 Jamz, now WHTD-FM HOT 102.7, a local urban radio station. This gave Jinx a chance to shine on special occasions, such as Summer Jamz 2005 and *The Holiday Mix Tape*. In 2006 the station contacted Jinx and asked him to come onboard.

In his spare time, Jinx loves collecting and watching DVDs, hanging out with family and friends, and perfecting his skill.

C arolyn Johnson-James is program director for WGPR "The Rhythm" 107.5 FM in Detroit. She has been with WGPR for more than 17 years.

Carolyn is the person who decides the broadcast content of a radio station. Typically, this person will decide what selections to make based on a target demographic. In a radio station, a program director could also be responsible for maintaining station identity. Carolyn is responsible for the sound on the radio station at all times and for the content of the station's broadcast day, including which announcers work there and what they say. Her job is to make sure that the station sounds as good as it can, since everything comes down to survey ratings. This career can be snuffed out in a heartbeat if the director's work does not produce good radio survey ratings for the company, but Carolyn knows her music.

Born in Detroit, Carolyn is married with four children.

Keith Jones

On-Air Personality
WHTD-FM HOT 102.7
Radio One Detroit

Catherine Kelly

Publisher
Michigan Citizen

Keith Jones began his career at the young age of 11 years old by singing in the youth choir. Shortly thereafter he was introduced to hip-hop. He immediately took a liking to working as a disc jockey (DJ), making mix tapes for his buddies while in junior high school and spinning at school dances.

Keith continued to work as an emcee and DJ until his true calling presented itself in the form of a Cleveland on-air personality by the name of Lynn Tolliver. He would listen to Lynn faithfully, and soon decided he wanted to be an on-air talent like his idol. Upon high school graduation, Keith enrolled at Columbus State Community College, majoring in business management with aspirations to own and run his own radio station. In the fall of his sophomore year, he began his internship with a local Ohio radio station.

Keith is a member of Alpha Phi Alpha Fraternity, Inc. His community service includes speaking to students as well as working with less-privileged families.

Keith is also a devoted husband and father.

Catherine Kelly is the publisher of the *Michigan Citizen* newspaper. The *Michigan Citizen* is a black media company focused on art, information, technology, social, environmental and economic justice.

At the age of 33, Catherine has had years of media experience. She was the managing editor for Russell Simmons' *Oneworld* magazine and entertainment editor for the now defunct African-American lifestyle publication *Savoy*. She has freelanced for a diverse set of magazines, including *Interview*, *The Source*, *Heart and Soul*, *Complex* and worked for *Vibe* magazine during its launch.

In the 1990s, Catherine was the technology editor for the urban business-to-business publication *Impact247*, and was the director of retail operations at Platform.net. At Platform, she managed international hip-hop and skate brands, such as Ecko Unlimited, Triple 5 Soul and Pervert.

Catherine graduated from Renaissance High School in Detroit and Eugene Lang College of the New School for Social Research in New York City. The *Michigan Citizen* was founded by her parents Charles and Teresa Kelly in 1978.

Lady BG

Assistant Program Director &
On-Air Personality
WDMK 105.9 Kiss FM
Radio One Detroit

Valerie D. Lockhart

Publisher & Executive Editor
Detroit Native Sun

Lady BG joined the Radio One family at the inception of Kiss FM in August of 1999 as an on-air personality and assistant program director. She has lived and worked in the industry in Detroit for more than 12 years.

Lady BG was born and raised in Institute, West Virginia, a small college community that surrounds West Virginia State University (WVSU). She always had a passion for music, and was bitten by the radio bug long ago. After graduating from WVSU with a bachelor's degree in mass communications, she pursued a career in radio.

Her 21-year radio career has taken her to numerous cities across the country. In addition to her radio career, Lady BG has done an incredible amount of voiceover work. Her voice has been heard on commercials throughout the country on radio and television. Additionally, she is a member of the Screen Actor's Guild. You can catch Lady BG on 105.9 Kiss FM weekdays from 3 p.m. – 7 p.m.

Lady BG is also a recent newlywed.

Seeking to enlighten the African-American community with insightful news and information, Valerie D. Lockhart founded the *Detroit Native Sun* in October of 2005. There, she serves as publisher and executive editor, giving a voice to both the young and old in the community.

Born and raised in Detroit, Lockhart was educated in the Detroit Public Schools system, and graduated, with honors, from the University of Detroit with a Bachelor of Arts degree in communications.

With more than 20 years of journalism experience, Lockhart has been recognized for her community service, creativity and accuracy in reporting. Awards received include the Lincoln University Unity in Media award, the American Red Cross Community Service Award and the James Tatum Foundation of the Arts Award. Likewise, she has received the Xavier University Parents Association Community Service Award for assisting local Hurricane Katrina victims, and awards from the big three automakers.

Karen A. Love

Chief Operating Officer
Michigan Chronicle

Jamillah A. Muhammad

Program Director
WMXD Mix 92.3 FM

Karen Love is chief operating officer of the *Michigan Chronicle*, and chief operating officer and publisher of *The Michigan FrontPage*. As chief operating officer, she is responsible for local and national advertising sales, and is the liaison to other African-American newspapers and related organizations across the country. She has been responsible for overseeing the daily operations of the company since 1989.

With more than 32 years of newspaper experience, Karen has received numerous awards, including the *Chicago Tribune* Black Achiever Award, the National Political Congress of Black Women (Detroit) Woman of the Year, the American Diabetes Association Awareness Award, MPRO & MDCH 2004 Pillar Awards of Excellence and the SCLC 2006 Print Media Award. Additionally, the Michigan Senate presented her with a proclamation recognizing her as one of Detroit's outstanding leaders. In 2007 she was elected first vice chairwoman of the National Newspaper Publishers Association. She is also founder of Project LoveSHARE.

Karen graduated, with honors, with a bachelor's degree in Christian education from the Eastern North Carolina Theological Institute, and is also a graduate of Wayne County Community College.

Jamillah A. Muhammad, affectionately called "Jam," is the program director for WMXD Mix 92.3 FM. She is also the president of Image First Productions, Inc., an up-and-coming production company.

Jamillah started her radio career 16 years ago at WGCI-AM in Chicago. She later moved to Milwaukee, where she was music director, then assistant program director for WVAZ-FM. She went on to program for WKKV-FM, taking the station's Arbitron ranking from No. 8 to No. 1.

During her early years in radio, Jamillah also worked as an assistant for the Mayor's Office of Special Events, helping coordinate the Chicago Gospel Festival and other special projects. She is a member of the Chicago Chapter of The Recording Academy, the National Association of Black Female Executives and the National Association of Black Journalists.

Jamillah has won various community and industry awards, including Urban Adult Contemporary Program Director of the Year Awards from Radio & Records and the Urban Network. She was nominated to be featured in *Crain's Detroit Business'* 40 Under 40. A resident of Southfield, she is single with no children.

Delvis Paul Nixon

GSM Station Manager &
Sports Director
News Talk 1200 WCHB AM
Radio One Detroit

Sarah Norat-Phillips

President & General Manager
WMYD-TV 20 Detroit

Passion and versatility describe Delvis Paul Nixon, GSM manager of News Talk 1200 WCHB AM and innovator of the sports department for WCHB. He is directly responsible for pulling two major power moves that have elevated the station to become a major player in the Detroit market. He accomplished this by signing a blockbuster deal with the University of Michigan Sports Network to broadcast University of Michigan sports for the first time in Radio One Detroit's history, and by recruiting the highly acclaimed sports show *Parker & the Man* to helm the nighttime airwaves.

Delvis continues to lead WCHB to record revenue levels by creating nontraditional revenue events, such as The CEO to CEO Seminars, The 2 Live Stews and Globetrotter Tour and The Les Brown Speaker Series, to name a few. A native Detroiter, he enjoys hosting a weekly sports show on WCHB, shopping, hanging out with family and friends and traveling.

In May of 1998, Sarah Norat-Phillips was named president and general manager of WDWB-TV, currently known as WMYD-TV 20 Detroit. In doing so, she became the first black female to head a major television station in Detroit. Since her appointment, she has committed herself to improving the station's market share, delivering quality programming and building stronger ties with the Detroit community.

Under her leadership, WB20 became one of the nation's strongest performing WB network affiliates, experiencing both ratings and revenue growth while building a solid foundation and track record of service. Norat-Phillips was successful in acquiring the broadcast rights to the Detroit Pistons after nearly 30 years on WKBD.

Throughout her career, Norat-Phillips has been honored with numerous awards, including the 40 Under 40 Award from *Business First Magazine* and several New York State Associated Press Awards. She is an Emmy Award-winning television writer and producer. She is also a graduate of Leadership Buffalo VI and Leadership Detroit XXII. Involved in various community organizations, Norat-Phillips serves as vice chair of the Arts League of Michigan.

A.J. Parker

On-Air Personality
WDMK 105.9 Kiss FM
Radio One Detroit

Al Payne

Operations Manager
Radio One Detroit

Known to listeners as "The Diva," A.J. Parker is a 27-year radio veteran.

A dynamic public speaker, A.J. calls her start in radio a fluke, after landing an on-air spot while she was a student at Michigan State University. However, her father was already in radio; that is no fluke, that is good genes, and being in the right place at the right time. A.J. cites her father, Al Benson, "The 'Ole Swingmaster," as her inspiration. He was on the air from 1950 to 1975.

Gaining experience in various markets before landing in Detroit, A.J. co-hosted the nationally syndicated Jerry Springer talk show, and facilitated the nightly Illinois State Lottery drawing on the Superstation WGN before the Chi-town wind blew her into WDMK 105.9 Kiss FM. Luckily it did, because the "Best of the 70s, 80s and Motown" would be incomplete without The Diva's infectious laughter and shining personality.

A.J. is the proud parent of one son.

Al Payne started his illustrious career in radio in high school, staying in the game through college at The University of North Carolina. After college, he began his professional career at WLBJ-A in Laurens, South Carolina. He has worked at WLWZ in Greenville, South Carolina; WFXC in Raleigh; WQMG in Greensboro; KRNB in Dallas, Cumulus in Beaumont (including KTCX); and Cumulus in Wilmington (including WMNX and WKXS). He is currently at Radio One, and Detroit is excited to welcome him as its newest tastemaker to the scene.

Al has been influenced by nearly everyone with whom he has worked. Citing listening to "Brother" Bill Prather on the air as the defining moment that made him realize radio was definitely it for him, he goes as far as to say that even if he won the lottery, he would still work.

F. Carlton Peeples

Owner
Carlton Signature Publishing & PR

Charles Pugh

Newscaster
FOX 2

F. Carlton Peeples is owner of Carlton Signature Publishing & PR, a premier firm focused on providing strategic business solutions through marketing and ad campaigns, including development, sales and purchasing, as well as fundraising and event planning. Carlton Signature also provides dynamic content for various publications, Web sites and search engines.

As a writer, Peeples has provided ink for several national publications, including *XXL*, *African Americans OnWheels*, *Savoy* and *Venhue* magazines, just to name a few. His subject matter ranges from urban culture to the auto industry, as well as being an advocate for the rights of fathers, the education of African-American male youth, and the economic empowerment of women and minorities. Peeples' first stage play/book, "Fatherless Sons," is set to debut in June of 2008.

Peeples is a member of Phi Beta Sigma Fraternity, Inc., Rho Nu Chapter at the University of Detroit Mercy. He later joined the alumni chapter of Nu Alpha Sigma, and is also a member of the National Association of Black Journalists, Adcraft Club and several other prominent organizations.

Born and raised in Detroit, Charles Pugh is a newscaster, talk show host, commentator, public speaker, college instructor and business owner. He started Charles Pugh Productions in 2006.

Born on August 3, 1971, Pugh grew up on the west side in a community called Research Park. His parents were George and Marcia Pugh. He was raised primarily by his grandmother, Margaret Pugh, after the deaths of his parents. Pugh attended Balch Elementary, Edmonson Elementary, Pelham Middle School and Murray-Wright High School. He graduated from the University of Missouri – Columbia with a degree in broadcast journalism in 1993.

One of very few openly gay African-American journalists in America, Pugh has reported and anchored at KOMU-TV in Columbia, Missouri; WIBW-TV in Topeka, Kansas; WKJG-TV in Fort Wayne, Indiana; and WAVY-TV in Norfolk, Virginia. In Detroit, he has worked for WJBK-TV, WCHB-AM and WJLB-FM.

Pugh has guest lectured at several universities, including the University of Michigan and Hampton University. He also taught class at Wayne County Community College.

Pugh has one brother, one sister, two wonderful nieces and one marvelous nephew.

Suga Rae

On-Air Personality
WHTD-FM HOT 102.7
Radio One Detroit

Scheherezade "Sherri" Redmond

Promotions Coordinator
Radio One Detroit

Starting her career with Radio One Detroit as a high school reporter, Suga Rae's talent, strong personality, will, drive and determination soon led her to an on-air position with the company's urban mainstream station. After advancing from a night-time gig to morning show, Suga Rae is showing the city how the ladies do it, holding down her own slot during the day with the famed *Suga's House*.

Suga Rae's hobbies include traveling, reading, and listening to her favorite artist, Common. A self-proclaimed shopaholic, Suga loves perusing through vintage stores for pieces that complete her unique style. She is truly a trendsetter. A powerhouse in the clubs, Suga is frequently requested as host and emcee for various events throughout the city.

With show staples that will keep her audience laughing and informed at the same time, Suga Rae "will get you through your day" with "Suga's Celeb News," "Gimmie 5" and more. She can be heard weekdays from 10 a.m. to 2 p.m.

Scheherezade "Sherri" Redmond holds the position of promotions coordinator for Radio One Detroit. She hails from Western Michigan University as the special events announcer for 89.1 WIDR, and is a product of their Audio Engineering Program. Her accomplishments include joining Lambda Pi Eta Communications Honors Society, earning the Bronze Test Judge appointment with the United States Figure Skating Association and being a member of Zeta Phi Beta Sorority, Inc. After receiving a degree in film, video and media studies, she aspired to take the Detroit media market by storm.

Sherri began working for Radio One Detroit in 2005 as a promotions assistant, and eagerly began learning the ins and outs of the radio world. She was trained to produce multiple programs, including *The Wendy Williams Experience*, *The Russ Parr Morning Show* and *The Tom Joyner Morning Show*. Sherri is currently striving to realize her dream of becoming a full-time on-air personality.

Rochelle Riley

Columnist
Detroit Free Press

Cedric Scott

Promotions Director
WHTD-FM HOT 102.7
Radio One Detroit

Rochelle Riley writes an op-ed column for the *Detroit Free Press*, and co-hosts a weekly talk show on Detroit Public Television called *Am I Right?* She also offers commentary on National Public Radio and MSNBC.

Rochelle has been nominated four times for the Pulitzer Prize, and the Michigan Press Association has twice named her the state's Best Local Columnist. She has won writing awards from the Charles E. Scripps Award Foundation, the Society of Professional Journalists, the Detroit Press Club Foundation, the National Association of Black Journalists, the Michigan Associated Press and the American Association of Sunday and Feature Editors. In 1996 her debut column for *The Courier-Journal* in Louisville, Kentucky, helped spur an $80 million campaign to build a museum honoring boxer and humanitarian Muhammad Ali. It opened in November of 2005 in Louisville, Ali's hometown.

Rochelle earned a journalism degree from The University of North Carolina at Chapel Hill. She is a member of Delta Sigma Theta Sorority, Inc., and is completing her first novel. She is the proud mother of a 18-year-old actress and future pre-school teacher.

Cedric Scott, currently the promotions director for Radio One urban outlet WHTD-FM HOT 102.7, comes to Detroit from his native South Carolina. He has worked at various radio stations since 1996, which included stops in Greenville and Myrtle Beach, South Carolina. His most recent stop was Flint, Michigan, where he doubled as the station's first promotions director and the No. 1-rated afternoon on-air personality, "Ced Lover."

Cedric received an undergraduate degree in advertising from the University of South Carolina. His accomplishments included serving as president of the student activities governing board for two years, the founding member of Dance Marathon and the first chairman of the Russell House University Union Advisory Board. He was also honored as an American Advertising Federation's Most Promising Minority Student for two consecutive years. He recently completed the requirements for a Master of Business Administration degree in marketing from the University of Phoenix with a 3.8 grade point average.

Smiley

Music Director & On-Air Personality
WHTD-FM HOT 102.7
Radio One Detroit

Solomon Spann III

NTR/Special Events Director
WHTD-FM HOT 102.7
Radio One Detroit

Smiley, Detroit's very own female emcee, has been with WHTD-FM HOT 102.7 for four years, but she has 15 years under her belt for length of time in the entertainment industry.

If one listened to Detroit hip-hop in the late 80s, one would probably remember the line, "Smiley...but I'm not friendly, for the simple fact that it's just not in me..." That was from this industry veteran's first rap single, "Smiley, But I'm Not Friendly," released in 1989 and certified gold.

In addition to listening to her funny wit and charm over the airwaves, a person can also watch Smiley in action on the television screen every Saturday at noon. She is the executive producer/editor and host of Detroit's No.1 music video show, *The Smiley Show*. Every local and national artist or group passing through town stops by *The Smiley Show*. She is always out and about, covering every hot event blazing the city streets.

Smiley can be heard Monday through Thursday from 10 p.m. – 2 a.m., and on Sunday from 10 a.m. – 2 p.m.

Solomon Spann III is NTR/special events director for WHTD-FM HOT 102.7, a Radio One property. In this position, he is charged with the task of generating revenue for special events and the Internet, often creating win-win relationships with metro Detroit businesses and the community.

Solomon is a 16-year communications veteran who has extensive expertise in advertising and marketing. His collegiate internship was done in Charlotte, North Carolina, for WBTV. He started his career in Columbia, South Carolina, at WWDM-FM as an on-air personality. Solomon was the top salesperson for WHXT-FM Rainbow Radio in Columbia, South Carolina. In 2002 he went to work for Time Warner Cable in cable ad sales. Solomon moved to Detroit in 2005, where he has been welcomed by the Detroit community. He is also president of an Internet-based travel agency.

Solomon is a graduate of Georgia Southern University, where he majored in broadcast journalism. He sits on the board of Commonwealth Academy, and is an active member of Word of Faith International Christian Center.

Spudd

Program Director &
On-Air Personality
WHTD-FM HOT 102.7
Radio One Detroit

Leland Stein III

Sports Columnist
Michigan Chronicle

Socially conscious, fiercely dedicated and undeniably gifted, Spudd is the program director and afternoon drive personality at WHTD-FM HOT 102.7. He is a major influence on what is hot in Detroit's music scene.

Spudd listens when the streets are talking, translating records and urban lifestyle into ratings. Consistently No. 1 in his time slot, listeners turn to him for everything ranging from politics to entertainment. He is informative and entertaining, often raising thought-provoking topics. As program director, Spudd leads a creative team of on-air personalities and mixers. "Every program director wants to be number one in the market, and I'm no exception, but my ultimate goal in this position is to make radio legends, personalities that go on to do great things for the community and the music industry," he says.

Hailing from Junction City, Kansas, Spudd has been with Radio One since 1998. His radio career spans 15 years and various cities. He has one son, and credits his mother and grandmother, who played major roles in shaping his life, with the old school lessons he has learned.

Leland Stein III has written for the *Los Angeles Sentinel*, *Black Voice News*, the *Chicago Defender* and the *Michigan Chronicle*. He has been published in *BlackSports*, *Michigan Sports Hall of Fame* magazine, MyBrotha.com, and the *National Alliance of African American Athletes* (NAAAA), *John R. Wooden Classic Commemorative*, *Star Athlete* and *U.S. Olympic* magazines. He was also a contributor to the *Major League Baseball All-Star Program*, the *NCAA Final Four Program* and the Commemorative Centennial Celebration of African Americans in the Olympics.

Leland has won numerous awards and was appointed to the U.S. Olympic Committee. He has covered two Olympic Games (Atlanta & Sydney), Super Bowls, NBA All-Star weekends and finals, NCAA Final Fours, Rose Bowls, the World Series, championship boxing, tennis and golf. He was appointed to the NAAAA board of directors, is its media relations manager, and is on the Michigan Sports Hall of Fame Selection Committee.

Leland received a Bachelor of Science degree in engineering from Michigan State University. A native of Detroit, he is married to Helen, and they have three children, Candace, Leland IV and Leighton, attending college.

Wax Tax-n Dre

WHTD-FM HOT 102.7
Radio One Detroit

James W. Thomas

Account Manager
WWJ Newsradio 950 AM
CBS Radio

With experience that spans from working as a disc jockey (DJ) to promotions to production, Wax Tax-n Dre began his career thinking that working a DJ was just a hobby. But soon, people insisted that he DJ parties for them.

After nervously auditioning for a local radio station while spinning live on the air at a club, he waited for a call back, only to learn that the station had already created a commercial announcing Wax Tax-n Dre as their newest DJ. "The World Famous" Wax Tax-n Dre has been with Radio One, Inc. – Detroit for 11 years.

Wax Tax-n Dre is multitalented. As a prominent cast member of *Switch Play TV*, a sketch/comedy show, he has discovered another love – acting.

A self-proclaimed "tech freak," he also loves video games. A native of Ecorse, Michigan, Wax Tax-n Dre graduated from Ecorse High School and the Detroit Business Institute.

He has won numerous awards and clawed in major DJ battles. He is looking forward to his next phase in life, where he figures he will make his own video game.

James Thomas is an account manager for WWJ Newsradio 950 AM, Detroit's CBS affiliate. In this position, he plans and directs advertising programs to create extra interest in the purchase of a product or service for a department, an entire organization or on an account basis.

In 1997 James retired from federal law enforcement to form Thomas, Wright & Associates, a firm of criminologists specializing in fraud detection and deterrence.

James is a frequent panelist, lecturer and speaker. He earned a bachelor's degree from the University of Maryland. A native of Alabama, James has two children, Jasmine and Michael.

Tune Up

On-Air Personality
WHTD-FM HOT 102.7
Radio One Detroit

Krafus Walker

Business Manager
Michigan Chronicle Publishing Company

Tune Up embodies the dynamic power and energy that is radio. The HOT 102.7 on-air personality has been with Radio One, Inc. in Detroit since 1998.

A native Detroiter, his professional radio career began as an unpaid college intern. Tune Up graduated from Northern Michigan University with a degree in language arts and journalism. While working nights for a pop station, he worked another full-time job from 8 a.m. to 5 p.m., until his break came when a local urban radio station offered him the traffic reporter/producer position for a popular morning show. From there, the personality "Tune Up Man" was born.

Tune Up is in constant demand from retailers, businesses and clubs. Loyal listeners "tune in" to HOT 102.7 as his energy, passion and laughter radiate over the airwaves. And if anyone happens to meet him while out and about, either at a live broadcast, appearance or club, one will be quickly pulled into his intense enthusiasm – it's infectious.

Tune Up says his inspiration for reaching to newer heights stems from his wife and two sons.

Krafus Walker is business manager at the *Michigan Chronicle* and *The Michigan FrontPage* newspapers. In this position, he manages the financial and technology affairs of one of the top African-American publications in America.

Krafus received a Bachelor of Science degree in electrical engineering technology from Purdue University in West Lafayette, Indiana. He developed his business skills while starting several small businesses in the services industry.

A native of Inkster, Michigan, Krafus is the husband of Darlene Cassell Walker and the father of Malika Walker. He is very active in the community and with his Church of God in Christ church organization.

Kebina S. Young

Marketing Director
Radio One Detroit

Kebina Young, a native of Detroit, is marketing director for Radio One Detroit. In her day-to-day operations, she works closely with both the sales and programming departments to create promotions that maximize the stations' exposure, while increasing revenue and ratings.

A graduate of Clark Atlanta University, Kebina earned a Bachelor of Arts degree in mass media arts with a concentration in radio, television and film. She began her career in television news in Miami, Florida, before moving to Lansing, Michigan.

Kebina left news in 2000, accepting a position with the Wayne County Community College District (WCCCD). She was soon promoted to marketing director of the Workforce Development and Continuing Education Division, where she was instrumental in creating and overseeing numerous programs that opened up the college's services to the community.

After four years with WCCCD, Kebina took her passion for marketing to an entirely different industry: radio. With a knack for promotions and her love for music and entertainment, she was hired into the family of Radio One, Inc.

Kebina is single with no children, and resides in Detroit.

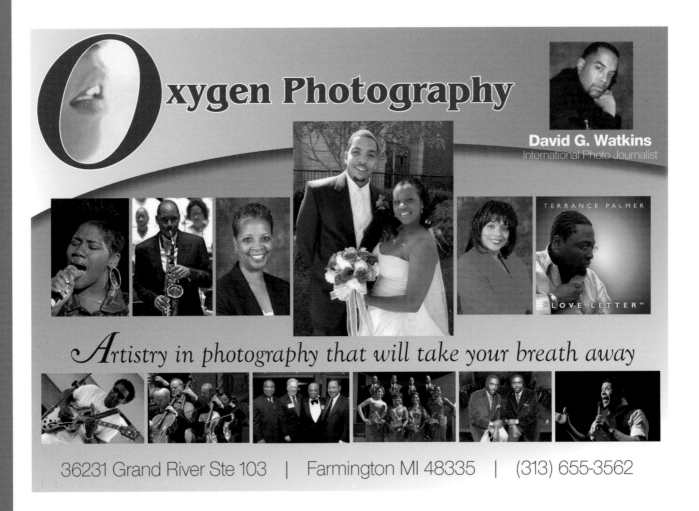

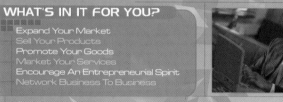